GUIDE
TO THE
CONTINENTAL
DIVIDE
TRAIL

GUIDE
TO THE
CONTINENTAL
DIVIDE
TRAIL

Volume 1:
Northern Montana

James R. Wolf

CONTINENTAL DIVIDE TRAIL SOCIETY
BETHESDA, MD 20824

Library of Congress Cataloging-in-Publication Data

Wolf, James R.
    Guide to the Continental Divide trail / James R. Wolf. —
Rev. ed.
       p.   cm.
    Includes bibliographical references.
    Contents: v. 1. Northern Montana.
    ISBN 0-934326-01-0
    1. Continental Divide National Scenic Trail — Guide-
books.
2. Hiking—Continental Divide National Scenic Trail—
Guide-books.
3. Natural history—Continental Divide National Scenic
Trail—Guide-books.   I. Title.
GV199.42.C84W64   1991
917.3'04928—dc20   91-31384
                                     CIP

Guides to the Continental Divide Trail
are published by
CONTINENTAL DIVIDE TRAIL SOCIETY
P.O. Box 30002
Bethesda, Md. 20824

Behind me lay the forests hushed with sleep;
  Above me in its granite majesty,
Sphinx-like, the peak thro' silent centuries
  Met the eternal question of the sky.
Victor at last—throned on the cragged height—
  I scan the green steeps of the mountain side
  Where late I toiled.

Between two silences my soul floats still
  As any white cloud in this sunny air.
  No sound of living breaks upon my ear,
No strain of thought—no restless human will—
  Only the virgin quiet, everywhere—
  Earth never seemed so far, or Heaven so near.

Preface

The backbone of North America, the Continental Divide, is a world of mountains, forests, grassland, and desert. Its scenery is grand and often inspiring, its wildlife and flowers exceedingly diverse, its landmarks reminders of our country's turbulent history.

The concept of a foot trail close to the Continental Divide has excited the imagination of hikers for years. In 1976, when the first edition of this guidebook appeared, such a trail was just an idea. In the last fifteen years, however, it has become a reality in Montana and work is progressing along its length all the way from Canada to Mexico.

The descriptions in this book include the route which has been selected as the official location for the Continental Divide Trail. As a general rule, the location is an exceptional one; but there are a number of deviations that would enhance your enjoyment, and these are recommended in the text.

The recommended route is described in Roman type, like this. It is suitable for backpackers, during the summer months, but some portions may not be safely negotiable by people traveling with pack animals.

Alternate routes—including some parts of the officially designated trail—are described in this distinctive typeface. An effort has been made to provide enough comparative information to aid in selecting the way that is best for you.

The text is based primarily upon my field work in 1973 and 1989. But I have also relied upon the numerous trip reports that members of the Continental Divide Trail Society have provided over the past several years. The recent observations of members Dan Smith and Karen Berger, who field-tested the manuscript in 1991, have been especially helpful. If you make a trip, please send the Society an account of your experiences—including any comments, suggestions, or corrections that might be of benefit to others.

As noted in the first edition, a number of agency personnel provided advice, information, and support in 1973—especially Bud Powell, Lloyd Reesman, Cal Tasinari, C.R. Morey, and T.W. Smith. Patti Johnston and Terri Marceron of the Rocky Mountain Ranger District extended similar cooperation as this revision took shape. In Glacier National Park, I had not only the encouragement and suggestions of Backcountry Supervisor Jack Potter, but also the pleasure of his company for the section south of Many Glacier.

Special thanks go to the staff of the Forest Service for their leadership and cooperation in the designation of the route in Montana and Idaho. Foresters Wendell Beardsley and Chuck Neal, who worked tirelessly and with great sensitivity, were key to this effort; their persistence and attention to detail led to the selection of the outstanding route you will enjoy. Regional Forester John Mumma and Recreation Director John Drake provided the support that made it all possible. Tim Love in the Lewis and Clark National Forest and Fred Flint in the Flathead National Forest read over a draft of portions of the text and provided helpful comments and suggestions—though of course any errors or oversights are my responsibility alone.

Please respect the land and living things of the backcountry. Take nothing but pictures, leave nothing but footprints. Know how to keep a clean camp, avoiding pollution, litter, and damage to vegetation. Be sure you are familiar with precautions for travel in bear country; and carry gear, appropriate to your hike, to guard against the serious risks of hypothermia.

Please enjoy the Trail thoroughly, and safely, but let those who follow find it as natural and clean as it was when you were there.

Happy hiking!

Jim Wolf
Bethesda, Maryland
September 1991

Contents

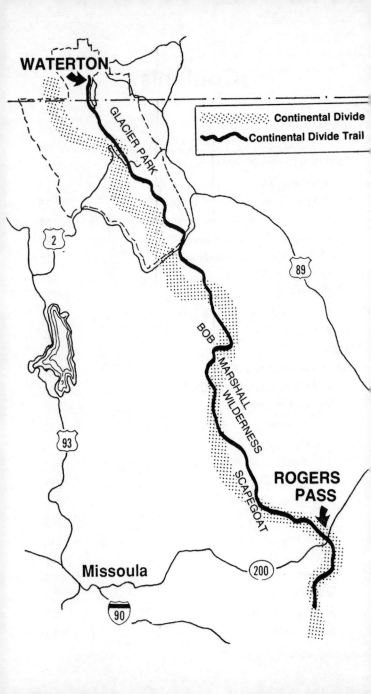

Introduction

The Trail begins at the Canadian border on the west shore of scenic Waterton Lake, where there is easy trail access from the Waterton Lake townsite in Alberta.

The first segment, of 114 miles, follows a winding course through the alpine terrain of Glacier National Park. This is rugged land, with bold contours and beautiful vistas everywhere. Wildlife is protected, with mountain goats and other unfamiliar mammals to add to the hiker's pleasure.

Most of the next segment is in the Bob Marshall Wilderness. This segment extends another 106 miles from the south edge of Glacier National Park at Marias Pass, on U.S. Highway 2, to a roadhead and supply point at Benchmark, east of the Divide. The Trail is generally lower and more forested, the mountains less imposing. Nevertheless, limestone cliffs that rise steeply from high meadows, and panoramic viewpoints along the Trail, provide many magnificent moments. This attractive land is not so heavily traveled, and it retains superb wilderness values.

The Scapegoat Wilderness makes up most of the final 52-mile segment, from Benchmark to paved highway at Rogers Pass. Drier and less forested than the more northern portions of the Trail, it is in some ways the most interesting. Here it is possible to walk along the crest of the Continental Divide for long distances, in solitude, enjoying the mountain vistas in every direction. Along Alice Creek one is reminded of Captain Lewis' explorations in 1806 as well as Isaac Stevens' railroad survey 50 years later.

The tables on pages 4 and 5 details the segments and sections of the primary route that is recommended in this guidebook. The figures for "auto road" (passable by car as well as jeep) and "cross-country" involve sometimes arbitrary judgments; they are intended merely to suggest the kind of hiking to be expected in a section. (The official route is considered for this purpose as an established trail even though it may not yet be cleared and marked.) Mileages are generally calculated with the aid of a map-measurer (a calibrated wheeled device); they are conservative and may not allow completely for minor shifts of direction or for extra length resulting from elevation changes.

Waterton Lakes National Park (4.7 Miles)

Waterton Lakes National Park in Alberta is a land of high mountains, lakes, and prairies of exceptional grandeur. Threading its heart are the Waterton Lakes—notably, spectacular fjord-like Upper Waterton Lake, which extends across the international boundary into Montana.

The view from the Prince of Wales Hotel, overlooking the Waterton Park townsite and the ribbon-like expanse of the upper lake, is justly renowned. The townsite itself, on the flat delta of Cameron Brook, offers a wide variety of tourist services, including motels, restaurants, post office, and stores.

The hiker picks up the approach trail at Cameron Falls, near a large public campground. The scenic route follows the west side of Upper Waterton Lake, sometimes in forest and sometimes near the shore, with a couple of fine views. This leads, after 4.7 miles, to the well-marked international boundary and the start of the Continental Divide Trail.

The only problem that may be anticipated is interruption of bus service between Glacier National Park and Waterton Lakes. Should this occur, it will be necessary to make bus connections by way of Calgary or Lethbridge. Also, northbound travelers should be sure to inquire about customs and immigration requirements.

In 1932, Waterton Lakes National Park and contiguous Glacier National Park were officially designated the Waterton-Glacier International Peace Park. This action, "for the purpose of permanently commemorating the long-existing relationship of peace and good will existing between the people and Governments of Canada and the United States," was the first of its kind in the world.

Glacier National Park (114.0 Miles)

The Trail carves through the heart of 1600-square-mile Glacier National Park, set apart in 1910 "as a public park or pleasure ground for the benefit and enjoyment of the people," subject to regulations providing "for the preservation of the park in a state of nature so far as is consistent with purposes of this Act, and for the care and protection of the fish and game within the boundaries thereof."

From the Canadian border, the Trail follows the shores of mountain-rimmed Waterton Lake and the narrow valley of the Waterton River. At 9.7, the Trail begins to climb steeply, crossing a first divide at 13.0 and the Continental Divide at 15.2. Hugging steep cliffs on the western slopes of the Lewis Range, the Trail remains mostly above timberline, with spectacular views of the peaks of the Livingstone Range, to Granite Park (26.0).

The route crosses the Continental Divide a second time, at 26.7, before descending to Many Glacier, in a lovely setting of lakes and glaciers, at 34.1. A climb past waterfalls—over Piegan Pass at 42.7—leads on to Going-to-the-Sun Highway, the one road that cuts across the Park, at 47.4.

After skirting Saint Mary Lake for several miles, the Trail doubles back to Red Eagle Lake at 61.2. A long climb in meadows ablaze with flowers and hemmed in by cascaded cliffs approaches the triple divide separating the waters of Hudson Bay, the Atlantic, and the Pacific. From Triple Divide Pass, at 69.3, the route makes a long detour east before ascending once again to the Continental Divide.

Pitamakan Overlook, a high point at 79.1, offers thrilling views. The rugged terrain finally leaves the high mountains, dropping to the blue waters of Two Medicine Lake. After crossing another ridge, the Trail comes to the town of East Glacier Park at 99.6. The last stretch, to the Burlington Northern railroad tracks and U.S. 2 along the southern boundary of the Park, is relatively uninteresting.

The route is easily followed throughout, except for a few miles in the Blackfeet Indian Reservation near East Glacier and some overgrown and poorly blazed bits in the last section near the southern edge of the Park.

East Glacier, with post office and stores, is the most important supply point in this segment, though additional supplies are available at Swiftcurrent (near Many Glacier) and Two Medicine Lake.

The principal problems to be considered are (1) snow, which may keep the best parts of the Trail closed until early July and then block them again in mid-September, (2) exposure to

Summary: North-to-South

	From	To	Total	Road	X–C	Elev. Gain
Glacier National Park						
Section 1	International Boundary	Many Glacier	34.1	0.5	0.0	6000
Section 2	Many Glacier	Going-to-the-Sun Road	13.3	0.0	0.0	2650
Section 3	Going-to-the-Sun Road	Pitamakan Pass	31.2	0.0	0.0	6350
Section 4	Pitamakan Pass	Two Medicine	10.6	0.5	0.0	850
Section 5	Two Medicine	East Glacier Park	10.4	1.0	0.0	2400
Section 6	East Glacier Park	Marias Pass (U.S. 2)	14.4	0.1	0.0	1700
		Subtotal	*114.0*	*2.1*	*0.0*	*19950*
Bob Marshall Wilderness						
Section 1-A	Marias Pass (U.S. 2)	North Badger Creek	17.1	0.3	0.0	1450
Section 1-B	North Badger Creek	Badger Pass	10.2	0.0	0.0	1650
Section 2	Badger Pass	Kevan Mountain	25.3	0.0	0.0	2350
Section 3	Kevan Mountain	Spotted Bear Pass	19.2	0.0	0.0	3350
Section 4	Spotted Bear Pass	Indian Point Guard Station	17.6	0.0	0.0	2550
Section 5	Indian Point Guard Station	Benchmark	17.0	0.4	0.0	2800
		Subtotal	*106.4*	*0.7*	*0.0*	*14150*
Scapegoat Wilderness						
Section 1	Benchmark	Green Fork	10.0	0.5	0.0	800
Section 2	Green Fork	Whitetail Creek	12.6	0.0	0.0	900
Section 3	Whitetail Creek	Scapegoat Boundary	13.0	0.0	2.5	4800
Section 4	Scapegoat Boundary	Rogers Pass (Mont. 200)	16.5	0.0	0.0	3700
		Subtotal	*52.1*	*0.5*	*2.5*	*10200*
		Total (CDT)	272.5	3.3	2.5	44300

4

Summary: South-to-North

	From	To	Total	Miles Road	X-C	Elev. Gain
Scapegoat Wilderness						
Section 4	Rogers Pass (Mont. 200)	Scapegoat Boundary	16.5	0.0	0.0	6250
Section 3	Scapegoat Boundary	Whitetail Creek	13.0	0.0	2.5	2000
Section 2	Whitetail Creek	Green Fork	12.6	0.0	0.0	1600
Section 1	Green Fork	Benchmark	10.0	0.5	0.0	50
		Subtotal	*52.1*	*0.5*	*2.5*	*9900*
Bob Marshall Wilderness						
Section 5	Benchmark	Indian Point Guard Station	17.0	0.4	0.0	2800
Section 4	Indian Point Guard Station	Spotted Bear Pass	17.6	0.0	0.0	3950
Section 3	Spotted Bear Pass	Kevan Mountain	19.2	0.0	0.0	3400
Section 2	Kevan Mountain	Badger Pass	25.3	0.0	0.0	1850
Section 1-B	Badger Pass	North Badger Creek	10.2	0.0	0.0	1100
Section 1-A	North Badger Creek	Marias Pass (U.S.2)	17.1	0.3	0.0	1000
		Subtotal	*106.4*	*0.7*	*0.0*	*14100*
Glacier National Park						
Section 6	Marias Pass (U.S.2)	East Glacier Park	14.4	0.1	0.0	1200
Section 5	East Glacier Park	Two Medicine	10.4	1.0	0.0	2850
Section 4	Two Medicine	Pitamakan Pass	10.6	0.5	0.0	3250
Section 3	Pitamakan Pass	Going-to-the-Sun Road	31.2	0.0	0.0	4000
Section 2	Going-to-the-Sun Road	Many Glacier	13.3	0.0	0.0	2300
Section 1	Many Glacier	International Boundary	34.1	0.5	0.0	5300
		Subtotal	*114.0*	*2.1*	*0.0*	*18900*
		Total (CDT)	272.5	3.3	2.5	42900

5

chilling rain and cold weather, (3) spacing and availability of authorized campsites, and (4) the remote possibility of an untoward encounter with a grizzly bear. It would be a good idea to write in advance to Glacier National Park for current regulations and brochures. Also, refer to the alternate-route descriptions in the text below; the alternates (from the Canadian boundary to Many Glacier and from Pitamakan Pass to Two Medicine Lake) can be negotiated for a somewhat longer season.

Bob Marshall Wilderness (106.4 Miles)

Bob Marshall (1901-1939), for whom this 950,000-acre wonderland is named, is a legendary figure in the wilderness movement. Superbly trained, with graduate degrees in forest and plant physiology, Marshall was rapidly rising in the ranks of the Forest Service, where he headed the Division of Recreation and Lands at the time of his premature death. In this position he was tireless in his efforts to identify roadless areas to be classified as primitive and protected as wilderness. But it is the personality and enthusiastic spirit of this far-sighted public servant that keeps his memory alive. For Marshall was an indomitable hiker, whose record of wilderness hikes—routinely over 30 miles in a day—staggers the imagination; and, more importantly, he knew, and he knew how to express, the conviction that an encounter with wilderness is modern man's best restorative.

The northern section in this segment, though not part of the Bob Marshall Wilderness, has to date been managed as a roadless area. The land, acquired from the Blackfeet Indians in 1896, might well have been included in the Wilderness were it not for purchase restrictions reserving to the Indians the right "to cut and remove...wood and timber for agency and school purposes, and for their personal uses for houses, fences, and other domestic purposes." Because of the suspected presence of subsurface oil and gas resources, exploration and development of this Badger-Two Medicine area may take place in coming years—though, it is to be hoped, well removed from the location of the Trail along the Continental Divide.

The last part of the segment is largely in the Scapegoat Wilderness, but it is more conveniently described with the Bob

Marshall so as to emphasize Benchmark's importance as a division between segments.

From Marias Pass on U.S. 2, the route drops to Sawmill Flats, on the South Fork of Two Medicine River, at 2.5. A gradual ascent leads to a low saddle, at the head of the valley, at 11.5. Continuing in the Badger Creek basin, the Trail follows steep-walled North Badger Creek to the base of the Continental Divide. After crossing a pass at 19.0, the Trail follows the remote valleys of Elbow and Muskrat Creeks, remaining close to the Divide.

Entering the Bob Marshall Wilderness at Badger Pass, at 27.4, the route makes a long and easy descent, first through high meadow and then forest, along Strawberry Creek. Leaving the valley at 38.5, the Trail climbs to Sun River Pass, 43.5, and on to a magnificent overlook on the Divide, at 54.3, near Kevan Mountain. After a drop of nearly 3000 feet in the next five miles, it follows Pentagon Creek down to the Spotted Bear River and then climbs along the river through forest to Spotted Bear Pass at 71.8.

The Trail soon comes to the spectacular centerpiece of the segment—a hike through richly-flowered meadows at the base of the thousand-foot cliffs of the Chinese Wall. Leaving the Wall at 81.6, one once again descends, to the West Fork of the South Fork of the Sun River. The recommended route abandons this stream, at 89.4, so as to enjoy the high country near Hoadley Reef.

Crossing from the Bob Marshall Wilderness to the Scapegoat Wilderness at 97.1, the vista southward is particularly impressive. From here the route drops into forest and continues to the end of the segment, at Benchmark, at 106.4.

The route outlined above, which is the recommended way to go, follows existing trail for its entire length, though some important junctions may not be marked. Other options, including some that are officially designated (and signed) as the Continental Divide Trail, are described in the more detailed text that follows. As indicated in that text, the alternatives are not yet constructed (Section 1-A), circuitous (Section 3), or scenically second-best (Section 5).

Travel may be difficult until late June, owing both to snow at higher elevations and high water at the numerous stream crossings. Campsites and water sources can be located without serious inconvenience (except that camping may be restricted or prohibited along the Chinese Wall). The absence of resupply points dictates that the hiker start out with a heavy pack—enough for ten days at the author's pace.

Scapegoat Wilderness (52.1 Miles)

The general character of this segment is well described in a committee report accompanying the 1972 legislation establishing the 240,000-acre Scapegoat Wilderness:

"...it is characterized by spectacular scenery, unique and interesting geologic formations, unspoiled streams and small lakes, and broad expanses of alpine and subalpine country that display sparse vegetation as a result of long winters, deep snows, and steep and rocky terrain. Interspersed are broad mountain valleys with some heavy stands of timber and scattered mountain meadows and parks. Scapegoat Mountain, rising to an elevation of over 9,000 feet, is a key attraction of the area. Glaciation has been a key geologic force in shaping the land forms....Wildlife is abundant and varied."

From Benchmark, the Trail gradually ascends Straight Creek to its head, at Straight Creek Pass, at 13.8. For miles on both sides of the pass, the route winds through a forest that was devastated by the 1988 Canyon Creek fire. The route descends the valley of the Dearborn River, on the Welcome Creek tributary to 16.4 and then along the main stem. This easy stretch is followed by a fairly steep climb from the river, at 24.0, to the Continental Divide at 26.4.

A scenic cross-country walk along the crest of the Divide occupies much of the way to the Valley of the Moon, a small water source at 32.6, at the base of Caribou Peak. Leaving the Scapegoat Wilderness at 35.6, the Trail picks up an old mining road that descends to Alice Creek. A short rise then leads to historic Lewis and Clark Pass at 45.1. The remainder of the segment follows the Continental Divide ridgeline quite closely, descending rapidly at the end to Rogers Pass, on Montana Highway 200, at 52.1.

While a hiker in this segment will need to use compass and maps for orientation at times, little difficulty should be expected either in finding or following the proper route. Much of the segment is at high elevation; and while this adds a great deal to the scenic interest, it also means that water sources (and good campsites) are relatively infrequent. Although portions of the Scapegoat Wilderness receive heavy use, the Trail gets little traffic (except, perhaps, during hunting season). Note that the recommended route, as summarized above, departs occasionally from the designated one. The reason for the deviation is that the official route is roundabout and less scenic (Section 1 and part of Section 3) or requires further construction (Section 4).

Daily bus service provides access to the Trail at Rogers Pass. Benchmark, to the north, is at the end of a dirt road; if possible, supplies should be left or sent there in advance, to lighten the load that would otherwise have to be carried at the start of the 158-mile stretch between Glacier National Park and Rogers Pass. (See Adresses section for details.}

Some General Information

This guidebook assumes that the user is familiar with backcountry techniques and etiquette. However, it is important to supplement such background information with knowledge about the specific conditions likely to be encountered along the Trail in northern Montana—in particular, the potential of encounters with bears. Both the Park Service and the Forest Service provide visitors with brochures that contain the latest advice on the subject, and they should be studied with care.

Although the maps published in this guidebook are designed to identify the route clearly, they are not detailed. They can be supplemented by the U.S. Geological Survey 7.5-minute topographic maps that are listed in the text (1:24000 scale). Alternatively, and at less expense, you can use a commercial topographic map for Glacier National Park and a Forest Service map of the Bob Marshall Wilderness Complex. (These are available from the Society.)

For those who may continue past Rogers Pass, the guidebook for southern Montana remains useful. There will, however, be important relocations. Some of these are well underway or completed, including: (1) alignment closer to the Divide between McDonald Pass and Delmoe Lake, (2) following the Divide more closely west of the Anaconda-Pintler Wilderness to Chief Joseph Pass, (3) routing via Jahnke Lake (bypassing the Van Houten detour), (4) remaining on national forest lands from Morrison Lake to Medicine Lodge Pass, and (5) keeping to the Divide between Garfield Peak and Monida Pass. The Society intends to supplement the guidebook to provide details as this work progresses.

Trail Description

North-to-South

Monuments marking the boundary of Canada and the United States — the start of the Continental Divide Trail.

APPROACH TRAIL
WATERTON TO INTERNATIONAL BOUNDARY
4.7 Miles

Mountain-rimmed Waterton Lake is splendid hiking country. The Trail parallels the western side of the lake, generally some distance back from and above the shoreline. Although there are some small rises and dips, the elevation changes are nowhere of any consequence. While much of the route is in lodgepole pine forest, there are several viewpoints. The Section begins at a bridge over Cameron Brook, immediately below the notable Cameron Falls, at the western edge of Waterton Park Townsite, Alberta.

The entire Section lies within Waterton Lakes National Park, which is administered by the Department of Indian Affairs and Northern Development. The headquarters for the Park is on Mount View Road, on the northern edge of town, about half a mile from the trailhead. Inquire there about any customs or immigration formalities that may apply to your situation. (Be sure to carry personal identification documents, which will be needed for entry into the United States.)

Water is available from streams. There are two primitive campsites, available by prior registration with the Park Superintendent.

There is daily bus service during the summer to Waterton Park from East Glacier Park (with an intermediate stop at Many Glacier). This scenic coach route drops its passengers off at the Prince of Wales Hotel, just north of the townsite, from which there is a commanding view over the entire seven-mile length of Upper Waterton Lake. Additional summer bus or limousine service may be available from Calgary and Lethbridge.

The town has numerous motels and restaurants, as well as a large trailer campground. Various publications, including a Park brochure, list of accommodations, map of the townsite showing the trailhead, and topographic map of the national park can be obtained (though they are not needed) by writing the Park Superintendent.

Detailed Trail data are:

Begin the approach to the Continental Divide National Scenic Trail at the bridge over Cameron Brook, directly below Cameron Falls on the western edge of the town. Following a map on a sign here, leave paved Cameron Falls Drive and take a parallel, higher, secondary road southward. Pass by the start of the Carthew Trail, which goes off to the right at 0.1.

Cut off to the right on an excellent trail at 0.3. There is a good view down Waterton Lake at 1.1. Keep left immediately thereafter, at the junction where the Bertha Lake Trail leads off to the right.

After descending, cross Bertha Brook on a bridge at 1.7. The lakeside campsite at 1.9, with fine scenery, may be available with advance permission from the Park Superintendent. Climb again, crossing a short scree slide and following an undercut and exposed trail, to a high point at 2.3.

The Trail drops down to the lake at 3.0, but only briefly. Pass a small brook at 3.3 on the way to a crest at 3.5, and then descend once more, with switchbacks, to the shore. There is a final rise to 4.3.

The Section ends at the international boundary, which is marked by two obelisks. A locked cabin is located on the Canadian side. Camping is authorized here, at a grassy campsite next to a creek, if a permit has been obtained in advance.

Distances and elevations are:

0.0	Cameron Brook	4250
0.1	Carthew Trail Junction	4300
0.3	Trail	4300
1.1	Bertha Brook Trail Junction	4550
1.7	Bertha Brook	4200
1.9	Waterton Lake	4200
2.3		4500
3.0	Waterton Lake	4200
3.3	Brook	4300
3.5		4350
3.8	Waterton Lake	4200
4.3		4300
4.7	International boundary	4200

GLACIER NATIONAL PARK SEGMENT
Section 1
INTERNATIONAL BOUNDARY TO MANY GLACIER
Designated (Waterton) Route: 34.1 Miles
Interim (Chief Mtn.) Route: 28.0 Miles

The designated route for this Section provides an exceptional backpacking experience. Its superb alpine scenery and tundra flora are unequaled anywhere along the Trail in Montana. But severe snow and ice conditions limit travel there to a few weeks—early July to early September; at other times it is best to use the alternate (interim) route described below.

The Trail is practically level as it proceeds down the full length of Waterton Lake to Goat Haunt Ranger Station at 3.9. There is a modest rise from there along the east bank of the Waterton River. Then, from 9.7 to 13.0, the Trail climbs steadily along the flanks of Cathedral Peak. After a slight dip across tundra to Fifty Mountain Camp at 14.2, the Trail reaches its high point on the Section as it crosses the Continental Divide below Mount Kipp at 15.2.

The route (the Highline Trail), usually with unobstructed views, contours on a high shelf beneath towering cliffs. Cattle Queen Creek and Ahern Creek have cut deep side valleys that are traversed at about 19.1 and 21.7, respectively. The route leaves the Highline Trail at 26.0, just before the Granite Park Chalet. There is another climb, over Swiftcurrent Pass at 26.7 and then down Swiftcurrent valley past a chain of lakes. The Trail goes through Swiftcurrent village, with all services, just before the end of the Section, at the Grinnell Glacier Trailhead, at 34.1.

The views are magnificent, especially along the Highline Trail. Snow-topped Vulture, Longfellow, and Heavens Peaks are perhaps the most prominent, but the number of summits is beyond counting. Side trails provide access to additional spectacular observation points on the Continental Divide—above Sue Lake (15.2) and on Swiftcurrent Mountain (26.6).

The heavy winter snowfall makes normal backpacking impractical outside of a few weeks in summer. There is a permanent snowbank at 23.1 that is steep, hazardous to cross until a good path has been cut, and not readily avoided by detour. This is the Ahern Drift, and until it has been worked on in early July you may be discouraged or prohibited from going through (though allowance can be made for experienced hikers equipped with ice axe). By the time the Ahern Drift is open, snow elsewhere should be limited to small patches. Use caution, though, if snow covers a streambed—especially at Cattle Queen Creek—as you could plunge through a weak spot. (Streams are otherwise bridged, where necessary, and should not pose any problem.)

The Section is entirely in Glacier National Park. A party is required to have a permit for each night in the backcountry, and camping is only allowed at designated campgrounds. (In this Section, these are at Waterton River, Goat Haunt, Kootenai Lakes, Fifty Mountain, and Granite Park—wood fires not allowed at the last two.) Through hikers will also be allowed to stay overnight at the developed Many Glacier Campground, near Swiftcurrent. Although the Park Service tries to accommodate CDT hikers, a party may on occasion find it impossible to cross the Section without some inconvenience or delay. (The earliest you can obtain permits is the day before you set out, and the most popular campsites are then often reserved quickly, so it's best not to dally.) It would be advisable to obtain current regulations by writing the Park Superintendent. Permits are issued at ranger stations throughout the Park, including the one at Goat Haunt (on Waterton Lake). Water sources are frequent throughout the Section.

Important: it is illegal to enter the United States from Canada without meeting a customs officer. Glacier Park rangers are authorized to act in this capacity, so plan to stop at Goat Haunt Ranger Station on your way south. (Rangers are on duty from early May to October, so you should have no difficulty.) Be sure to carry personal identification.

Meals, lodging, groceries, telephone, and laundry are available at Swiftcurrent. You can buy a good trail lunch at the Granite Park Chalet during its season (July 1 to Labor Day); don't count on spending the night at the 75-year-old chalet, though, as it starts taking reservations at New Year's and quickly fills its books for the entire season. Sometimes they have a cancellation, so you might contact them to inquire (see address for Belton Chalets in background information). Public transportation (tour bus service) is available at Many Glacier, a short distance from the end of the Section.

U.S.G.S. Maps: **Porcupine Ridge**, **Mount Geduhn**, **Ahern Pass**, and **Many Glacier**.

Also: our Maps **1** and **3**.

Detailed Trail data are:

From the monuments at the international boundary, continue southward along the shore. Pass signs indicating the start of the Waterton Lake Trail and prohibiting camping and the making of fires. The Trail soon forks to the right (left fork leads to a horse ford). Cross Boundary Creek at 0.3 on a sturdy footbridge. The creek here shoots with impressive force through a narrow notch.

Stay left at the junction at 0.4, where the North Boundary Trail turns off to Cameron Lake in Canada. Follow the Waterton Lake Trail, which has no significant rises or drops. Pass small side creeks at 1.9 and 3.0.

Turn right at the junction at 3.1. (The trail straight ahead passes the grassy Waterton River Campground at 0.2, just before a horse ford.) The Boulder Pass Trail continues west, away from the lake, at the junction at 3.2; instead, turn left so as to cross the Waterton River by a suspension bridge at 3.5. (Another spur trail leads directly from the campground to the bridge.) Across the river, a side trail to the right leads 0.4 mile to Rainbow Falls. As the Trail returns to the lakeshore, the horse trail joins from the left at 3.7. Cross Cleveland Creek at 3.8.

Come to the Goat Haunt Ranger Station at 3.9. (Following the shoreline another 0.2 mile east, a paved path leads to a boat landing and exhibit area; nearby are two cabins, each divided into several concrete-floored open-faced hikers' shelters equipped with picnic table and fireplace.)

Continue south from the ranger station, using the Waterton Valley Trail, soon crossing several creeks. Small wet meadows occasionally break the forest. At 6.3, just past Camp Creek, a side trail leads 0.3 mile to the right to a campground on one of the Kootenai Lakes; moose are often observed nearby. The Trail goes by a marsh outlet via a low bridge at 6.9. Look backward from time to time to Mt. Cleveland, the highest mountain in Glacier National Park (10,466 feet). An opening on the right of the trail at 7.2 affords good views up Valentine Creek, backed on the north side by Porcupine Ridge (which terminates in the four jagged pinnacles known as Citadel Peaks). Continue with minor elevation changes; formerly the Valentine Fire Trail led off to the right at 7.6, and traces may still be visible.

Reach a junction with the Stoney Indian Pass Trail (which ascends to the left) at 8.6. Keep going straight, descending and crossing Pass Creek, as it tumbles over the colorful red boulders of the Grinnell Formation, at 8.8. Follow the narrow gorge carved by cascades of the Waterton River from 9.1 to 9.5. Cross a side stream at 9.5, just below a small waterfall.

Bear left at a junction at 9.7 and begin a continuous ascent for the next three miles. (An abandoned trail straight ahead continues up the valley.) The Trail is mostly in scrub growth from 10.0 to 11.3. Cross a good creek just below a waterfall, at 10.5, with several smaller seeps or rivulets higher up. Vulture Peak is prominent to the southwest. Climb in subalpine forest from 11.3. Cross a creek (which may be dry in late summer) at 12.1 and again at 12.3. Patches of snow may linger, but should present no difficulty in July.

The Trail reaches the crest of a spur ridge at 13.0. Keep to the right, hiking across delightful grassy slopes to Fifty Mountain Campground at 14.2. (At one time there was a shortcut that bypassed the campground, but it has been blocked off and is no longer in use.) Fifty Mountain Camp has magnificent views—perhaps even 50 summits—as well as good water and some trees for shelter. An intersecting trail from here crosses Flattop Mountain and then descends to Going-to-the-Sun Road in the upper part of the McDonald valley.

Follow the Highline Trail, ascending from Fifty Mountain Camp, through tundra carpeted with glacier lilies. Switchback up to the right at 14.6. (A former bypass trail may be seen joining from the left.)

Come to a small saddle and the Continental Divide, below Mt. Kipp, at 15.2. Mt. Carter, Vulture Peak, Mt. Geduhn, Longfellow Peak, Heavens Peak, and Mt. Cannon, as well as many more mountains, provide an unexcelled panorama. Small snowpatches may be encountered, but again are unlikely to present any difficulty. At the Continental Divide, a

Ahern Drift.

marked trail leads off to the left, ascending 0.4 mile to the Sue Lake Observation Point (elevation 7750, with excellent views of jagged Stoney Indian Peaks and Mt. Merritt, as well as Pyramid Peak and Mt. Cleveland; Sue Lake is directly below.) Continue in open country, overlooking the attractive glacial valley of upper Mineral Creek. Pass another side stream at 16.5.

Beginning at 17.9, make a circuit around Cattle Queen Creek. There are several runoff streams along the way. Cattle Queen Creek itself, at 19.1, may be covered by a snowbank; be careful, as the surface may have been so undercut by the flowing water that it can support little weight. Across the Mineral Creek valley, two impressive high waterfalls can be observed on the flank of Flattop Mountain.

The Trail, having dipped to a low point at 18.8, climbs steadily to 20.5, where it crosses a ridge and starts a three-mile circuit of Ahern Creek. Once again there are fine views of the high peaks in the northwest part of the Park and also mountains to the west and south; the Ahern Drift stands out as a white stripe crossing the cliffs on the far side of the cirque.

A small stream at 21.2 plummets down the hillside over black rock steps, presumably an outcrop of the igneous Purcell Sill. The principal branch of Ahern Creek is at 21.7; here a signed trail leads off to the left 0.4 mile to Ahern Pass (elevation 7100), which looks out over Helen Lake and the Belly River country.

The Trail passes under a sheer cliff at 23.1. The Ahern Drift here is a permanent steep snowbank. Even after it is opened for travel—some time in the first half of July—hikers will need to tread carefully when traversing it. During the summer it is necessary from time to time to cut new crossings as the snow gradually moves down the slope. Leave Ahern Creek basin at 23.4 and continue in open country, crossing a short stretch of talus at 24.2.

With the Granite Park Chalet visible ahead, a side trail descends from a junction at 25.6 to the Granite Park Campground. (It is 0.4 mile to the campground, which is sheltered among scattered trees at an elevation of about 6450 feet; about halfway there you walk to the right of a patrol cabin, where you can obtain water from a reliable creek. To return to the CDT from the campsites, either retrace your steps or continue another 300 yards at contour to an intersection with the Granite Park Trail and then, turning left, climb 0.4 mile to the Highline Trail at the Granite Park Chalet.) Cross a creek at 25.9, passing a onetime—but now closed—route from there to the campground.

Leave the Highline Trail at the junction at 26.0. Turning left, climb in subalpine meadows toward Swiftcurrent Pass. There are flowers aplenty—globeflowers, glacier lilies, springbeauties, cinquefoils, purple mountain heath (a shrub), shootingstars, false asphodel, veronica, Sitka valerian, and penstemons. Along the way you can enjoy the view past the chalet and upper McDonald valley towards snowy Heavens Peak. According to all reports, the 1.4-mile side trip from the junction at 26.6 to Swiftcurrent Lookout (8436 feet) ought not to be missed; its 3000-foot plunge to Windmaker Lake must be a dizzying sight. (An alternative is to continue 8.0 miles on the Highline Trail from Granite Park to Logan Pass, and then descend 4.7 miles along Going-to-the-Sun Road to rejoin the Trail; the alternative is shorter and quicker, but the highway location is undesirable.)

Granite Park Chalet, with Heavens Peak beyond.

A large cairn at 26.7 marks Swiftcurrent Pass. There is no view to the east until about 26.9, where you step over a couple of spring-fed creeks. Drop down into a little basin, where there is a small pond, and boulderhop the shallow creeks there at 27.2. Switchback right at 27.6. Below, you can pick out Many Glacier Hotel on Swiftcurrent Lake, with Lake Sherburne in the valley beyond it and Duck Lake way out in the haze on the plains. Step over the creek at 27.8.

Swing sharply around a spur ridge—called the Devil's Elbow because of the bend and the steep dropoff below—at 28.0; over a thousand feet downhill lies Windmaker Lake. The hillside is rocky, and marmots abound. The Trail descends from here with a series of long switchbacks, starting (just before a pair of high cascading streams) with one to the left at 28.4. Occasionally there are some stunted subalpine fir, but for the most part the terrain is completely open. The grotesquely contorted strata of the headwall are worthy of note

21

at 29.1, where the Trail makes its next switchback to the left. The small lakes strung out in the valley ahead add to the scenic charm.

After reaching the valley floor at 29.6, the route parallels Swiftcurrent Creek for the remainder of the Section. It crosses a couple of side creeks as it circles north of Bullhead Lake. It might be wise to make some noise to alert bears that sometimes frequent the area, as the scrubby growth may block your view until you come upon them; the vegetation consists largely of aspens and small conifers that have grown up since a devastating fire in 1936. A pool of eddying waters—a local ranger called it The Giant Jacuzzi—is at 31.6, just above the pretty cascades of Redrock Falls. A good place to look out over Redrock Lake is at 32.2, where the Trail uses a plank bridge to cross a side stream. The rest of the way, past Fishercap Lake, is of little interest. Pass a register box (and a pack trail to the left) at 33.4. Cross Wilbur Creek, with another bridge, at 33.5.

The footpath ends at Swiftcurrent village at 33.6. On the left are the store, coffee shop, and lodgings. Continue past the parking area toward Many Glacier. The ranger station and campground are off to the right at the side road at 33.8. The Section ends in the picnic area, at the trailhead for the Grinnell Glacier Trail, at 34.1. Grinnell named many park features, including Swiftcurrent Lake, and is memorialized by his Indian appellation—Fishercap—as well as his own proper name. As he wrote with passion, perhaps with this valley in mind:

> "...No words can describe the grandeur and majesty of these mountains, and even photographs seem hopelessly to dwarf and belittle the most impressive peaks."

Distances and elevations are:

0.0	International boundary	4200
0.2		4250
0.4	North Boundary Trail Junction	4200
1.9	Creek	4250
3.1	Waterton River Campground (0.2 mile)	4200
3.2	Boulder Pass Trail Junction	4250
3.5	Waterton River	4250

3.9	Goat Haunt Ranger Station	4200
6.3	Camp Creek	
	(Kootenai Lakes Campground 0.3 mile)	4400
7.6	Trail junction	4450
8.0		4400
8.6	Stoney Indian Pass Trail Junction	4550
8.8	Pass Creek	4500
9.7	Trail junction	4600
10.5	Creek	5250
10.7	Enter Mount Geduhn Quadrangle	5450
12.1	Creek	6450
13.0	Ridge (enter Ahern Pass Quadrangle)	7000
14.2	Fifty Mountain Campground	6700
14.6	Switchback	7000
15.2	Continental Divide (Sue Lake Trail Jct.)	7450
18.8		5800
19.1	Cattle Queen Creek	6000
20.5	Ridge	6800
21.7	Ahern Creek	6650
22.5		6500
23.1	Ahern Drift	6600
23.4	(6765)	6750
23.8		6700
24.1		6800
24.6		6550
25.3		6800
25.6	Trail junction (campground 0.4 mile)	6650
26.0	Swiftcurrent Pass Trail Junction	6750
26.7	Swiftcurrent Pass (7185)	7200
27.2	Basin	6850
27.8	Creek	6550
28.0	Devil's Elbow	6500
28.6	Enter Many Glacier Quadrangle	6000
29.6	Valley floor	5300
31.8	Redrock Lake	5050
32.2	Creek (5078)	5100
33.5	Wilbur Creek (4928)	4950
34.1	Grinnell Glacier Trailhead	4900

Interim (Chief Mountain) Route

The Chief Mountain alternate route has some noteworthy charms—especially the glacier views from Redgap Pass—but, for southbound travelers, its only real advantages are its longer season and convenient access.

You would start at the boundary at the customs station on the Chief Mountain Highway (Mont. 17). The Trail descends a couple of miles, in forest, to the Belly River. It then proceeds up the valley, where meadows often permit you to view sheer-walled mountains, to lovely Elizabeth Lake at 9.8; along the way is Dawn Mist Falls, a cataract of tremendous power. A steady ascent, much of it above timberline, leads to Redgap Pass, at 14.2. The remainder of the Section is pleasant enough, but without distinction. The route makes a wide sweep to the east, to get around Apikuni Mountain; along the way, it descends the valley of Kennedy Creek past Poia Lake, at 20.0, and then crosses low Swiftcurrent Ridge, at 22.3, before dropping to Many Glacier. The Section ends nearby at the Grinnell Glacier Trailhead, at 28.0, where it meets the principal route.

Water crossings should present no problem, as all the larger streams have bridges in place. Snow will persist at Redgap Pass into June, and can be expected again in September, but the grades are moderate and should be easier to negotiate than those south of Many Glacier.

Every party is required to have a permit for each night in the backcountry, and camping is allowed at designated sites only. (In this Section, these are in the lower Belly River valley—at Threemile and the Belly River Ranger Station—and at Elizabeth Lake and Poia Lake.) Through hikers will also be allowed to stay overnight at the developed Many Glacier Campground, near Swiftcurrent at the end of the Section. Permits must be secured ahead of time, as there is no ranger station at the border.

Public transportation (tour bus service) is available each morning—but only during the tourist season—from East Glacier (with a stop at Many Glacier) to the trailhead. (This is the bus that continues to Waterton.) See the introduction, above, to the principal route description for additional information.

U.S.G.S. Maps: **Gable Mountain, Many Glacier,** and **Lake Sherburne.**

Also: our Maps **2** and **3.**

24

Detailed Trail data are:

Welcome to the Continental Divide Trail at the boundary between Canada and the United States. Walk south on the Chief Mountain International Highway (Montana Route 17), passing the U.S. customs station at 0.1. Locate the trailhead at the parking lot, on the west side of the highway, at 0.2. Take the trail toward Belly River, in forest, descending. Walk through a young aspen thicket at 1.0, with views southwest toward Mt. Merritt (10,004 feet).

After crossing several little side creeks on short bridges, reach the valley of the Belly River at 2.2. For hikers, a wooden causeway has been provided across a wet place; there is also a parallel route with a ford, as marked by signs, for use with horses. The valley soon becomes a broad open bottom with a wide path (the Belly River Trail) for travel. It is especially nice once the vegetation turns to grassy meadows (without rank herbs such as cow parsnip), around 3.0.

The small Threemile Campground, along the Belly River, is to the right of the Trail at 3.2. Walk close to the stream, especially near its bends at 3.4 and 3.6. There are some overgrown stretches, but the grassy meadows at 4.1 afford excellent views up both the Belly (south) and Mokowanis (southwest) valleys. Also note landmark Chief Mountain to the east. There are some wooded stretches, with log bridges over side creeks, before the Trail passes within 100 feet of another river bend, at 5.0.

Pass, at 6.1, through an opening in the Belly River Ranger Station perimeter fence. Keep going at the junction at 6.2, where the Cosley Lake Cutoff Trail turns sharp right. Remain to the right of the Ranger Station, outside the fence enclosing its pasture.

After turning the corner of the fence, pass (at 6.5) the side trail that drops to the Belly River Campground along the river's edge; off to the west you have a view of the sheer ramparts of Glacier Park's highest mountain, Mt. Cleveland (10,466 feet). Continue in mixed forest, with minor elevation changes; along with thimbleberry and white geranium, you might watch for queencup, sweetpea, vetch, and—in deep shade by a side creek—a pink pyrola or two. And bunchberry, a diminutive dogwood with showy white bracts, has a limited distribution in Glacier in places such as this.

Turn right at the next junction, at 7.7 (avoiding the route straight ahead to a horse ford), so as to cross the Belly River by suspension bridge at 7.8. Fifty feet past the river, turn left (on the Ptarmigan Trail) toward Elizabeth Lake. The side trail from the horse ford comes up from the left at 8.1, after you've passed a pretty bend in the river.

Dawn Mist Falls soon announces its presence with the roar of rushing water. Don't fail to take the side trail at 8.3, which leads (after 0.1 mile) to its base. Dawn Mist Falls is a greater cataract than any that can be found along the entire length of the proper Continental Divide Trail route—not the highest, perhaps, but the most powerful. The Belly River is about 25 feet wide at the brim of the falls; there the water tumbles about 60 feet in a single leap, with a couple of shorter steps below that. Returning to the main trail, climb in forest (with another view at the top of the falls, at 8.5). You might keep an eye and ear cocked for signs of the winter wren, cedar waxwing, and red-breasted nuthatch as you approach Elizabeth Lake.

The campground at the foot of Elizabeth Lake, at 9.8, has a magnificent view south toward the Ptarmigan Wall; it is a popular spot, so permits may be hard to come by. Turn left at the junction here and continue along the Ptarmigan Trail. Use the suspension bridge, over the calm Belly River, at 9.9. Climb in forest at a moderate grade. With rising elevation there are good views— over Elizabeth toward Helen Lake and Ahern Pass (on the Continental Divide). The scree slope at 11.6, where mountains in every direction tower above you, is a particularly fine vantage point; along with the scrubby aspen you will find stonecrop and spotted saxifrage.

Taking the left fork at the junction at 11.8, continue on the Redgap Pass Trail. (For hikers, though, it would be better to keep right and proceed on the Ptarmigan Trail, through the Ptarmigan Tunnel, to Many Glacier; but here it is assumed that most people taking this route will be traveling during the snowier months, when the Ptarmigan Tunnel is closed.) A snowbank at 12.5 may linger well into July, but should not be an obstacle. The Trail climbs past stunted growth to reach timberline. The gully at 13.3 affords a good chance of finding water; it is spring fed, and you cross it again, after several switchbacks, at 13.6. As can be surmised from the name of the pass ahead—Redgap—the soil and rock all about are rusty in color.

Another several switchbacks lead to the crossing of Redgap Pass at 14.2. The scene to the west is spectacular. Two glaciers are prominent—Ahern on the left and Old Sun (on the slopes of Mt. Merritt). Farther to the right is Mt. Cleveland, with bands of snow along its horizontal rock bands. Elizabeth Lake sits in the valley 2500 feet below, though only its lower half is in clear view. An idol-like rock formation known as Ruggles of Red Gap is said to smile on the west side of the pass, but Ruggles eluded this observer. The flowers sparkle in their customary variety—moss campion, sky pilot, white dryad, fernleaf candytuft, sandwort, mountain forget-me-not, alpine crazyweed, cinquefoil, silky phacelia, and cutleaf daisy among them.

Leaving Redgap Pass, descend gradually along the south slopes of Seward Mountain. The valley ahead is far less interesting than the cirques and glaciers that have been left behind. The dominant feature is Apikuni Mountain—its rounded slopes bare at upper elevations, above the forested bottom of Kennedy Creek below. One nice feature, though, is the view south over the pristine little basin of Kennedy Lake to a snow-capped summit (Mt. Gould, probably) beyond. Water can be obtained from the creek at 14.6. The Trail then switchbacks down the mountainside, soon encountering whitebark pine and subalpine fir. Cross a cascading creek, near the upper end of its falls, at 16.1; and switchback three times over a second creek in the following quarter of a mile.

The Trail levels out by 17.0, on a bench above Kennedy Creek. It continues, dropping slightly more, to the bank of the stream at 17.4. Beavers may have flooded some of the path near here. A log bridge takes you over a side creek at 17.9. Break out of forest at 18.3 and proceed in the open, mostly on well-trodden path through grassy meadows.

After some willow thickets, skirt Poia Lake. Cross its outlet (Kennedy Creek) on a stout bridge at 19.8. Curving to the right, walk along the foot of the lake to the campground at 20.0. The campsite itself is in the trees and not attractive; but there is a nice view from the shore up the valley and to the glacier in the distance beyond Redgap Pass, and you may be serenaded by a shy hermit thrush.

The Trail keeps on going down the valley so as to pass the main mass of Apikuni Mountain. To the left, Kennedy Creek twists and cascades for a bit. Stonecrop, buckwheat, and gray daisies brighten the sunny slope. After passing a beaver pond at 20.7, begin the climb of Swiftcurrent Ridge. Step over a small creek at

21.1. A trail formerly led off to the left at 21.4, but it has been abandoned and is overgrown. The climb includes some short switchbacks, and at one point a nice patch of tall spruces and Douglas firs. Wet spots, where you will find bog-orchids, are crossed on boardwalks at 21.5 and 21.9.

The crest of Swiftcurrent Ridge, at 22.3, lacks a view. You may pause, however, along the shores of Swiftcurrent Ridge Lake, at 22.6 to admire the summits to the south. Continuing around the west end of the lake, at 22.7, drop to a junction at 23.1, where the Sherburne Cutoff Trail forks left. Keep straight, still on the Redgap Pass Trail, largely in meadow and often with good views. Cross permanent Windy Creek on a bridge of logs at 24.5. You might observe a varied thrush in the cottonwoods along the creek. Descend, sometimes in the open. Pass a section with several short boardwalks at 25.3. Gradually converge with the Many Glacier Road, enjoying the views ahead (toward Grinnell Glacier and The Salamander) as well as Lake Sherburne to the left.

Reach the Many Glacier Road at 26.2, the Grinnell Glacier observation point. Continue straight at 27.4, where a side road turns left to the Many Glacier Hotel. Swiftcurrent Lake is to the left for the next quarter of a mile. The Section ends at the picnic area at 28.0; this is also marked as the Grinnell Glacier trailhead. (It is another 0.3 mile on the road to the ranger station and campground, where some spaces are available for through hikers. Just beyond that is Swiftcurrent, with lodging, meals, a store, phones, and laundromat.)

Distances and elevations are:

0.0	International boundary	5300
0.2	Trailhead	5350
2.2	Valley	4550
3.2	Threemile Campground	4600
4.1	Meadow	4700
5.0	River bend	4650
6.2	Cosley Lake Cutoff Trail Junction	4650
6.5	Belly River Campground	4700
7.8	Belly River	4650
8.3	Dawn Mist Falls (0.1 mile)	4700
9.8	Elizabeth Lake Campground	4900

11.8	Redgap Pass Trail Junction	6050
12.5	Enter Many Glacier Quadrangle	6500
13.3	Gully	6850
14.2	Redgap Pass	7550
14.6	Creek	7400
16.1	Creek	6500
17.9	Creek	5900
18.7	Enter Lake Sherburne Quadrangle	5850
20.0	Poia Lake Campground	5800
20.1		5850
20.7	Beaver pond	5500
22.3	Swiftcurrent Ridge	6200
22.6	Swiftcurrent Ridge Lake	6100
23.1	Sherburne Cutoff Trail Junction	5900
24.5	Windy Creek	5400
25.8	Enter Many Glacier Quadrangle	5000
26.2	Many Glacier Road	4900
26.8	(4849)	4850
27.4	Many Glacier Hotel (0.3 mile)	4900
28.0	Grinnell Glacier Trailhead	4900

A rewarding full-day hike awaits the traveler in this Section. The layout is simple—from the Swiftcurrent valley the Trail climbs a high spur ridge and then drops abruptly to the St. Mary drainage. There are opportunities aplenty to enjoy scenery and wildlife, but the absence of authorized campsites dictates a steady pace.

The Section starts out with a long walk, with little rise, up the narrow valley of Cataract Creek. Indeed, falls are especially worthy of note—lacy Feather Plume Falls at 4.4 and the more vigorous Morning Eagle Falls at 5.3. The Trail then climbs with switchbacks, traversing long-lasting snowbanks. The high point, Piegan Pass at 8.6, is hemmed in. The views are better before and after it, especially in the meadows of Preston Park at 10.4. The last part of the Section is a steady descent, in forest, to the Going-to-the-Sun Road (Jackson Glacier Overlook) at 13.3.

Because campsites are unavailable in the Section, the best plan is to spend the night before the hike at Swiftcurrent (either at the Many Glacier Campground or in the cabin or motel lodgings—which are priced moderately in comparison to the elegant Many Glacier Hotel) and then to continue on to camp on Reynolds Creek in Section 3. (Another possibility is to hitchhike to Rising Sun, where lodgings and meals can be obtained; but the inconvenience of getting there hardly justifies the effort. Returning to the Trail from Rising Sun would be easier, as the morning tour bus could drop you off at the trailhead.)

U.S.G.S. Maps: **Many Glacier** and **Logan Pass**.

Also: our Map **3**.

Detailed Trail data are:

Leaving the road at the picnic area east of the Many Glacier Ranger Station, pick up the Grinnell Glacier Trail. Cross Swiftcurrent Creek by bridge at 0.3 and then skirt the south

Lake Josephine.

end of Swiftcurrent Lake. As this is part of a nature trail, common shrubs such as menziesia, alder, and snowberry are identified by signs. Turn left at the boat dock at 0.7, continuing along the lake shore. (*Note:* according to the topographic map, it would be just as convenient to turn right and travel along the west shore of Lake Josephine, then continue to Grinnell Lake, and return to the official trail at 4.4, below Feather Plume Falls.) This leads to a large bridge over Cataract Creek and the junction just beyond it at 0.9. Take the right fork. (The left fork continues around the lake to Many Glacier Hotel.) Walk upstream, intersecting a larger trail, which comes in from the left, at 1.1.

Stump Lake, to the right, is mostly blocked by trees. Remain in the valley at 1.4, where a connecting route turns uphill to the higher branch of the Piegan Pass Trail. There is a fine view of Grinnell Falls and The Salamander at 1.5, where a short side trail bears right to the outlet of Lake Josephine.

Hike well back from the shore, sometimes on boardwalks, occasionally crossing side creeks. Take the left fork (the horse trail) at 2.3, just a hundred yards before the Oastler Shelter (a leanto to provide cover for persons waiting for the Lake Josephine boat). Keep left again in 200 feet (where the right fork continues to Grinnell Glacier) and left again after another 100 feet (at a junction with a cutoff trail that goes downhill to the dock).

Climbing, reach the Piegan Pass Trail at 2.6 and turn right. Head up the valley of Cataract Creek, in forest. Soon there is a view, to the right, of Grinnell Glacier, with the Garden Wall behind it. Farther up the valley, delicate Feather Plume Falls sprays its water in ribbons that drop hundreds of feet down the cliff face. Near the base of these falls, cross a side creek at 4.1 and Cataract Creek at 4.5.

Cross Cataract Creek again at 5.0. (Although there are bridges over Cataract Creek, these are removed during the winter and put back in place after the peak of the snowmelt; early in the season it may be necessary to ford the icy water.) As the Trail approaches impressive Morning Eagle Falls, it switchbacks sharp left. Higher up, where there are several more switchbacks, the route traverses fairly steep slopes; snow will persist into July and then will require some care (perhaps even an ice axe if the surface is hard and icy).

Approaching timberline, boulderhop a fork of Cataract Creek at 6.6. This is a pretty area, with picturesque cascades and chutes along the stream, and with polychromatic rocks—blue, green, orange, and red layers, along with the broad black band of igneous rock that circles around, high on the Garden Wall, beneath the Continental Divide. Continuing climbing, in open terrain, with some smaller creeks and a few switchbacks. The flowers are magnificent, of course—limestone columbine, sky pilot, white dryad, creeping sibbaldia, fernleaf candytuft, moss campion, mountain forget-me-not, and homely buttercups among them. Inspect the basin below carefully; it's a good place to observe mountain goats.

Reach Piegan Pass, in the igneous band, at 8.6. Despite the elevation, snow is unlikely to linger, except in patches, past the end of June. The views at the pass itself are restricted, so follow the footpath as it traverses east beneath Cataract Mountain and Mt. Siyeh. The basin of Siyeh Creek, below, is frequented by bighorn sheep and mountain goats. Around 9.8 you will be able to pick out thin, high Piegan Falls tumbling down the side of Piegan Mountain.

Cross the little log bridge in Preston Park, at 10.4, and then keep straight at the trail junction. (The Siyeh Pass Trail, a high route from St. Mary Lake, joins from the left.) This is the best place to take in Blackfoot Glacier, to the south, though much of it is obscured by the nearer bulk of Citadel Mountain; on the Continental Divide beyond the glacier you can pick out pointed Mt. Logan as well as massive flat-topped Blackfoot Mountain and Mt. Jackson. Walk in forest, with some white-bark pines mixed in with the spruces and firs. A bridge with handrails marks Siyeh Creek, at 10.7, where the water steps down several flat limestone ledges. A large avalanche chute opens the forest at 11.4. Keep descending past the junction at 12.0, where the Siyeh Bend Cutoff Trail turns off to the right. The next mile receives little use and may be poorly maintained.

The Trail tunnels beneath the Going-to-the-Sun Road at 13.2 and then curves left, below the roadway, to the end of the Section, at the Jackson Glacier Overlook, at 13.3.

Distances and elevations are:

0.0	Grinnell Glacier Trailhead	4900
0.9	Cataract Creek	4900
2.6	Piegan Pass Trail Junction	5100
4.5	Enter Logan Pass Quadrangle	5200
5.0	Cataract Creek	5300
6.6	Creek	6300
8.6	Piegan Pass (7570)	7550
10.4	Preston Park (Siyeh Pass Trail Junction)	7000
10.7	Siyeh Creek	6850
12.0	Siyeh Bend Cutoff Trail Junction	6300
13.3	Going-to-the-Sun Road	5250

The Triple Divide—where the watershed of Hudson Bay abuts those of both the Atlantic and the Pacific—is the major landmark of this rugged Section. The terrain is so difficult, in fact, that the route must deviate from the Continental Divide, descending far down into the St. Mary and Cut Bank valleys. Although there are few spectacular vistas, the lakes, waterfalls, flowers, and wildlife make this Section a rewarding one.

From the Jackson Glacier Overlook, the trail descends in forest to the upper end of St. Mary Lake, at 2.4. St. Mary Falls and Virginia Falls are notable attractions of the area. It is then necessary to follow the lakeshore for several miles, as a chain of peaks makes it impractical to turn south any sooner. Circuiting the mountains, the Trail enters the Red Eagle valley, crossing the creek there at 11.4 and reaching Red Eagle Lake at 13.8. After skirting the east shore of the lake, the Trail climbs more than 2500 feet as it ascends the valley of Hudson Bay Creek to Triple Divide Pass at 21.9.

Leaving the Hudson Bay drainage, the Trail descends steadily to the confluence of Atlantic Creek and the North Fork of Cut Bank Creek at 25.1. The remainder of the Section is another climb, with some small lakes along the way, to Pitamakan Pass—on another spur ridge—at 31.2.

Campgrounds have been established at Red Eagle Lake (foot of lake at 13.8, head of lake at 14.7), on Atlantic Creek (24.8), and at Morning Star Lake (27.8). Through hikers from Many Glacier may obtain special authorization to camp along Reynolds Creek, near the start of the Section, at 1.3.

The closest developed facilities are the motel and cabins at Rising Sun (on Going-to-the-Sun Road). Also at Rising Sun are a campground, restaurant, and general store. If space is available, the morning tour bus from Rising Sun will drop you off at the start of the Section.

U.S.G.S. Maps: **Logan Pass**, **Rising Sun**, **Saint Mary**, **Mount Stimson**, and **Cut Bank Pass**.

Also: our Maps **3** and **4**.

Detailed Trail data are:

From the lower end of the Jackson Glacier Overlook, continue on the Piegan Pass Trail in the direction of the Gunsight Pass Trail. Hike downhill through damp forest. At 1.2, the Trail is close to Deadwood Falls, where Reynolds Creek cuts a narrow channel through a resistant band of the Grinnell Formation.

Continue straight at the junction at 1.3, where the Gunsight Pass Trail turns right and promptly crosses the creek. (There is a campsite, just past the bridge, that is reserved for through hikers. It is the only campsite between Many Glacier and Red Eagle Lake; be sure to keep it clean and observe all regulations scrupulously, so as to help ensure its continued availability.)

The footway splits at 2.4, with the path to the left leading back up to the paved road and the one to the right—which is our route—skirting the south shore of St. Mary Lake. Having turned to the right, descend and cross the St. Mary River on a solid wooden bridge at 2.7. Immediately upstream, St. Mary Falls shoots through a red mudstone bed in two powerful fifteen-foot leaps. Early morning should be the best time for pictures.

From 2.9, the Trail closely follows Virginia Creek and passes a series of pretty cascading drops. A sturdy bridge crosses Virginia Creek at 3.4 near the base of Virginia Falls, with a principal drop of about 80 feet. This is another morning photograph shot.

For the next several miles, the Trail (the Saint Mary Lake Trail) contours along the slopes above the lake with little change of elevation. Stretches of Douglas fir woods alternate with open patches overgrown (as this stretch is very lightly traveled) with cow parsnip and other plants, including stinging nettle.

There are two good creeks crossing the Trail—the first at 5.1 (with Going-to-the-Sun Point opposite on the north shore of the lake) and the second at 6.4 where a small shaded island between two forks of the stream makes an inviting spot for a rest.

The Trail is close to St. Mary Lake as it approaches the Narrows. Going-to-the-Sun Mountain is prominent to the west. The long spit extending into the lake is known as Silver Dollar Beach. (There is no obvious access to the spit; a switchback trail which cuts down a scree slope at 7.8 may follow the shore and end up there.)

Passing Silver Dollar Beach at 8.1, the Trail rises and then descends, crossing more scree at 9.1 and 9.3 and approaching the shore closely at 9.5. A few feet out in the lake at 9.6 are the remains of a boat landing. (Before construction of the St. Mary Lake Trail, hikers would arrive here by launch to begin a hike to Red Eagle Lake.) Ducks seen during the summer from this point are probably Barrow's goldeneyes. Although the beach consists of rounded stones rather than sand, the view westward and the pleasant cottonwood shade make this a good lunch stop.

Leaving the shore of St. Mary Lake at the landing, the Trail goes over a ridge into the Red Eagle Creek drainage. After some descent, the Trail approaches Red Eagle Creek and makes a sharp turn to the left at 10.7. (Disregard the former route, now blocked, that descends directly to the stream; fording there could be difficult at times of high water.) Continuing on the designated route, which may be obscure at places, rise a bit to reach a high bluff, overlooking Red Eagle Creek, at 11.1. Descend by switchbacks.

Turn right at the junction at 11.4. Follow the Red Eagle Trail, promptly crossing Red Eagle Creek on a wide bridge. Ascend through alternating stretches of woods and meadows, with occasional minor side creeks.

Reach the foot of Red Eagle Lake, an authorized campsite, at 13.8. The lakeside setting, with precipitous Split Mountain and the Continental Divide as a backdrop, makes this an exceptional place to stop.

Take the Triple Divide Pass Trail around the east shore of Red Eagle Lake to another campground, at its head, at 14.7. As the winding tread emerges from forest at 15.4, enjoy the falls upstream on Red Eagle Creek. Ignore the trail which forks back acutely to the left at 15.5.

Cross Red Eagle Creek by bridge at 15.8. After more bends and a rise of land, cross the creek by bridge a second time at 16.5. Just beyond is a junction with the abandoned Red Eagle Pass Trail.

Red Eagle Lake.

Turn left at the junction and ascend the valley of Hudson Bay Creek. Triple Divide Peak comes into view at the head of the valley. The Trail crosses a creek on a collapsed log at 18.8. The source of the water is a cascade of perhaps a thousand feet down the sheer eastern wall of Split Mountain.

Still ascending, and passing minor creeks, the Trail crosses Hudson Bay Creek at 20.3 by means of a straightforward boulderhop. This is another delightful spot, with several waterfalls dropping into the green basin from the shelf below Norris Mountain.

The Trail continues steeply to Triple Divide Pass, at 21.9. Mountain goats haunt this rugged open terrain. To the right, Triple Divide Peak rises another 600 feet; from its slopes Hudson Bay Creek, Atlantic Creek, and Pacific Creek start their journeys to far-separated waters by way of the Nelson, Mississippi, and Columbia Rivers. To the south, the Continental Divide follows the level top of a long straight cliff which has the fitting name of Razoredge Mountain.

The descent toward Atlantic Creek is a long gradual drop along a narrow footway constructed on the open slopes of

37

Mount James. There are a number of steep creek beds, but some (or all) may be dry. One of the more likely water sources is a spring at 22.1. Medicine Grizzly Lake appears on the floor of the valley far below.

Medicine Grizzly Trail comes in from the right at 24.5. (The former Medicine Grizzly Campground, 1.4 mile by side trail, has been closed because of bear feeding in the area.) Continue straight, passing a campground on Atlantic Creek at 24.8.

Turn right on the Pitamakan Pass Trail at the junction at 25.1. (To the left, it is about four miles to the Cut Bank ranger station and campground.) Cross Atlantic Creek by bridge at 25.4. Atlantic Falls is immediately upstream. Proceed up the valley of the North Fork of Cut Bank Creek. Descend to the meadow at 26.3, passing small creeks there and at 26.9.

After crossing the North Fork at 27.7, follow the east shore of Morning Star Lake. The lake, in a lovely setting beneath steep slopes, is an authorized camping area. Climbing again, approach the creek at a waterfall at 28.7, with several ledges farther upstream. Cross the outlet of Katoya Lake, using logs or boulders, at 28.9.

Reach Pitamakan Lake, a splendid tarn with green meadow and patches of pine and subalpine fir, at 29.8. Above the snowbank on the far shore rises treeless Mt. Morgan on the Continental Divide. Camping is not permitted at this beautiful and fragile spot. Cross the outlet, being sure to obtain water if you intend to continue by way of Dawson Pass. Lake of the Seven Winds lies about 200 feet to the right of the Trail at 30.2, but is not directly accessible.

Pass treeline and switchback up to the trail junction in Pitamakan Pass, at 31.2, on a saddle between Mt. Morgan and a small summit. There are fine views of the valleys—Cut Bank to the north and Dry Fork (and distant plains beyond) to the east. The prominent concave-sloped mountain to the south, on the Continental Divide, is Flinsch Peak.

Distances and elevations are:

0.0	Jackson Glacier Overlook	5250
1.3	Gunsight Pass Trail Junction	4650
1.8	Enter Rising Sun Quadrangle	4600
2.4	Saint Mary Lake Trail Junction	4550

2.7	Saint Mary River (Saint Mary Falls)	4500
3.4	Virginia Creek (Virginia Falls)	4800
		4750
		4850
5.1	Creek	4650
		4800
6.4	Creek	4750
7.2	(4552)	4550
8.6	(4690)	4700
9.6	Red Eagle Landing (St. Mary Quadrangle)	4500
10.3	Ridge	4800
10.7	Sharp turn	4700
11.1		4750
11.4	Red Eagle Trail Junction (Red Eagle Creek)	4600
12.1		4700
12.4	(4673)	4650
13.7	Enter Rising Sun Quadrangle	4800
13.8	Red Eagle Lake (foot)	4750
14.7	Red Eagle Lake (head)	4750
15.8	Red Eagle Creek	4800
16.3	Rise	4900
16.5	Red Eagle Creek (Red Eagle Pass Tr.Jct.)	4850
17.5	Enter Mt. Stimson Quadrangle	5100
18.8	Creek	5300
20.3	Hudson Bay Creek	5900
21.9	Triple Divide Pass (7397)	7400
22.5	Enter Cut Bank Pass Quadrangle	6900
24.5	Medicine Grizzly Trail Junction	5450
24.8	Atlantic Creek Campground	5450
25.1	Pitamakan Pass Trail Junction	5350
25.4	Atlantic Creek	5350
26.1		5500
26.3	Meadow	5450
27.6		5800
27.7	North Fork, Cut Bank Creek	5750
27.8	Morning Star Lake	5750
28.9	Katoya Creek	6350
29.8	Pitamakan Lake	6800
30.2	Lake of the Seven Winds	7000
31.2	Pitamakan Pass	7600

Flinsch Peak. From Mt. Morgan, the Trail follows the crest of the Continental Divide along the ridge at the left of the picture.

GLACIER NATIONAL PARK SEGMENT
Section 4
PITAMAKAN PASS TO TWO MEDICINE
Recommended (Dawson Pass) Route: 10.6 Miles
Designated (Dry Fork) Route: 8.5 Miles

This is the Continental Divide Trail as we like to imagine it—a thin line at the very crest of the continent, with breathtaking vistas from a perch just below the clouds. This magnificent route is not the official one, though, as it is always closed to horses; and, when snow conditions or bad weather are a factor it is not good for hikers either. (The alternate route, described below, is the officially-designated location.)

The first part of the Section gives it its distinction—along the rocky west slopes of Mt. Morgan and Flinsch Peak and the narrow hogback between them. The Trail leaves the Divide at Dawson Pass at 3.5. After descending steeply to upper Two Medicine valley, it skirts the north shore of Two Medicine Lake to 10.0, where it meets the alternate route. The Trail then follows a paved campground road to the end of the Section, at the Two Medicine Road, at 10.6.

The one backcountry campground in the Section is at No Name Lake (on a short spur from the Trail at 5.5). However, through hikers who are continuing on to East Glacier can arrange to include a pleasant overnight stop at the Two Medicine Campground in their permit. Apart from snowmelt, which is not always available, water may not be found before the side creek at 5.7.

Tour buses run twice a day, in each direction, between Two Medicine and East Glacier. There are no lodgings at Two Medicine—but you will find, in addition to the ranger station and campground, a general store (with snack bar).

U.S.G.S. Maps: **Cut Bank Pass**, **Mount Rockwell**, and **Squaw Mountain**.

Also: our Map **5**.

Detailed Trail data are:

Beginning at Pitamakan Pass, take the Dawson Pass Trail, which ascends to the right. Bear slightly left at the trail

41

junction at 0.2. (Straight ahead a track leads to Cut Bank Pass and continues to the Nyack valley by way of a steep scree-covered descent; though little used these days, the path was once the Indians' principal route of travel across the Continental Divide.)

Reach Pitamakan Overlook on the Continental Divide at 0.5. This is the highest point on the Continental Divide Trail in Glacier National Park. It is also an exceptional viewpoint. Triple Divide Peak is clearly visible, partially obscuring Mt. Siyeh. Beyond Tinkham Mountain in the foreground, the spectacle to the west includes Blackfoot Mountain, Mt. Thompson, 10,142-foot Mt. Stimson (second highest in the Park), and flat-topped Mt. Pinchot.

The Trail contours along the northwest slope of Mt. Morgan, possibly affording a chance to view the fleet prairie falcon. Coming around the west spur of the mountain at 1.0, abruptly change direction and head southeast. The upper Nyack valley and the spire of Mt. St. Nicholas are notable new landmarks.

Between 1.5 and 1.9, the Trail lies on or close to the Continental Divide in the saddle separating Mt. Morgan and Flinsch Peak. To avoid sharp drops, the Trail sometimes stays to the right (west) side of the ridge. Continuing around the west slope of Flinsch Peak, the Trail gradually ascends on narrow rocky footing until it again reaches the Divide at 2.9. The peaks around Mt. St. Nicholas are especially prominent.

Descend by switchbacks and reach Dawson Pass at 3.5. Here leave the Continental Divide, and descend eastward toward the Bighorn Basin. Farther on, Two Medicine Lake can be seen curving around the base of Rising Wolf Mountain. The grade is quite steep for the first mile. At 5.5, a trail leads 0.1 mile to the right to No Name Lake, where there is a campground. Starting at 5.7, cross several small creeks that lie quite close together. Pass Pumpelly Pillar, which rises just to the right of the Trail, and leave the Bighorn Basin.

Take the left fork, continuing in forest on the Dawson Pass Trail, at the junction at 6.9. (The trail to the right follows the south shore of Two Medicine Lake instead of the north shore, is less direct, and has a bit of climbing.) Cross a small creek at 7.7. Beyond the lake, come to a fork at 9.8. (The right fork is a shortcut to the campground by way of a knee-deep horse ford.) Take the left fork and continue around Pray Lake.

Intersect the alternate route at the junction at 10.0. Turn right and cross a concrete and wood bridge over Two Medicine Creek. From the bridge, continue around Pray Lake to the paved road that runs through the vast Two Medicine Campground. The horse ford is on the right at 10.4. Follow the road past the picnic area to the ranger station, at 10.6.

The Section ends, a few feet farther on, at the junction with Two Medicine Road. (To the right, 250 yards away, is the Two Medicine General Store, which carries a line of hikers' foods and other supplies. There is counter service, limited pretty much to hot dogs and pie. The store commands a magnificent view past Two Medicine Lake up to the Continental Divide.)

Distances and elevations are:

0.0	Pitamakan Pass	7600
0.2	Trail junction	7700
0.5	Pitamakan Overlook	8100
1.0	Contour Mt. Morgan	8000
1.5	Continental Divide	7950
1.9	Continental Divide	7850
2.0		7900
2.2	Enter Mount Rockwell Quadrangle	7800
2.9	Continental Divide	7950
3.5	Dawson Pass (7598)	7600
5.5	No Name Lake Trail Junction	6000
5.7	Creeks	5900
6.9	Trail junction	5250
7.2		5200
7.7	Creek	5250
8.0		5200
8.2		5250
9.4	Enter Squaw Mountain Quadrangle	5200
10.0	Pitamakan Pass Trail Junction	5150
10.6	Two Medicine Road (5199)	5200

Designated (Dry Fork) Route

This designated route involves a nice walk down the narrow Dry Fork valley. It is well sheltered and usable in June and into the fall, when the more exposed Dawson Pass route may be hazardous.

The Section begins with a switchbacking descent to the cirque at the head of Dry Fork. The Trail then drops down the valley, much of it burned in a 1929 fire, through alternating patches of forest and meadow. After crossing Dry Fork at 5.7, it rises over a low ridge to 7.9, where it meets the recommended route, continuing then through the developed campground to the Two Medicine Road at 8.5.

There is a scenic backcountry campsite, at Oldman Lake (a detour from the Trail at 1.6). See the introductory text for the recommended route for additional information concerning Two Medicine.

U.S.G.S. Maps: **Cut Bank Pass, Kiowa,** and **Squaw Mountain.**

Also: our Map 5.

Detailed Trail data are:

The designated route descends from Pitamakan Pass, with long switchbacks, reaching (at 1.3) the cirque of Oldman Lake at the head of Dry Fork. A side trail to the right, at 1.6, leads (in 500 yards) to the campsite on Oldman Lake. It is worth a detour to visit, even if you do not plan to camp there, for the lakeside view of towering Flinsch Peak. You can then rejoin the main trail (after another 1000 yards) at a junction at 2.2.

Continue down the valley, among the firs and whitebark pines, on excellent footpath, with occasional creeks. The gully at 2.9, a tumble down contorted layers of red shale, is a curiosity; likely to be dry in the morning, it turns into a graceful cascade as the midday sun melts the snow in the basin above it.

Much of the valley is open, affording further fine views back toward Flinsch Peak and Mt. Morgan. The Trail keeps well up the hillside, but the 25-foot falls of Dry Fork are clearly in sight, to the right, at 4.3. Use a short plank bridge, at 4.5, to cross a side creek that rushes down a slickrock chute. There are several more side creeks, as the Trail keeps descending at an easy grade through alternating bands of young lodgepole and meadow; the largest of these, at 5.6, is fed by some waterfalls off to the left.

Turn right at the signed junction and follow the path, to the right, to cross Dry Fork on a narrow bridge, with handrail, at 5.7. The cottonwoods, winding stream, and pyramidal mountains make a pleasant prospect upstream. In the gravel along the creek you can find both whiteleaf and silky phacelia, showy Jacob's-ladder, yarrow, field chickweed, stonecrop, woolly groundsel, sandwort, and sticky cinquefoil.

Leaving the valley at 6.3, climb to a bench at 6.6. Step over a small creek here; high to the right is a narrow waterfall that, in a few leaps, drops down the thousand-foot rock wall from hidden Sky Lake. Cascading Two Medicine River, and Lower Two Medicine Lake, are on the left as the Trail swings clockwise at 7.0. After descending nearly to the water, go over one more rise before reaching the signed junction, at 7.9, with the recommended route from Dawson Pass. Turn left, crossing Two Medicine River on a bridge after 200 feet. There turn right and follow the paved campground road along the water, to the Two Medicine Ranger Station, at 8.5. The Section ends at the road junction here. To the right 250 yards is the Two Medicine General Store, where you can obtain snacks, film, and a limited supply of groceries. The view up Two Medicine Lake is imposing.

Distances and elevations are:

0.0	Pitamakan Pass	7600
1.6	Trail junction (Oldman Lake 0.3)	6800
2.2	Trail junction (Oldman Lake 0.6)	6500
4.5	Creek	5700
5.7	Dry Fork	5500
5.9	Enter Kiowa Quadrangle	5500
6.3		5450
6.6	Bench	5550
7.3	Enter Squaw Mountain Quadrangle	5300
7.7		5150
7.8		5200
7.9	Dawson Pass Trail Junction	5150
8.5	Two Medicine Road (5199)	5200

GLACIER NATIONAL PARK SEGMENT
Section 5
TWO MEDICINE TO EAST GLACIER PARK
10.4 Miles

The Trail from Two Medicine to East Glacier Park is an easy one-day hike. It is a marked contrast to the previous sections, being relatively dry and overlooking the flat plains to the east.

The Section starts at the Two Medicine Road, at the ranger station. Leaving the road at 0.3, the Trail climbs with long switchbacks and gains 2200 feet of elevation over the next three miles. From the high point, there are excellent views over Two Medicine Lake.

After following the open top of a prominent ridge down to 5.2, the Trail descends more gradually, leaving Glacier National Park at 6.9. After Bald Hill (7.4), the route follows a mixture of jeep tracks, dirt roads, and trail. The lack of signs outside the Park can result in some confusion. The populated portion of East Glacier begins at 10.0; the East Glacier Ranger Station, which is not on the Trail, is 0.3 mile away. The Trail skirts the west edge of the Glacier Park Lodge golf course and drops down to cross Midvale Creek on a bridge at 10.4, at the end of the Section.

Although camping is not restricted outside the Park boundary, most parties cross the entire Section without stop. In any event, the absence of water between Two Medicine and Fortymile Creek (5.5) makes most of the Section unsuitable for camping. It is advisable to carry a good drinking supply from Two Medicine.

East Glacier is on the main Amtrak line between Chicago and Seattle, with daily train service in each direction. During the summer, scenic tour buses connect East Glacier with Two Medicine and other points in the Park as well as Waterton Townsite in Canada.

East Glacier offers a wide range of tourist services. The elegant Glacier Park Lodge provides the most convenient lodging; more simple accommodations are available in the center of East Glacier. Other facilities in the village are groceries, laundry, shower (at trailer campground), post office, and various shops. As mentioned above, there is a ranger station (on State Route 49) half a mile north of the Lodge and center of town. Additional services are available in the town of Browning, site of the Blackfoot Museum, 12 miles to the northeast by road.

The campground is the only place to spend the night at Two Medicine. (To assure space, through hikers should include a stop there in the permit obtained before setting out.) The general store at Two Medicine carries a line of trail foods and has limited counter service.

U.S.G.S. Maps: **Squaw Mountain** and **East Glacier Park**.

Also: our Map **5**.

Detailed Trail data are:

The Section starts at the entrance to Two Medicine Campground. Head east, away from the lake, on Two Medicine Road. Canteens should be filled before setting out, as there is no water on the mountain until Fortymile Creek (at 5.5). Appistoki Creek is a few yards to the right of the road at 0.2. Turn right on a service road at 0.3; and then, after 50 feet, immediately turn left and enter the signed trail toward Scenic Point and East Glacier.

A short side trail continues ahead, from a junction at 0.8; it leads to Appistoki Falls. Bear left at this junction, and soon pass an overlook over the narrow gorge of Appistoki Creek. Ascend with long switchbacks. Gnarled limber pine and low mats of common juniper will be encountered from 1.6 on. With increasing elevation, the views back across Two Medicine Lake toward Dawson Pass and the peaks on and beyond the Continental Divide become continuously more impressive. Much of the terrain is completely open, so the vista is unobstructed.

The Trail reaches a ridge at 2.9 and stays a few yards to the right of the crest. Sky pilot, stonecrop, forget-me-not, lupine, and many other flowers line the way. The Trail, marked with some small cairns, contours to the north of a minor summit at 3.2 and then continues on the top of a spur leading to the jutting prominence of Scenic Point. Very suddenly, the panorama of the endless plains to the east comes into view.

At 3.7, Scenic Point is about 300 yards up the hill to the left; from its summit, you can enjoy a last view of Two Medicine and the Glacier high country. Follow a long curving shoulder that descends to the east. After approaching a headwater stream at 5.0 and 5.2, the Trail reaches thicket-lined Forty-mile Creek at 5.5. This is the first good water supply since Two Medicine.

Cross Fortymile Creek on a log bridge and ascend slightly, passing a high point under The Head (the northeast buttress of Bison Mountain) at 5.9. Follow an eroded trail through open country down toward Fortyone Mile Creek. Cross the creek at 6.7 on a log bridge and continue through aspen, lodgepole, and spruce woods.

Beyond the Glacier National Park boundary, at 6.9, the Trail continues in the Blackfeet Indian Reservation. A beaver pond is to the right at 7.2. At 7.4, the Trail comes to the edge of Bald Hill near its open top, with views to East Glacier and the mountains of the Lewis and Clark National Forest south of the Park. Here an obscure trail turns to the right and climbs slightly before rejoining the principal route.

After a short fairly steep descent down Bald Hill, the Trail becomes a jeep track and then an ungraded dirt road. At an open field with a lone aspen, at 8.5, take the trail that turns right and leaves the road. Descend through pleasant aspen-lodgepole woods with a small creek to the right. Look for the orange metal blazes along the way, especially at the junctions at 8.9 and 9.0 where there are alternate paths off to the left. (Consult the topographic map if the blazes have disappeared.)

The Trail reaches a graded dirt road at 9.7, at a prominent sign indicating a route to Scenic Point and Two Medicine. Follow this road to the left along a fenced field. At the first intersection, mile 10.0, turn right on Clarke Drive, passing private residences. (If proceeding to the ranger station, continue straight to Montana Highway 49 instead of turning right; the office is in the second block south on the highway.) Squaw Mountain, to the right, is named for the Old Squaw rock formation on the talus slopes below the summit; from this perspective you might imagine her, with a papoose on her back, to be scanning the scene to the south.

The Glacier Park Lodge golf course is on the left at 10.2. Past the golf course, at 10.3, you can walk up to Glacier Park Lodge; from there it is 300 yards to East Glacier Park, using the Highway 49 underpass under the Burlington Northern tracks. Descend along the dirt road, crossing Midvale Creek on a bridge at 10.4, the end of the Section.

Distances and elevations are:

0.0	Two Medicine Road (5199)	5200
0.3	Trailhead	5250
0.8	Appistoki Falls Trail Junction	5450
2.9	Ridge	7250
3.2	High point of Section	7450
3.8	Scenic Point (summit 7522)	7400
5.5	Fortymile Creek	6000
5.9		6150
6.7	Fortyone Mile Creek	5750
6.9	Park boundary	5700
7.4	Bald Hill	5500
8.5	Trail cutoff from road	5200
8.9	Enter East Glacier Park Quadrangle	5100
9.7	Graded dirt road (4865)	4850
10.0	Road intersection	4850
10.4	Midvale Creek	4750

GLACIER NATIONAL PARK SEGMENT
Section 6
EAST GLACIER PARK TO MARIAS PASS (U.S. 2)
14.4 Miles

This Section has none of the grandeur of the more northern portions of Glacier National Park. The Trail gets relatively little use and in parts is badly overgrown. Still, it provides a serviceable connection between East Glacier Park and the Continental Divide to the south of U.S. Highway 2.

From East Glacier, the route heads southwest toward Squaw Mountain, entering the park at 2.0 on the Autumn Creek Trail. From 3.8, where a side trail leads off to the higher open slopes of Squaw Mountain, to the intersection with the Firebrand Pass Trail at 6.7, the route is sometimes obscure as it passes through interspersed woods and meadows with rank vegetation. It continues by contouring along the flanks of Calf Robe Mountain and Summit Mountain, generally in forest. The Section ends on the Divide, at Marias Pass, at 14.4.

As it is reasonably short and involves little climbing, the Section requires less than a day to complete. There are no authorized campsites, and for that matter it would be hard to find any place that one would like to pitch a tent. Plan to spend the night before the hike in or very near East Glacier Park (as discussed in the text) and then go on at least as far as Marias Pass the next day.

The two branches of Railroad Creek (at 5.2 and 5.3) are the only reliable water sources for the first several miles, so a canteen would be welcome. Beyond Railroad Creek, water should be readily available.

See the introduction to Section 5 for information concerning services and transportation at East Glacier Park.

U.S.G.S. Maps: **East Glacier Park**, **Squaw Mountain**, and **Summit**.

Also: our Map **6**.

Detailed Trail data are:

The Section begins at the vehicular bridge crossing Midvale Creek, behind and below Glacier Park Lodge. There are no signs to point the way. So, upon crossing the bridge, bear left and rise to 0.1, and there locate an orange blaze (tacked to a tree) on the right side of the road. The Trail leaves the road here and proceeds along the path to the west.

It would be possible to spend the night in this area—either where the Trail leaves the road at 0.1 or a bit farther on, in the extensive meadows at 0.3. (If you do camp, it would be prudent to secure water from a safe source—not Midvale Creek.)

Walk through the flat meadows at 0.3. Take the left fork where the tread divides at 0.5. (The right fork leads, after 0.3 mile, to Midvale Creek.) Continue on unused road, climbing slightly and passing to the left of a beaver pond at 1.3.

Enter Glacier National Park at 2.0. Where a side road turns right through the lodgepole forest near here, continue straight on the Autumn Creek Trail. The wide path—a fire road or former logging road—ends at 3.3. The Trail bears to the right and ascends somewhat more steeply.

Keep going straight, on the less used path, at 3.8. (The more heavily used route makes a right-angle bend to the right toward the open slopes of Squaw Mountain, from which good vistas can be obtained.)

The next three miles may be hard going. Dense patches of cow parsnip, as well as other tall growth, may cover the tread and require some effort to negotiate. The Trail may be completely obscured for short stretches, and blazes or posts to point the way may be few and far between.

Cross the north and south forks of Railroad Creek at 5.2 and 5.3, respectively, just above their confluence. Railroad Creek is the first reliable water supply since East Glacier Park. Boulderhop the two forks and proceed, after a short switchback, with little elevation change.

Turn left at the junction in the meadows at 6.7. Continue from here on the merged Firebrand Pass and Autumn Creek Trails. (To the right, Firebrand Pass is 2.4 miles.)

Make a sharp right bend at the junction at 7.5, continuing on the Autumn Creek Trail. (The Firebrand Pass Trail descends straight ahead, reaching U.S. Highway 2 in 1.6 miles.) Walk in forest, with frequent metal blazes to mark the way. Cross a number of small creeks, including Coonsa Creek at 7.8. There is little of special note, but one landmark is at 9.3, where the Trail (in meadow) crosses a creek just below a miniature waterfall. Then, after a climb, the route passes the confluence of two forks of another small creek—again, in a meadow—at 10.0. Off to the left lies the long valley of the South Two Medicine River.

The remainder of the Section trends downhill, still mostly in forest and with frequent rivulets draining from the Continental Divide above. You may recognize one of these creeks, at 10.6, by walking along it a few feet before dipping down to cross it and then rising on its far bank. There are some wet spots not far beyond, where you might watch for green bog-orchid and blue camas. After descending some more, switch-back left at 11.5 and walk downhill along another creek; bend right and cross it without difficulty at 11.7, directly below Summit Mountain (which is visible upstream). The route continues with little elevation change, with occasional meadows and more small creeks.

Keep straight at the junction with the Summit Trail at 13.2. (Leave the Autumn Creek Trail, which turns right and proceeds west.) This is a remarkable point on the Continental Divide, which drops down to low Marias Pass instead of following the high ridges along the skyline. Follow the Divide, aiming southeast and descending a bit through stands of beargrass to Three Bears Lake at 13.6. The low dike at the west end separates the Atlantic-bound lake waters from the creek, just a few feet away, that flows to the South Seas. Keep straight at 14.0, along a wide abandoned road, as a snowmobile trail crosses at an angle. Enter Marias Pass, where a sign marks the trailhead, at 14.3. Turn left and walk 200 feet along the railroad tracks to an orange blaze on a tree on the park boundary. Cross the tracks and reach U.S. 2, atop the Continental Divide, at 14.4. A tall granite obelisk on the south side of the highway memorializes the contributions of Theodore Roosevelt to the conservation of America's forests. Alongside is a statue of John Stevens, who established the existence of this low crossing of the Rocky Mountains.

Distances and elevations are:

0.0	Midvale Creek	4750
0.1	Trailhead	4800

0.5	Trail divides	4850
1.3	Beaver pond	5000
1.5	Enter Squaw Mountain Quadrangle	5050
2.0	Glacier National Park boundary	5150
3.3	Road end	5450
3.8	Squaw Mountain side trail	5750
5.2	Railroad Creek, north fork	5450
5.3	Railroad Creek, south fork	5450
5.4		5550
5.5		5500
5.9		5550
6.7	Firebrand Pass Trail Junction	5500
7.0		5450
7.3		5550
7.5	Firebrand Pass Trail Junction	5500
7.8	Coonsa Creek	5500
8.0	Enter Summit Quadrangle	5550
9.3	Creek	5750
10.0	Creeks	5950
11.7	Creek	5500
13.2	Summit Trail Junction	5400
13.6	Three Bears Lake	5300
14.4	Marias Pass (U.S. 2)	5250

BOB MARSHALL WILDERNESS SEGMENT
Section 1-A
MARIAS PASS (U.S.2) TO NORTH BADGER CREEK
Interim (Valley) Route: 17.1 Miles
Designated (Divide) Route: 15.1 Miles

When the designated route is actually located and marked, this Section should prove to be an excellent skyline hike, with fine panoramas. In the interim, though, the Trail climbs, quite pleasantly, up the wooded valley of a mountain stream.

The interim Trail starts in Marias Pass, on U.S. Highway 2, and crosses over a minor ridge to ford the South Fork of the Two Medicine River, at Sawmill Flats, at 2.5. The travelway proceeds up the winding valley, with additional fords (which could prove to be difficult in spring, when the snow is melting). Whiterock Creek Camp, at 11.0, is a good place to spend the night. Beyond an inconspicuous divide at 11.5, the Trail dips to the Badger Guard Station, at 12.8. It then forks off to the right, ascending the valley of North Badger Creek to 17.1, where the designated route will meet it.

The Section is closed to vehicles (except for a bit near Sawmill Flats). It receives little backpacking use, because of the distance between U.S. 2 and the popular parts of the Bob Marshall Wilderness. There does seem to be a fair amount of horse travel, though, on the valley trails, which are in good condition.

The Section is situated in the Rocky Mountain Ranger District of the Lewis and Clark National Forest. Water is readily available, and it should not be difficult to find a satisfactory place to camp. (No camping is permitted, though, in the immediate vicinity of the Badger Guard Station.)

Hiking from U.S. 2 to Benchmark, at the end of the Segment, should take about nine or ten days at a moderate pace, so a heavy pack will be required at the outset. For that reason, it might be helpful to do the section from East Glacier Park to Marias Pass as a day hike, unencumbered, and then start out afresh from Marias Pass the next day. (Unfortunately there is no public transportation, but if you stay at a motel the proprietor may offer to give you a lift.)

U.S.G.S. Maps: **Summit**, **Hyde Creek**, and **Crescent Cliff**.

Also: our Map **7**.

Detailed Trail data are:

Beginning at the crest of Marias Pass, walk a bit east to enter the Summit Campground. Take the first campground road to the left and follow it until, at 0.3, it hairpins back around to the right. From this point, the route (marked by a post) is a foot trail, Summit Cutoff Trail No. 133. After 200 feet, step over a little creek. Take the right fork at the trail junction at 0.4 and climb moderately. The Trail, reaching a bench at 0.7, merges with a cleared pipeline swath. Pick up a jeep trail here and follow it east as it angles right, crossing the pipeline, reentering forest before 0.8. The path, a former logging road, splits and then rejoins between 0.8 and 0.9, dipping a couple of times at small drainages. A side trail (a shortcut to U.S. 2) is supposed to take off to the left near the small meadow at 1.4, but it was not observed. Descending, come to a signed junction in the meadow at 2.0. (Elk Calf Mountain Trail No. 137 joins from the right; it's a viewless up and down slog and should be avoided at all costs.)

Descend to reach Sawmill Flats—the broad bottom along the South Fork of the Two Medicine River—at 2.5. Ford the stream, which in July is likely to be about a foot deep and up to 15 feet wide. Angle right toward the upper end of the meadow, at 2.6, intersecting the old road that runs up and down the valley. (Jeep traffic is now prohibited.) Follow the path—Two Medicine Trail No. 101—through lodgepole pine forest. There are some pretty viewpoints between 2.6 and 3.0, a stretch in which the South Fork, joined by the tumbling waters of Pike Creek, cascades down a narrow gorge. A pipe barrier formerly gated the road at 3.1.

There are frequent fords as the Trail heads upstream, starting with crossings at 4.0 and 4.2. (*Note:* according to reports, no more fords are required after 4.2. There is said to be a marked route that leaves the valley at 4.5 and contours along the hillside above the right, i.e. north, bank for the next two miles; the author missed that route and suspects that others, as well, may do so.) Don't be too concerned if you lose track of any marks: just keep following the river farther upstream, fording several times, particularly where the slopes drop down steeply all the way to water level. This will lead you back to the north bank by 6.4. (At 6.8, Trail No. 136 should turn right, heading west toward Elkcalf Mountain, but the junction was not observed.) The travelway will be recognized beyond here as a onetime jeep road. Pass a small side creek at 7.3.

Proceed through the fence gate, at 8.4, to the trail junction 50 yards beyond it. (This is the south terminus of the miserable Elk Calf Mountain Trail No. 137—which crosses the river but, contrary to the maps, does not climb Elkcalf Mountain.) Continue ahead on the jeep road. Pass a creek (actually, it's the East Fork of the river) at 8.8. At 9.6, a brief crossing can be avoided by following the footpath on the right (north) bank. There are small ponds in a marshy area to the right of the Trail at 10.5.

Come to Whiterock Creek Camp (a good campsite, with ample room for several parties) at 11.0. Here cross Whiterock Creek and continue straight on jeep trail, ascending through mixed fields and woods and reaching the high point on the divide between the Two Medicine and Badger drainages at 11.5.

After passing a wet area (off to the right), the Trail reaches a signed jeep road intersection at 12.2. Continue on Trail No. 101, bearing right. (The left fork is Trail No. 102, the Little Badger Creek Trail, which goes to Palookaville by way of Whiterock Creek.)

Badger Guard Station, a locked cabin, is on the left at 12.8. Camping is not permitted nearby.

Leave Trail No. 101, which passes through the guard station grounds. Instead, continue on the jeep road, going through a barbed wire fence and proceeding ahead on Trail No. 103, the North Badger Trail. Cross a small creek. As you travel, enjoy the pleasant views overlooking the Badger valley to the southeast.

At 13.0, the dirt road forks. Take the right fork, ascending slightly through a field. The signed Lee Creek Trail No. 141 is an obscure footpath which takes off to the right at 13.4. Continue on the jeep road, which crosses Lee Creek at 13.8 and swing back to the left.

Descend toward North Badger Creek and the talus slopes of rugged Goat Mountain ahead. (The Goat Mountain area may contain valuable oil or gas resources, and proposed exploration there is a matter of controversy as of this writing). A camp could be made as the trail turns up the valley. For a short distance, at 14.6, follow an axe-blazed path to avoid a wet spot in the road. After passing a pole fence, approach North Badger Creek closely at a rocky overlook at 15.8, below the cliffs of Running Owl Mountain. This is a pleasant rest stop, and just about the only good view up and down North Badger Creek. The scramble down to the creek to get water is quite steep, so caution should be exercised. With luck, a golden eagle may be seen soaring along the cliffs above the Trail.

The interim route terminates at the trail junction at 17.1, where Kip Creek Trail No. 142 (designated to be the future CDT route) ascends the slope to the right.

Distances and elevations are:

0.0	Marias Pass (U.S. 2)	5250
0.3	Trailhead	5250
0.7	Pipeline	5450
1.4	Meadow	5500
2.0	Elk Calf Mountain Trail (137) Junction	5300
2.5	Sawmill Flats (South Fork, Two Medicine River)	5050
4.2	South Fork, Two Medicine River (5184)	5200
6.6	Enter Hyde Creek Quadrangle	5350
8.4	Elk Calf Mountain Trail (137) Junction	5500
8.8	East Fork, Two Medicine River	5550
9.6	Bypass ford	5600
11.0	Whiterock Creek Camp (5749)	5750
11.5	Two Medicine-Badger Divide	5800
12.2	Little Badger Creek Trail (102) Junction	5700
12.8	Badger Guard Station	5500
13.4	Lee Creek Trail (141) Junction	5600
13.9	Enter Crescent Cliff Quadrangle	5500
14.4	Enter North Badger valley	5350
15.8	Overlook	5500
17.1	Kip Creek Trail (142) Junction	5700

Designated (Divide) Route

This should be a very fine Section, especially along the skyline south of Elkcalf Mountain. The description is based upon detailed planning maps prepared by the Lewis and Clark National Forest, not personal observation. Even though the designated route is more direct than the interim route, don't expect to save any time by following it. (There is some question whether—in view of concerns recently expressed by members of the Blackfeet Nation—the designated route will ever be constructed.)

From Marias Pass, the Trail will climb past the first minor summit, Flattop Mountain, skirting a little pond (probably the best campsite) at 2.2. It will reach the Continental Divide at 2.9 and follow it south, often on the actual crest, beyond Elkcalf Mountain. Once past Running Crane Mountain, the route will leave the Divide at 10.1 and descend to the headwaters of Lee Creek, at 11.4, perhaps the first source of water in nine miles. It will then turn south, rising over a low spur ridge before dropping down to North Badger Creek, and the intersection with the interim route, at 15.1.

As the Section tracks the Continental Divide at the outset, portions lie in both the Hungry Horse Ranger District of the Flathead National Forest (west slope) and the Rocky Mountain Ranger District of the Lewis and Clark National Forest (east slope).

U.S.G.S. Maps: **Summit, Hyde Creek,** and **Crescent Cliff.** Also: our Map 7.

Detailed Trail data are:

The Section starts at the crest of Marias Pass. Proceed south, climbing to the dirt Pike Creek Road at 0.3. Cross the road and climb, fairly steeply at places, to a bench at 0.8. Continue with little elevation change to a small creek at 1.2, after which the Trail climbs once again. Disregard the road that intersects the route at 1.3; just keep climbing.

Watch for the junction, at 1.9, where there are two options—straight (along the Divide over Flattop Mountain) or angling to the right and traversing below Flattop. The CDT takes the tread to the right, so as to skirt a pond (campsite) at 2.2. The route then ascends along the west slopes of Flattop, converging with the Divide and the alternate trail, at 2.9. Keep to the left of the next knoll, to a saddle at 3.4.

The Trail follows the well-defined ridgeline of the Divide east toward Elkcalf Mountain, but then at 4.2 contours around on the Flathead (west) side of the summit. Return to the crest at 4.7, at the head of the Townsend Creek basin, and descend to a gap at 5.5. Continue the pleasant hike, with easy grades, mostly just to the west of the crest. There is a high point at 6.7, with switchbacks before and then after it, dropping to a narrow gap at 7.6. After skirting a knoll to the top of a headwall, bypass the next high summit by contouring to 9.3; similarly, from there to 10.1, contour around Running Crane Mountain. (Each of these contours is to the west, as the eastern side is nothing but cliffs.)

Leave the Continental Divide at 10.1, at the head of Sidney Creek. Following the general southeast course of the mountain, angle gradually downhill to cross little Lee Creek, where water can be obtained, at 11.4. Turn right at 11.8, at the junction with Lee Creek Trail No. 141. Climb to the saddle between Bullshoe Mountain and Running Owl Mountain, at 12.1, where the tread becomes Kip Creek Trail No. 142. Descend in the Kip Creek drainage, at first fairly steeply and then at a moderate grade, crossing feeder creeks at 12.5 and again at 14.0 and another one at 14.5. The Section ends at the junction with North Badger Trail No. 103, at 15.1, in the deep valley of North Badger Creek.

Distances and elevations are:

0.0	Marias Pass (U.S. 2)	5250
0.3	Pike Creek Road	5300
1.3	Road	5700
1.9	Trail junction	6250
2.1		6300
2.2	Pond	6250
2.5	Flattop Mountain (summit 6650)	6550
2.9	Trail junction	6450
3.1		6550
3.4	Saddle	6450
4.5	Elkcalf Mountain (summit 7607)	7250
5.5	Gap	6900

6.7	High point (summit 7370)	7300
7.6	Gap	7050
8.3	Top of headwall	7300
9.0	Enter Hyde Creek Quadrangle	7200
9.3	Enter Crescent Cliff Quadrangle	7150
10.1	Continental Divide	7300
11.4	Lee Creek	7150
11.6		7000
11.8	Lee Creek Trail (141) Junction	7050
12.1	Saddle	7200
12.5	Creek	6850
14.0	Creek	6100
14.5	Creek	5950
15.1	North Badger Trail (103) Junction	5700

NORTH BADGER CREEK TO BADGER PASS
10.2 Miles

The Trail in this Section, largely in wooded valleys, includes a brief excursion into the Bob Marshall Wilderness.

The Trail continues the ascent of North Badger Creek for a mile and then enters the South Badger drainage at a minor ridge at 1.9. After descending to Elbow Creek, at 4.3, there is an easy walk up to Muskrat Pass, on the Continental Divide, at 8.1; from there to 9.3, the route is on the west slope (in the Bob Marshall Wilderness). The Section ends soon thereafter, at 10.2, at Badger Pass (also on the Divide).

Convenient water sources are infrequent beyond Elbow Creek. Campsites are available at several locations, including Lost Horse Camp (4.3) and Badger Pass.

The Section lies mostly in the Rocky Mountain Ranger District of the Lewis and Clark National Forest; the mile west of the Divide, though, is in the Spotted Bear Ranger District of the Flathead National Forest.

U.S.G.S. Maps: **Crescent Cliff** and **Morningstar Mountain**. Also: our Map **8**.

Detailed Trail data are:

The Section commences at the junction of the designated and interim routes, where Kip Creek Trail No. 142 intersects North Badger Trail No. 103. Proceeding up the valley on the latter, cross Kip Creek after 50 yards and bend back to the left. The summit on the Continental Divide, up Kip Creek and beyond Running Owl Mountain, is Bullshoe Mountain. Pass small creeks at 0.6.

Come to a junction in a meadow at 1.0. Instead of continuing straight ahead on Trail No. 103 to the Continental Divide at Big Lodge Mountain, turn left on a single-file path on Elbow Creek Trail No. 145. Pass a campsite on the right of the Trail and cross North Badger Creek at 1.2.

Ascend through forest by switchbacks on a well-used pack trail, reaching a saddle at 1.9. To the north are the almost bare

Bruin Peaks. The Trail breaks out of forest at 3.3, and this affords a clear view up the valley of Muskrat Creek to the Continental Divide. Where the Trail forks near here, take the left fork and continue descending (right fork quickly degenerates).

Reach the confluence of Elbow Creek and Muskrat Creek at 4.3. Curly Bear Mountain appears down the open valley of Elbow Creek. This area, known as Lost Horse Camp, was once a wide flat grassy bench suitable for camping, with wild strawberries as an extra bonus; reportedly, though, it has been flooded out within the past few years, and rock and timber debris may still be scattered about.

Leave Elbow Creek Trail No. 145 (which descends to the left) at the marked trail junction at Lost Horse Camp. (The U.S.G.S. map places this junction at 4.0; but that doesn't square with our observations.) Continue on Muskrat Creek Trail No. 147, which immediately crosses willow-lined Elbow Creek and Muskrat Creek just above their confluence. This should be a simple boulderhop. Carry water from here, as it is several miles to the next water along the Trail.

Ascend, well up on the flank of Elbow Mountain and above Muskrat Creek, occasionally circuiting small slides. For the most part, the route is through forest without much of scenic interest. There is a trail intersection at 6.4, shortly after crossing a muddy spot on a low horse bridge. The main trail appears to bend to the left; instead take a sharp right, heading in a southerly direction (still on Trail No. 147).

After a short descent, climb again. At 7.2, Blue Lake may be seen, 100 feet below, by stepping a few feet off the Trail to the right. It is a pretty spot, with the Continental Divide as a backdrop; but because of the steep slope and probable insect problems, it is not recommended for camping. One of the headwaters of Muskrat Creek, at 7.6, may produce a small flow. An obscure unmarked trail comes in from the left at 7.8.

Reach Muskrat Pass at 8.1. Cross the Continental Divide here, in a flat meadow with scattered spruces and firs. Enter the Flathead National Forest and Bob Marshall Wilderness.

There seems to be some confusion about the junction at 8.5. The best option appears to be to keep going straight, soon passing a small pond on the right. (Thus, disregard the trail—even though a sign indicates that it is the way to Badger

Pass—that makes an acute turn back to the right and around the west shore of Beaver Lake.)

There is another trail junction at 8.8. Here bend to the left around a large lonesome spruce instead of proceeding straight on Trail No. 175. (Trail 175 crosses a small stream in meadow in about 50 yards and then continues around the east side of Beaver Lake and descends Cox Creek.)

Soon pass a small campsite and corral and ascend on pack trail, which may be overgrown, to the Continental Divide at 9.3. (Avoid the apparent foot trail that rises abruptly from the campsite; author took it and bushwhacked a considerable distance before rejoining the broad route.) Beaver Lake, to the south of the Trail, is visible as you gain elevation; you would not have seen it before unless you had detoured to camp alongside it. New footway—presumably the connection with the marked route from 8.5—joins from the right at the crest.

Leaving the Bob Marshall Wilderness temporarily, continue with little elevation change to the trail junction at 10.2, just north of Badger Pass. A good camp be made immediately before the junction, on a headwater of South Badger Creek.

Distances and elevations are:

0.0	Trail junction	5700
1.0	Elbow Creek Trail (145) Junction (5797)	5800
1.2	North Badger Creek	5750
1.9	Saddle	6250
4.3	Lost Horse Camp	5500
4.7	Enter Morningstar Mountain Quadrangle	5600
5.3		5950
5.4		5900
5.6		5950
5.8		5900
6.4	Trail junction (5943)	5950
6.8		5850
7.2	Blue Lake overlook (5940)	5950
8.1	Muskrat Pass (Continental Divide)	6000
8.5	Trail junction	5950
8.8	Cox Creek Trail (175) Junction	5950
9.3	Continental Divide	6300
10.2	Trail junction	6250

BOB MARSHALL WILDERNESS SEGMENT
Section 2
BADGER PASS TO KEVAN MOUNTAIN
25.3 Miles

This Section proceeds through the uncrowded northern portion of the Bob Marshall Wilderness to the high country overlooking the magnificent Chinese Wall. Several parks break up the forest, affording pleasant places to pause and enjoy the trip.

The first part is a long, gradual descent along Strawberry Creek. At 11.0, the route turns up Bowl Creek and climbs to viewless Sun River Pass (on the Continental Divide) at 16.2. The next several miles, to Round Park at 19.6 and then in the lower reaches of Open Creek, involve little elevation change. The last mile, though, is a climb near Kevan Mountain, to a trail junction at 25.3, at the north end of the Chinese Wall. (More commonly, this is known as the North Wall—reserving the "Chinese Wall" designation for the cliffs of Section 4—but the overall appearance and geology is much the same.)

The route described below is the designated CDT. But there is a good alternative beyond the Bowl Creek junction at 11.0. The alternative continues downstream to Gooseberry Park and then turns south along Clack Creek Trail No. 160. This hike features the cliffs of the Trilobite Range and Pentagon Mountain, the latter a commanding backdrop for alpine Dean Lake. It rejoins the designated route at Switchback Pass in the next Section. The alternative is especially worth considering if you decide to continue south via Pentagon Creek and the Spotted Bear River, but in that case you might make a short detour from Switchback Pass to the Divide so as take in the North Wall views from Kevan Mountain.

There are adequate sites available for camping as far as Round Park at 19.6. Water supplies are good throughout. Heavy pack use has damaged the treadway, all too often making it a quagmire. Since it is about ten miles or more from any point within the Section to the nearest vehicle access, resupply here is not practical.

As far as Sun River Pass, the Trail is in the Spotted Bear Range District of the Flathead National Forest; the remainder

Entering the Bob Marshall Wilderness at Badger Pass.

is in the Rocky Mountain Ranger District of the Lewis and Clark National Forest. All of the Section lies within the Bob Marshall Wilderness.

U.S.G.S. Maps: **Morningstar Mountain, Gooseberry Park, Pentagon Mountain**, and **Porphyry Reef**.

Also: our Maps **8** and **9**.

Detailed Trail data are:

The Section begins at the junction of Trail No. 121 (North Fork of Birch Creek Trail) and Strawberry Creek Trail No. 161, marked with an attractive Bob Marshall Wilderness boundary sign. A small camp can be made near here, with water from the creek just to the west.

Follow Trail No. 161 (which may be unsigned) southward into the Wilderness, crossing the Continental Divide at 0.1. Here, in Badger Pass, the terrain is flat open meadow and the

65

precise location of the Divide is not obvious. There is a little open water to the left, and ahead are the rocky slopes of Mt. Field. (Mt. Field is a misnomer; it memorializes Joseph and Reuben Fields, a couple of brothers with Lewis and Clark. Two nearby summits, Mt. Drewyer [Drouillard] and Mt. Patrick Gass, are named for other members of the expedition.)

Descend gradually through pleasant woods, crossing to the right bank of Strawberry Creek (here only three feet wide and a couple of inches deep) at 1.4. The Trail remains mostly in forest, usually a considerable distance from Strawberry Creek. There are a number of small tributaries and an occasional mucky spot. Where the path divides from time to time, keep to the uphill route.

The Trail crosses to the left bank by easy boulderhop at 3.7. It continues through spruce forest with small side streams. In a small clearing at 5.1, the minor East Fork Trail (No. 371) bears to the left, to ascend the East Fork of Strawberry Creek. Continue straight ahead, coming to the boulder-strewn channel of the East Fork at 5.5.

After crossing East Fork, continue parallel to the left bank of Strawberry Creek. The forest for the first mile is young lodgepole, then mixed spruce, fir, and lodgepole. Small side streams are passed on bridges made of short cross-logs.

Reach a marked trail junction at a T-intersection at 7.9. The Gateway Trail (No. 322) turns left and ascends. (A couple of miles from the junction, it passes through the Gateway Gorge, a marvelously tight passage between 1000-foot cliffs.) Here turn right and continue on the Strawberry Creek Trail in the direction of Gooseberry Cabin.

Strawberry Creek is immediately to the right of the Trail at 8.2. This is a good place to camp, with grassy flat ground and an unobstructed view up the valley. Just beyond, cross Strawberry Creek without difficulty. Pass some side creeks with bridges.

Disregard an unmarked path that crosses the route at about 9.5; this presumably affords a shortcut, to the left, to the Trail Creek Trail. Fifty yards beyond this point is a relatively high bridge over Grimsley Creek. Once again there are good places to camp near Strawberry Creek. Trail Creek Trail No. 216 makes an acute bend to the left at 9.9. Heavy pack use formerly made a quagmire of the route along Strawberry

Creek, but some minor relocations have corrected the problem, at least temporarily.

Turn sharp left at the trail junction at 11.0, descending on Bowl Creek Trail (No. 324) toward Strawberry Creek. (If you elect to hike the Clack Creek alternative mentioned in the introductory text, you would continue ahead toward Gooseberry Park.) Ford Strawberry Creek at 11.2—though about ten yards wide, it is only a few inches deep in July.

The Trail ascends gradually from Strawberry Creek to Sun River Pass, following Bowl Creek. (There have been reports of avalanche damage in recent years, but the footpath has been repaired and can be traveled without difficulty.) The Mt. May Trail (which leads 1.9 mile to a lookout) forks uphill at 11.6; take the lower fork, which descends to Bowl Creek. At one time it was necessary to ford across the stream and back (cautiously), but new treadway allows you to remain on the right (east) bank. Fast water such as occurs here is typical habitat for the ouzel, a gray chunky bird that dips to the stream bottom for tasty morsels.

Disregard Scalp Creek Trail No. 315, which cuts off to the right at 12.3, and the barely visible abandoned Basin Creek Cutoff Trail—also to the right—at 12.8. Continue straight, crossing a small creek at 13.2. There are short switchbacks at 13.5 and a stretch of scree overlooking Bowl Creek at 13.8. Enter the wet meadows of Grizzly Park around 14.3. A trail from Grimsley Park soon comes in from the slope on the left.

A camp can be made along the Trail, close to Bowl Creek, at 14.8. Leave Bowl Creek Trail No. 324, which forks left, at 15.0. Instead, proceed straight ahead on the marked Sun River Pass Trail. There are good grassy campsites at 15.1, where the route crosses to the left (south) bank of Bowl Creek. (It may be possible to boulderhop a few yards upstream.)

The trail junction at 15.4 may be obscure. The right fork, which is well defined, is the Basin Creek Trail. (It crosses Basin Creek about 100 yards from the junction and proceeds up a valley, parallel to the Continental Divide, for several miles toward Pentagon Mountain. Although some maps indicate a trail ascending the headwall of the valley toward Dean Lake, today there are few if any traces of a footway.) Taking the left fork at 15.4, ascend through a burned area. Cliffs and steep slopes can be seen to the west, with Pentagon Mountain especially prominent.

Sun River Pass, at 16.2, has no view. Cross the Divide into the Sun River drainage. This isn't the best part of the Trail—there are several short climbs and descents, the treadway suffers from heavy stock traffic, and the moist forest may seem unusually buggy. Cross a small creek at 17.7.

Turn right at the trail junction in a clearing at 19.3, and follow Open Creek Trail No. 116 westward. (The trail to the left leads to a roadhead at West Fork Guard Station, but it requires a 2000-foot climb over Washboard Reef.)

Enter Round Park on the far side of Fool Creek at 19.6. A camp might best be made at one of the sheltered sites here, as there are no satisfactory flat open sites with water in the upper portions of the Open Creek valley or for many miles on the west side of the Continental Divide. (However, if you continue in the next Section along the designated route, Lake Levale would be a fine place to stop.)

To continue from Round Park, head for the axe blazes to the southwest on the far side of the meadow. Then walk through spruce-fir forest, for the most part well back from Open Creek. There is an occasional view of Signal Mountain to the southwest, just on the other side of the valley. From time to time there may be more than one treadway, as new paths have been put in place to avoid eroded spots; look for recent axe blazes to point the right course. The Trail crosses small side creeks at 21.9 and several times thereafter over the next couple of miles.

The Trail is routed to the right (south) bank of Open Creek, though not for long, at 24.0. You can avoid the two fords by taking the obscure path that bears to the right about 50 feet before the first crossing; although this soon disappears, you can keep going, close to Open Creek, until you intersect the pack trail again at 24.2. There is a possible campsite, perhaps the last in the nearly-level bottomland, along the way.

After a good side creek at 24.6, the Trail begins to climb more steeply. Cross Open Creek, now much reduced, at 25.1. The snow-pocked cliffs of the Continental Divide tower overhead, the subalpine forests open up, and from here on wildflowers are abundant—paintbrush, yellow columbine, gentian, valerian, mariposa, stonecrop, American vetch, and many more, along with the beargrass and elk parsnip. The Section ends at the junction with Wall Trail No. 175, at 25.3.

Distances and elevations are:

0.0	Trail junction	6250
0.1	Badger Pass	6300
0.7	Enter Gooseberry Park Quadrangle	6250
1.4	Strawberry Creek	6100
3.7	Strawberry Creek	5850
4.0		5900
5.1	East Fork Trail (371) Junction	5750
5.5	East Fork, Strawberry Creek	5700
6.1		5600
6.4	(5647)	5650
7.9	Gateway Trail (322) Junction	5550
8.2	Strawberry Creek	5500
8.5		5600
9.5	Grimsley Creek	5500
9.9	Trail Creek Trail (216) Junction	5450
11.0	Bowl Creek Trail (324) Junction	5400
11.1	Enter Pentagon Mountain Quadrangle	5350
11.2	Strawberry Creek	5350
11.6	Mt. May Trail (256) Junction	5550
12.0	Bowl Creek	5400
12.3	Scalp Creek Trail (315) Junction	5450
14.3	Grizzly Park	5800
14.6	Enter Porphyry Reef Quadrangle	5750
15.0	Sun River Pass Trail Junction	5800
15.4	Basin Creek Trail Junction (5813)	5800
16.2	Sun River Pass (6251)	6250
16.6		6300
17.7	Creek	6150
19.3	Open Creek Trail (116) Junction	5800
19.6	Round Park	5800
21.0	Enter Pentagon Mountain Quadrangle	5850
24.0	Open Creek bypass	6150
24.6	Creek	6250
25.1	Open Creek	6600
25.3	Wall Trail (175) Junction	6750

KEVAN MOUNTAIN TO SPOTTED BEAR PASS
Recommended (Pentagon) Route: 19.2 Miles
Designated (Gates Park) Route: 26.1 Miles

A massive limestone ridge—a northern extension of the Chinese Wall—lies at the heart of this Section. Although the designated route does incorporate a fine stretch below this cliff face, it is so circuitous and fire-scarred that it cannot be recommended. The alternate route described below—along the valleys to the west—offers some rewarding, if less spectacular, scenery.

The highlights of the Section, on the recommended route, are at the start —first, the view south along the east face from the crest of the Divide (at 1.7) and then the vistas near Switchback Pass (at 2.4). Next comes a descent, losing some 3000 feet of elevation to the Pentagon Guard Station, by the Spotted Bear River, at 8.8. The Trail then ascends that river, heading up a narrow forested valley, all the way to the end of the Section, at Spotted Bear Pass (on the Divide), at 19.2. (The designated route, east of the Divide, is discussed below. According to some reports, it is also possible to make an exceptional cross-country skyline trek, of approximately 18.1 miles, but this has some very steep, often rocky, parts; it is also exposed, snow-covered at places in early summer, and requires about 2300 feet more elevation gain than the recommended route. Anyone attempting to hike cross-country should carry detailed topographic maps and observe grizzly bear precautions scrupulously.)

Water is available at frequent intervals except at the start of the Section. (The first 6.3 miles may be completely dry.) Locating a campsite with water is often difficult because of the slopes and dense vegetation; the best place is near the confluence of Pentagon Creek and the Spotted Bear River, not far from the Pentagon Guard Station. Although streams must be forded at several places, the only one that is likely to prove to be tricky is Pentagon Creek, just above this confluence.

Once again the Trail is located in both the Rocky Mountain Ranger District of the Lewis and Clark National Forest (to 1.7) and the Spotted Bear Ranger District of the Flathead National Forest. There is no road access within ten miles of any part of the Section.

U.S.G.S. Maps: **Pentagon Mountain, Trilobite Peak, Bungalow Mountain, Three Sisters,** and **Slategoat Mountain.**

Also: our Maps **9, 10,** and **11.**

Detailed Trail data are:

Starting at the junction of Open Creek Trail No. 116 and Wall Trail No. 175, return to the left (north) bank of Open Creek. Fill a canteen here, as it is six miles to the next reliable source of water.

The Trail may be obscure as it climbs through stretches of open country. Weave through some long-lasting snowpatches at 0.8. Reach a beautiful little basin, carpeted with buttercups, at the foot of cliffs at 1.1; the ground is spongy and wet, but there is no obvious source of drinking water.

Continuing close to the edge of an escarpment, enjoy views over Open Creek and toward the reefs and peaks to the east. Lake Levale is now visible to the southeast. Follow the cairns, bypassing a steep shortcut that rises on the left.

Reach the thin ridge of the Continental Divide at 1.7. The summit of Kevan Mountain, rising an additional 400 feet, is just half a mile to the north—and the panorama merits a side trip if your schedule permits. The Divide here is the type locality for the Pentagon shale formation, with its abundant trilobite fossils. Dryads and other alpine flowers abound.

Far to the west you can make out the Swan Range, including snow-covered 9255-foot Swan Peak. To the southwest and south, to the left of nearby Table Mountain, are Silvertip Mountain, Bungalow Mountain, and Larch Hill (which lies on the Trail in Section 4). Beyond the sheer cliffs of the Divide and Lake Levale to the southeast, it is about 15 miles to 9392-foot Rocky Mountain Peak on the eastern edge of the Bob Marshall (and the highest point in the Wilderness). To the east is the wide glacial valley of Open Creek, with a backdrop of Porphyry Reef, Wrong Ridge, and a string of summits beyond (probably including Mt. Patrick Gass, Mt. Wright, and Mt. Lockhart).

There is a path that drops down toward the west. This should be bypassed and, instead, follow close to the crest of the Divide and then swing right, around to the west of Kevan Mountain, before starting to descend. Although the route is sometimes obscure, the objective is the obvious high pass to the northwest.

Reach a trail junction in Switchback Pass at 2.4. The intersecting route to the right is the alternative Clack Creek route, mentioned in the introductory text for Section 2. (It is well worth walking the short distance to the dropoff to the right for the view overlooking the hanging valley and head-walls at the upper end of Basin Creek.)

Turn left at the junction in Switchback Pass. Descend on Basin Creek-Pentagon Cabin Trail No. 177, through spruce-fir forest (with Douglas fir at lower elevations), toward Pentagon Cabin. From about 2.9, the descent makes numerous switch-backs (hence "Switchback Pass"), providing a steady moderate grade. The Trail approaches a talus slide at 4.8.

Cross a good creek on moss-covered rocks at 6.3. This is the first water since crossing the Continental Divide. A camp can be set up just north of the creek. Continue close to the East Fork of Pentagon Creek to the confluence with Pentagon Creek proper at 7.1. (There is also a trail junction here, with Dolly Varden-Pentagon Trail No. 173 joining from the right.)

Continue downstream and cross Pentagon Creek at 7.3, possibly getting across a little way up the stream on a logjam. Proceed along the right bank of Pentagon Creek. At the crossing, Pentagon Mountain is prominent upstream, but then the trail continues in forest that cuts out any views. The tread, which is excellent here, maintains a rather constant elevation well above the right bank of Pentagon Creek. At 8.6, a side trail makes a 90° turn to the right and heads up toward Pot Mountain.

Pass a good established campsite on the left, on Pentagon Creek, at 8.8. Immediately beyond the campsite, reach a major trail junction, with the Pentagon Guard Station just ahead on the bank of the Spotted Bear River. This is a well-constructed wooden cabin, with privy and corral nearby.

Turn left on Spotted Bear River Trail No. 83 and immediately cross Pentagon Creek. This will probably require fording, and caution should be exercised. About 100 yards after crossing Pentagon Creek, continue straight where Trail No. 92 bears left to Hart Lake and the Continental Divide.

Walk through lodgepole forest. Pass a wilderness restoration area—perhaps some day once again open to camping—at 9.3. Boulderhop Hart Creek at 9.5. Continue ahead at 10.0 where the Lime Divide Trail bears right and descends toward the river. At 10.3, again take the left fork, ascending Trail No. 83 toward Spotted Bear Pass. (The Wall Creek Trail forks right and drops down to the stream.)

Step over a small creek, possibly with strawberries in fruit, at 10.5. There is room for a camp near the river. Although the Trail is generally screened by forest, there are occasional good views upstream; and as the Trail bends to a more southerly course, the peaks of the Three Sisters can be seen ahead.

Cross a side creek on a logjam or by boulderhopping at 12.0. Pass a landslide and a small creek at 12.3. Just beyond an unmarked straight cross-trail, come to the Spotted Bear River at 12.9. It is about five yards wide and calf-deep and most likely must be forded. (*Note:* the Forest Service map erroneously indicates that the trail cuts across the river farther upstream—above the confluence with Three Sisters Creek.) Campsites are almost nonexistent in the remainder of the Section.

Continue an easy gradual ascent through the forest parallel to the left (west) bank of the River, but well back of it. Streambeds, very likely dry, are at 13.0, 13.4, and 13.9. Above 13.4, where Three Sisters Creek joins the Spotted Bear River, the flow of the latter is much reduced.

From around 14.1 and continuing for about a mile, thousand-foot cliffs crowd the right side of the Trail. Cross Christopher Creek, which usually has water, at 14.4. Pass a small seep at 15.4. At 16.1, where the Trail approaches the river closely, an obscure track bears left between two large spruces and heads for the water in about 50 yards. A small party can make camp here, in dry weather, on some gravel patches.

Continuing among large spruces and firs, reach the Spotted Bear River at 16.6. A logjam a short distance upstream may provide a ready means to cross. Then climb more steeply, passing a small side stream at 16.9 and a muddy seep shortly thereafter. The Trail appears to fork at 17.5, but the left fork rapidly disintegrates. Take the right fork instead, immediately crossing a major feeder (with the aid of fallen logs, most likely), just below a pretty little waterfall. Although there are numerous small creeks and seeps for the next mile or more, the steepness of the terrain and the fallen timber make the area unattractive for camping. The stretch descibed in this paragraph needs maintenance—it is offten overgrown or very wet.

Nearing the head of the valley, enjoy occasional views northward. Then reach the Continental Divide once more, at Spotted Bear Pass, at 19.2. The Section ends here, at the junction with the designated route.

Distances and elevations are:

0.0	Wall Trail (175) Junction	6750
0.8	Snowpatches	7250
1.1		7450
1.7	Continental Divide	7950
2.0	Flank of Kevan Mountain	8050
2.4	Switchback Pass	7750
4.7	Enter Trilobite Peak Quadrangle	6350
6.3	Creek	5400
7.1	Dolly Varden-Pentagon Trail (173) Junction	5150
7.3	Pentagon Creek	5150
8.3	Enter Bungalow Mountain Quadrangle	5050
8.4		5100
8.6	Trail (359) junction	5000
8.8	Pentagon Guard Station	4850
9.5	Hart Creek	4900
10.0	Lime Divide Trail (349) Junction	4950
10.3	Wall Creek Trail Junction	5000
11.0	Enter Three Sisters Quadrangle	5100
11.6		5250
12.0	Creek	5200
12.3	Creek	5250
12.9	Spotted Bear River	5200
13.4	Streambed	5350
13.5		5300
13.9	Streambed	5350
14.4	Christopher Creek	5400

16.1	River access	5550
16.6	Spotted Bear River	5650
17.5	Creek	6100
18.4	Enter Slategoat Mountain Quadrangle	6350
19.2	Spotted Bear Pass	6700

Designated (Gates Park) Route

The first several miles of this route, on Wall Trail No. 175, are exceptional. The terrain is grassy, the views magnificent, and water supplies are frequent; the problem is that once you start along the base of the cliffs, the only practicable way to return to the high country requires a long detour far down to Gates Park; and the forest on the descent exhibits severe scars from the Gates Park Fire of 1988. In addition, unless you were to take a short side trip for the view, you would miss some of the scenery enjoyed at the start of the recommended route. *Note:* the following sketchy report is based exclusively on topographic maps, not field investigations.

U.S.G.S. Maps: **Pentagon Mountain, Three Sisters, Gates Park**, and **Slategoat Mountain**.

Also: our Maps **9**, **10**, and **11**.

Detailed Trail data are:

Leaving Open Creek Trail No. 116, make a sharp turn left and proceed on Wall Trail No. 175, rising. Pass the outlet of Lake Levale at 1.0. (It is 0.2 mile up the little valley to the lake, with places to camp, beneath a backdrop of cliffs.) Cross over a spur ridge at 1.5 and enjoy the view of the cliffs and valleys ahead. Continue in open country, circling around the head of the South Fork of Open Creek at 2.9. Climb a bit once again to the next spur ridge, at 3.3, where Trail No. 132 turns left, climbing the nearby minor summit known as Moonlight Peak.

Descend to a tarn, beneath cliffs, at 3.9. Go over another rise at 4.1. Trail No. 151 turns left, to go down the North Fork of Lick Creek, at 4.5. Continuing along the base of the cliffs, cross the North Fork at 4.9 on the way to the next ridge (at 5.5), separating its drainage from that of the South Fork.

The Trail remains close to the Wall, losing a bit of elevation to the head of the South Fork at 7.3 and then climbing a final spur ridge, at 8.3.

Once the Trail reaches Red Shale Creek, at 8.9, it abandons the Divide. (While the topographic maps suggest that one might walk south all the way to Rock Creek, two more climbs—500 feet and 900 feet—with roundabout route-finding would be required. Some of it, especially along Baldy Bear Creek, could end up with bushwhacking—all in all hardly to be recommended. It might be a bit shorter than the established designated route, but would certainly not save any time.)

Descend the burned valley of Red Shale Creek, crossing back to its left bank at 9.9. After the side creek at 13.0, keep well up the slope as the creek cuts through a narrow ravine. Stay to the right at 14.9, headed east, at the junction with Trail No. 161.

Enter the wide open flats of Gates Park, at 15.3, just to the south of the dirt landing strip. Turn right at the trail junction here, proceeding southwest on Trail No. 111 toward Rock Creek and the Chinese Wall. Rise a bit, passing a minor ridge at 15.8. The route descends to cross Red Shale Creek—perhaps a problematic ford in June—at 16.0.

The climb back to the Divide begins with a switchback out of the ravine, after which the route swings around Goat Ridge toward the valley of Rock Creek; along the way are a couple of tributaries—Horsey Creek at 18.0 and Miners Creek at 18.6. Finally reaching the valley of Rock Creek, the route dips a bit before leveling out at 19.2.

Cliff-lined ridges constrict the valley above Baldy Bear Creek, at 20.6. Rock Creek Guard Station is situated at the narrowest point, at 23.3. The Trail soon veers off to the right, climbing a side ravine to the end of the Section, at Spotted Bear Pass, at 26.1. The designated route meets the recommended one (Spotted Bear River Trail No. 83) at a signed junction here.

Distances and elevations are:

0.0	Trail junction	6800
0.2		6750
1.0	Lake Levale (0.2 mile)	7100
1.5	Spur ridge (7535)	7550

2.9	Enter Three Sisters Quadrangle	6850
3.3	Trail (132) junction	7100
3.9	Tarn	6650
4.1	(6700)	6700
4.5	Trail (151) junction	6450
4.9	North Fork, Lick Creek	6650
5.5	Spur ridge	7100
5.9		7000
6.0		7100
7.3	South Fork, Lick Creek	6450
8.3	Spur ridge (7220)	7200
8.9	Red Shale Creek	7000
9.9	Red Shale Creek	6600
12.0	Enter Gates Park Quadrangle	5900
13.0	Creek	5700
14.9	Trail (161) junction (5398)	5400
15.3	Trail (111) junction (Gates Park)	5350
15.8	Ridge (5443)	5450
16.0	Red Shale Creek	5350
17.4		5650
17.7	(5618)	5600
18.0	Horsey Creek	5650
18.6	Miners Creek	5750
19.2		5550
19.4	Enter Three Sisters Quadrangle	5550
20.1	Enter Slategoat Mountain Quadrangle	5500
20.6	Baldy Bear Creek (5561)	5550
22.9	Creek	5850
23.3	Rock Creek Guard Station	5800
26.1	Spotted Bear Pass	6700

BOB MARSHALL WILDERNESS SEGMENT
Section 4
SPOTTED BEAR PASS TO INDIAN POINT GUARD STATION
17.6 Miles

The Chinese Wall, a sheer limestone reef marking the Continental Divide, is the central feature of this Section. This best-known attraction of the Bob Marshall Wilderness, a full 20 miles or more from roads of any description, preserves a sense of solitude despite its deserved renown. In addition to the scenic quality of vast open country below the Chinese Wall, the hiker can enjoy the flowers and wildlife.

The Trail contours around to the south of Larch Hill. Stands of alpine larch, a distinctive lacy conifer that sheds its needles each winter, grow at My Lake, along the way at 1.2. After reaching the base of the Chinese Wall at 3.4, the route follows the cliffs south for several miles. The precipice—sometimes a thousand feet high—forms a backdrop to the west, while graceful glacial valleys complete the unobstructed view eastward. After veering off from the Wall at 9.8, the Trail descends through the sparsely timbered valley of Burnt Creek. From 11.5, the Trail drops much less steeply through the lodgepole forest along the West Fork of the South Fork of the Sun River, passing the Indian Point Guard Station at 17.4, to the end of the Section at 17.6.

Springs are abundant at the base of the Chinese Wall. However, owing to overuse in past years, severe camping restrictions may be in effect over its full length. Efforts are being made, however, to permit one-night stops (no wood fires) for small backpacking parties. For current status, contact the Rocky Mountain Ranger District (of the Lewis and Clark National Forest), which encompasses the entire Section.

U.S.G.S. Maps: **Slategoat Mountain**, **Amphitheatre Mountain**, and **Prairie Reef**.

Also: our Maps **11** and **12**.

Detailed Trail data are:

Having ascended the Spotted Bear River to the junction in Spotted Bear Pass, bear right in the direction of My Lake and

Larch Hill. Climb quite steeply, with a few switchbacks, through firs and pines. You can look out occasionally through clearings toward Three Sisters, to the north, and the Rock Creek valley to the south.

You have a choice at the junction at 0.9. The designated route follows the left fork (Trail No. 194, according to current maps), descending slightly to reach My Lake at 1.2. As of 1991, camping at the lake was prohibited. (The author took the right fork, now listed as Trail No. 176, which climbs the ridgeline for another half mile, then contours around to the north of Larch Hill, swings south through Larch Hill Pass, and rejoins the designated route. That way provides some outstanding views—to snow-dotted Silvertop Mountain to the northwest; far-distant peaks to the north, perhaps even Mount St. Nicholas and other mountains in Glacier National Park; the Three Sisters to the northeast; and the Chinese Wall to the south. And, according to some hikers' reports, the panorama becomes still more spectacular if you continue up the ridge to the summit of Larch Hill.)

An attractive feature of My Lake and the nearby forest is the alpine larch, a deciduous conifer that turns golden yellow in autumn. (Larches are uncommon along the CDT—they grow not far from the Trail in the Preston Park area of Glacier National Park and are encountered once again in the Anaconda-Pintler Wilderness of southern Montana.) There are also some pretty flowering shrubs, notably swamp laurel and purple mountain heath. From My Lake, the designated route proceeds around the south side of Larch Hill, going over a spur ridge on the way. It reaches the base of the Chinese Wall at 3.4, just below Larch Hill Pass. (The alternate route mentioned above rejoins the CDT here, at a triangular trail junction.)

Follow the glorious route south, along the foot of the Chinese Wall. This is extraordinarily scenic open terrain, beneath the cliffs, with numerous tiny creeks. If camping is allowed, one fine place would be in the fairly sheltered area, shortly before an obvious small rise, at 4.4. Enjoy the many flowers— elephantshead, Sitka valerian, Siberian chive, veronica, subalpine daisy, globeflower, elk thistle, yellow columbine, red-stemmed saxifrage, and willowherb among them. Golden eagles may soar along the cliffs; and rosy finches, mountain chickadees, and red-breasted nuthatches may be found close at hand. At about 5.5, the Trail bears left, away from the cliffs, descending to cross the headwaters of Rock Creek at 6.0.

Climb once again, reaching the divide between Rock Creek and Moose Creek, at the base of Salt Mountain, at 6.6. There are excellent photo opportunities here, as at almost any place along the Wall. Descend to a trail junction at 7.0 and continue ahead on Wall Trail No. 175 toward the West Fork of the Sun River. (Moose Creek Trail No. 131 turns left and descends to the North Fork of the Sun.)

Proceed along the base of the cliffs, with the rounded valley of Moose Creek to the left and Cliff Mountain ahead. Reach the source of Moose Creek, a small shallow pond with algal growth, at 8.0; a campsite formerly used by large parties shows severe damage.

Past the crest at 8.6, near the base of Cliff Mountain, bear off to the southeast. Take a breather here, as the last view of the high country is one of the best. Follow the well-defined right fork at an unmarked trail junction at 8.9. (The left fork leads, in about 100 yards, to a large campsite.) Reenter forest, for the first time in several miles, at 9.3, but emerge shortly thereafter into the basin of Burnt Creek, scarred by fire many years ago.

Bend to the left at 9.8 and head directly away from the Chinese Wall. There is a spring just to the left of the Trail at 10.2 and a small side stream at 10.3. Continue to descend, now in young lodgepole pine forest. Cross to the right bank of Burnt Creek at 11.0.

Reach the West Fork of the South Fork of the Sun River at 11.5. Boulderhop to the left bank and hike downstream. Cross to the right bank, possibly with the aid of a number of parallel poles, at 12.6, a short way below a prominent foot-high ledge in the stream.

Look out over the river, from a viewpoint at 13.1, toward Prairie Reef, the high burned mountain to the southeast. Cross the West Fork again at 13.7; it is only about ten feet wide, but may have to be forded. Pass a small tributary from No Name Gulch at 14.2. Rise a bit to contour some distance from the main stream. The cliffs of Red Butte are visible, high to the west, at 14.9. Descend fairly steeply, crossing Black

The Chinese Wall.

Bear Creek beneath the bare western slopes of Prairie Reef at 16.0.

Come to the junction with Indian Creek Trail No. 211, close to the gorge of the river, at 16.5. (This would be a very good small campsite, with a rivulet as a convenient water source; other places are available, however, farther north at various points near the West Fork.) Continue ahead, in pure lodgepole forest, on West Fork Trail No. 203. Disregard the left fork, at 17.2, that leads directly to the Indian Point Guard Station. Another path to the guard station (100 yards uphill, but not visible from the Trail) is at 17.4, at the crossing of a small creek.

The Section ends at 17.6, at a signed junction near the West Fork of the South Fork of Sun River. The flat meadows here are full of flowers, including meadow deathcamas, Columbia puccoon, nineleaf biscuitroot, and Baker's mariposa. There are ample places to set up camp closer to the stream.

Distances and elevations are:

0.0	Spotted Bear Pass	6700
0.5	Enter Amphitheatre Mountain Quadrangle	7200
0.9	Trail junction	7450
1.2	My Lake	7350
1.4		7450
1.7		7400
2.0	(7596)	7600
2.6		7300
3.4	Wall Trail (175) Junction	7500
4.4		7050
4.8	Spur	7250
6.0	Rock Creek	6950
6.6	Rock Creek/Moose Creek Divide	7350
7.0	Moose Creek Trail (131) Junction	7200
7.3		7100
7.8		7200
8.0	Moose Creek	7150
8.5	Enter Slategoat Mountain Quadrangle	7600
9.8	Leave Chinese Wall (6924)	6900
11.0	Burnt Creek	6200
11.5	West Fork of South Fork, Sun River	6050
12.6	West Fork (5797)	5800
13.4	Enter Prairie Reef Quadrangle	5700
13.7	West Fork (5662)	5650
14.9		5750
16.0	Black Bear Creek	5500
16.5	Indian Creek Trail (211) Junction	5400
16.8		5450
17.4	Indian Point Guard Station	5400
17.6	Ahorn Creek Trail (209) Junction	5300

This Section offers a choice—either an up-and-down hike to the cliffs below the Continental Divide or a water level walk in the valleys of the Sun River. The high route is recommended, because of the views; but the shorter riverside alternative would save some time.

The recommended route crosses the West Fork and proceeds south through forest along Ahorn Creek. From a junction at 3.6, it climbs with greater purpose along the East Fork of Ahorn Creek. There is a lovely high meadow, encircled by an amphitheater of high cliffs, at 7.1.

After a short steep climb to a high saddle at 7.7, the Trail leaves the Bob Marshall Wilderness and enters the Scapegoat Wilderness. Not only Scapegoat Mountain, but numerous other ridges and peaks near and far provide a grand vista to the south and east. The descent follows the valley of Hoadley Creek to its junction with the South Fork of the Sun River at 13.4. Here it makes a short detour away from the Continental Divide in order to reach the roadhead at Benchmark, where resupply arrangements can be made. The South Fork and a tributary are forded just before reaching the Benchmark administrative site, at 16.9, and the end of the Section at 17.0.

The Section is located in the Rocky Mountain Ranger District of the Lewis and Clark National Forest, with all but the last three miles lying in one of the wilderness areas as well as the Sun River Game Preserve. Water is generally available at short intervals in this Section, but good sites for camping are scarce. River crossings might be difficult during spring runoff, when the designated route would be more practical.

Forest Road 235, a high-standard gravel road maintained for use by passenger cars, connects Benchmark to Augusta, Montana. Augusta is an hour away, so it is more convenient to make arrangements to resupply at Benchmark Wilderness Ranch, which is located at the far end of the airstrip, about two miles from the Trail. (For a reasonable fee, the ranch will

83

hold parcels for arriving hikers. Cabins and showers are also available. To obtain current information, contact Beverly Heckman, Benchmark Wilderness Ranch, Box 190, Augusta MT 59410. You can also try calling 406-562-3336, a phone in Augusta. The assistance of outfitters along the Trail is greatly appreciated, so CDT users are urged to keep their requests as simple and straightforward as possible.)

U.S.G.S. Maps: **Prairie Reef**, **Trap Mountain**, and **Benchmark**.

Also: our Map **13**.

Detailed Trail data are:

The Section begins at a trail junction in the meadows along the West Fork of the South Fork of the Sun River. Leaving West Fork Trail No. 203, take a sharp right turn and proceed, toward Camp Creek Pass, on Ahorn Creek Trail No. 209. (This area is good for camping.) A cairn and blaze mark the way to the West Fork at 0.2. Ford the West Fork, which might be difficult (or even impassable) during spring runoff but ordinarily should present no problem.

Slightly upstream from the ford, continue through spruce and fir forest. Cross Blind Fork easily at 1.6. After a little rise, the Trail descends and crosses Ahorn Creek at 2.3; a fallen log may be available to bridge the stream. Pass some more small side streams, characteristically with brook saxifrage and arrowleaf groundsel nearby; and queencup's white flower dots the forest floor early in the year. Reach a junction at 3.6, after the Trail bends left. (Just before the junction, a short unmarked path to the right leads to a campsite by the East Fork of Ahorn Creek.)

Keep straight at this junction, ascending on East Fork Ahorn Trail No. 225 in the direction of Grizzly Basin and Hoadley Creek. (The continuation of Trail No. 209 forks to the right, crosses the East Fork in 100 feet, and then heads for Camp Creek Pass.) Ascend more rapidly, passing side creeks at 4.9, 5.3, and 6.2.

Climbing higher, you can look back over the Ahorn valley toward Red Butte. At 7.1, a trail blocked by small timber leads 50 yards or so to a beautiful meadow beneath the cliffs of the western extension of Hoadley Reef. A small stream, the source of the East Fork, meanders through the meadow; there may be bugs, but camping should otherwise be excellent. The climb from here is very steep, so pause from time to time to enjoy the scenery; and watch for mountain goats as well. Reach the edge of a talus-filled gully at 7.5 and ascend along it.

The crest, at 7.7, marks the boundary between the Bob Marshall Wilderness and the Scapegoat Wilderness. The superlative view of the island-like mass of Scapegoat Mountain to the south and of the mountains to the southeast, along the Continental Divide as far as Caribou Peak, rewards you for traveling this way instead of following the designated route in the valleys. The sheer cliffs to the right are Hoadley Reef.

The Trail descends along a narrow ridge (between Grizzly Basin on the left and the headwaters of Hoadley Creek) before turning to the right at 8.3. After crossing a small headwater at 8.6, proceed downhill through open country. There are blazes and cairns, but they may be obscure and hard to locate; if you lose the marks, keep going down the open slope on a course parallel to Hoadley Reef and a couple of hundred yards from the base of its cliffs.

Reenter forest and continue to descend. At switchbacks at 9.5, cross two branches of Hoadley Creek just above their confluence. Bear left at the trail junction at 10.5, descending Hoadley Creek Trail No. 226, in the direction of Benchmark. (The trail ascending to the right is a popular route of access from Benchmark to the southern part of the Bob Marshall Wilderness.) Cross to the left bank of Hoadley Creek at 10.6. There is room for a single tent at a campsite here. Densely forested creek bottoms such as this are good places to find winter wrens, golden-crowned kinglets, and other small birds.

Hike above the left bank of Hoadley Creek, crossing a small side stream at 10.9 and thereafter several other tributaries that are likely to be dry. From 12.9 to 13.1, Hoadley Creek runs through a small but pretty gorge that is headed by a narrow chute of falling water. Bend around to the left to the valley of the South Fork of the Sun River at the mouth of Hoadley Creek.

Intersect South Fork Trail No. 202 at 13.4. (Hoadley Creek Trail No. 226 terminates at the junction.) Continue straight, downstream, toward Benchmark. (If you elect to bypass Benchmark, turn right and continue up the South Fork on

Trail No. 202, on the designated route described in Section 1 of the Scapegoat Wilderness Segment.) A camp can be made along the river, on a gravel bank.

Pass a small meadow at 14.7, close to river level. Continue, with slight rises and dips, through lodgepole forest dating from a fire in 1910. Exit the Scapegoat Wilderness at a sign about 15.2. Boulderhop a wide but shallow creek at 15.5. The next half mile is excellent—flat and with frequent overlooks of the bending and rushing river. Leave Trail No. 202, just past a register box, at 16.0; bear right at the junction and descend to the South Fork on South Fork Cutoff Trail No. 255. (The officially designated route, using Trail No. 202, bypasses Benchmark.) Ford the South Fork at 16.1. During midsummer the river is about 10 yards wide and calf-deep; if the water is high, the ford can be avoided by following Trail No. 202 another 1000 yards to the bridge at 10.2 of the designated route.

After fording the South Fork, follow it briefly and then make a clockwise swing around a ridge into the Straight Creek valley. (The prominent peak to the north is Prairie Reef.) Reach Straight Creek at 16.5; it is about the same size as the South Fork and must also be forded. After another small creek, reach a roadhead by outfitters' large corrals.

Follow the road, bending to the left. After passing the entrance to the Benchmark administrative site at 16.9, come to the end of the Section at the road junction at 17.0. (The recommended route turns right, toward Augusta; the road from the left is the designated route from Indian Point.)

Distances and elevations are:

0.0	Ahorn Creek Trail (209) Junction	5300
0.2	West Fork of South Fork, Sun River	5300
1.6	Blind Fork (5438)	5450
2.1		5500
2.3	Ahorn Creek	5450
3.6	East Fork Ahorn Trail (225) Junction (5635)	5650
4.9	Creek (6400)	6400
6.7	Enter Trap Mountain Quadrangle	7050
7.1	Meadow	7250
7.7	Ahorn-Hoadley Divide	7800

8.6	Headwater	7150
9.4	Enter Benchmark Quadrangle	6550
9.5	Hoadley Creek	6500
10.5	Trail junction	6000
10.6	Hoadley Creek	5950
12.1		5700
12.3		5750
13.4	South Fork Trail (202) Junction	5450
13.6		5500
14.7	Meadow	5400
14.8		5450
16.0	South Fork Cutoff Trail (255) Junction	5300
16.1	South Fork, Sun River	5250
16.4		5300
16.5	Straight Creek	5250
16.6	Roadhead	5250
16.9	Benchmark Administrative Site	5300
17.0	Road junction	5300

Designated (Sun River) Route

The designated route is the primary travelway between the road at Benchmark and the Chinese Wall. It is very direct and uncomplicated. The first part is a walk down the left bank of the West Fork to 5.9, where there is a sturdy bridge over the stream. This stretch includes a number of nice open spots. Turning south, the route ascends the South Fork, though well up the slope above it, in forest. The Trail crosses the South Fork on another bridge at 10.2, reaching the road at 10.5. The designated route joins the recommended one at 11.2, near the Benchmark administrative site. (See introduction to recommended route for resupply and other information for Benchmark.)

Camping near the West Fork bridge is not allowed. The best campsites are at the very start of the Section, though there are a few other possibilities along the West Fork. Drinking water is generally available at frequent intervals (except for the three miles past the West Fork bridge).

U.S.G.S. Maps: **Prairie Reef, Pretty Prairie**, and **Benchmark**.

Also: our Map **13**.

Detailed Trail data are:

Beginning at the junction of West Fork Trail No. 203 and Ahorn Creek Trail No. 209, which is the recommended route, continue downstream along the West Fork.

Cross White Bear Creek at 0.1. At 1.2, a side trail (No. 224) goes off to the left to climb over 3000 feet to Prairie Reef Lookout. The sunflower-like balsamroot is conspicuous on the grassy south-facing slope near Reef Creek, which is boulderhopped at 1.5. Drop down in lodgepole forest, with occasional aspen clumps, passing several small creeks. There is easy access to the river and good ground for camping at 3.1. Then climb in forest, following the course of the valley as it bends left. Boulderhop a small creek at the rise at 3.3. Continue well above the river level, with some nice views and occasional creek crossings. The scenery (looking up the meandering stream toward the mountains) is especially fine from a high point at 4.7. This stretch is open country and very enjoyable, but ends with a return to forest at 5.4. After crossing Wapiti Creek at 5.6, come to a trail junction, where West Fork Trail No. 203 terminates, at 5.8.

Turning right (on South Fork Trail No. 202) at the junction, walk over the West Fork of the South Fork of the Sun River on the sturdy horse bridge at 5.9. (Camping is not permitted along the trail within 1/4 mile of the bridge.) Beyond the long flat meadow at 6.4, the Trail rises well above river level. The Low Water Trail to Pretty Prairie joins from the left at about 6.8. The route continues in forest, after a register box, with minor elevation changes. Bighead Trail No. 242 descends to the left from the junction at 7.9. Ford ankle-deep Deer Creek in a sunny patch at 8.9. The trees open up to provide a view over the bending river at 9.6. Boulderhop small Burned Creek at 9.7.

Approaching Benchmark, keep left at the (possibly unsigned) trail junction at 9.8 and drop down to the bridge over the South Fork at 10.2. (*Note:* the designated route is Trail No. 202, which remains on the west bank of the river; but let us assume instead that most hikers would prefer to detour to Benchmark in order to resupply. Trail No. 202 formerly forked right at the junction at 9.8, but now—since construction of the bridge—seems to do so at a second junction, at 10.2, just before the bridge.) Cross the bridge and follow the broad well-worn path to the Benchmark trailhead at 10.5. The Forest Service South Fork Campground is located nearby. Walk the high-standard gravel road, climbing to 11.0 and then dropping to a junction at 11.2, where the Section ends. (The entrance to the Benchmark administrative site is 0.1 mile on the side road.)

Distances and elevations are:

0.0	Ahorn Creek Trail (209) Junction	5300
1.2	Trail (224) junction	5400
1.5	Reef Creek	5350
3.1	Enter Pretty Prairie Quadrangle	5150
3.3	Creek	5250
4.4		5100
4.7		5150
5.6	Wapiti (Elk) Creek	5100
5.8	South Fork Trail (202) Junction	5050
5.9	West Fork of South Fork, Sun River	5050
6.8	Trail junction	5150
7.5	(5278)	5300
7.9	Bighead Trail (242) Junction	5250
8.9	Deer Creek	5200
9.7	Burned Creek (5219)	5200
9.8	Trail junction	5200
10.2	South Fork, Sun River (5208)	5200
10.5	Trailhead	5250
10.7	Enter Benchmark Quadrangle	5300
11.0		5350
11.2	Road junction	5300

SCAPEGOAT WILDERNESS SEGMENT
Section 1
BENCHMARK TO GREEN FORK
Recommended (Straight Creek) Route: 10.0 Miles
Designated (South Fork) Route: 14.5 Miles

Each of the routes involves a hike, largely in forest, up a valley. There is an occasional view, but the real attractions of the Scapegoat Wilderness lie ahead, farther to the south.

The recommended route is clearly superior with respect to both scenery and ease of travel. The only reasons to consider the designated route—other than the fact that it is the official one—are, first, proximity to the Continental Divide and, second, convenience for people who have crossed the Ahorn-Hoadley Divide and wish to bypass Benchmark.

From start to finish, the recommended route follows the banks of Straight Creek. There is plenty of water, of course, but desirable campsites are few—the best is at 3.9. The recommended and designated routes join at 7.1 and are identical for the remainder of the Section.

The Section is in the Rocky Mountain Ranger District of the Lewis and Clark National Forest, with all but the first three miles in the Scapegoat Wilderness as well. See the introductory text for the preceding Section for information concerning access to Benchmark and resupply there.

U.S.G.S. Maps: **Benchmark**, **Wood Lake**, and **Scapegoat Mountain**.

Also: our Map **14**.

Detailed Trail data are:

The Section begins at the intersection of the main road to Augusta with the spur to the Benchmark administrative site. The recommended route follows the main road south, toward Augusta. Turn right at the next intersection, at 0.2, following the sign for Benchmark Campground. (It is another two miles on the road to the Benchmark Wilderness Ranch, where supplies can be mailed in advance. See introductory text for preceding Section.) Follow the side road past Wood Creek and past the campground entrance.

90

Pick up Straight Creek Trail No. 212 at the parking area at 0.5, at the end of the road. Follow the pack trail up the valley of Straight Creek, through lodgepole forest; there are excellent views of Patrol Mountain and picturesque bends of the creek at 0.8 and 1.2. Continue straight at 2.8, where Patrol Mountain Lookout Trail No. 213 bears right, descending.

Enter the Scapegoat Wilderness at a sign at 3.1. Pass several creeks and seeps. Dry grassy flats line Straight Creek from roughly 3.8 to 4.1; this is the best place in the Section for camping, as for example near the register box at 3.9. Continue through forest, with occasional openings. The small side creeks, including Park Creek at 6.2, have bridges or culverts.

After closely following the bank of Straight Creek from 6.9 to 7.1, come to the junction with the designated route. (The designated route, Elbow Creek Trail No. 248, joins from the right after having forded the stream.) Soon cross a landslide that is dotted with penstemons of blue and purple. Straight Creek is much divided as it runs through gravel beds at 7.7. Cross a side creek at 8.2.

Crown Creek, marked with a sign at 8.8, is sometimes dry. Just past the creek, Petty-Crown Creek Trail No. 232 turns sharp left toward Petty Creek and Ford Creek. Pass the junction with Cigarette Creek Trail No. 247, which crosses Straight Creek, at 9.4. Continue ahead along the right (east) bank to the end of the Section, at the junction with Green Fork Trail No. 228, at 10.0.

Distances and elevations are:

0.0	Road junction (5291)	5300
0.2	Road junction (5298)	5300
0.5	Straight Creek Trail (No. 212)	5300
1.9	Enter Wood Lake Quadrangle	5450
2.8	Patrol Mountain Lookout Trail (213) Junction	5500
3.1	Enter Scapegoat Wilderness	5600
3.9	Register box	5550
7.1	Elbow Creek Trail (248) Junction	5750
8.8	Petty-Crown Creek Trail (232) Junction	5900
9.4	Cigarette Creek Trail (247) Junction	5950
9.5	Enter Scapegoat Mountain Quadrangle	6000
10.0	Green Fork Trail (228) Junction	6050

Designated (South Fork) Route

If you hike this way, you will have a longer trip, quite often with mucky spots, with more up-and-down and fords. Why bother (unless you are coming over the Ahorn-Hoadley Divide and bypassing Benchmark)?

The first part, including fords of Straight Creek and the South Fork of the Sun River—coincides with the end of the recommended route from Indian Point to Benchmark. (The formally designated route, Trail No. 202, avoids these fords; but anyone who comes this close to Benchmark will surely wish to detour to the road in order to resupply.) Beyond 3.6, and a second ford of the South Fork, the route enters new country as it heads upstream to 8.8. After a climb across a minor ridge, it descends along Elbow Creek. Fording Straight Creek again at 11.6, it converges with the recommended route (Straight Creek Trail No. 212) and continues along this trail to the end of the Section at 14.5. The fords can be an obstacle in high water: the current may be strong and thigh-deep through June and perhaps even into July.

Water and campsites are available as needed. There is one nice view—up Ellis Creek to Sugarloaf Mountain—but most of the way is densely forested, with only occasional meadows.

U.S.G.S. Maps: **Benchmark, Wood Lake,** and **Scapegoat Mountain.**

Also: our Map **14.**

Detailed Trail data are:

Leave the main Benchmark-Augusta road at the junction at the start of the Section, passing the entrance to the Benchmark administrative site at 0.1. Curve around to the right and pass outfitters' large corrals to the end of the road, at 0.4.

Pick up the pack trail (South Fork Cutoff Trail No. 255). After a small creek, ford Straight Creek at 0.5; during midsummer it is about ten yards wide and calf-deep. Make a counter-clockwise swing around a ridge into the valley of the South Fork of the Sun River. (The prominent peak to the north is Prairie Reef.)

Ford the South Fork—about the same size as Straight Creek—at 0.9. Rise to the junction, at 1.0, where the officially designated route (South Fork Trail No. 202) joins from the right. Sign in at the register box nearby and follow the river upstream.

The first half mile is excellent—flat and with frequent overlooks of the bending and rushing stream. Boulderhop a wide but shallow creek at 1.5. Enter the Scapegoat Wilderness at a sign about 1.8. The Trail proceeds with minor elevation changes. Much of the forest of lodgepole pines dates from a fire in 1910. Pass a small meadow at 2.3, close to river level.

Turn left at the junction at 3.6. (Hoadley Creek Trail No. 226, to the right, is the recommended route between Indian Point and Benchmark.) Promptly ford the South Fork, which is about ten yards wide. There are places to camp on both sides of the river.

Once across the South Fork, climb up the bank, crossing a side creek at 3.8 and leveling out at 4.0. After small ups and downs, dip to the streambank at 4.6; there is room for a little camp a few feet to the right, by the water. Returning to the hillside, walk carefully along the narrow ledge directly above the river's edge at 4.8. Step over a willow-lined creek at 5.0.

The scenic highlight of the Section is the view south southwest at 5.3, up Ellis Creek, toward flat-topped Sugarloaf Mountain, a cliff-sided summit on the Continental Divide. Proceed along the hillside, well above the river, passing a couple of small but vigorous side creeks.

Dip to the junction with Ellis Creek Trail No. 227, which bears right, at 5.6. Continuing along the South Fork, cross a large dry gully in another 100 feet. The Trail is mostly in forest, on the slope, but with occasional openings. Great stands of cow parsnip sometimes crowd the tread, which is mucky at spots.

Drop down close to water level by 6.6. There is access to the river, and campsites can be located. Probably the best place is about 7.7, as the Trail begins to veer back up the slope; there is a broad meadow extending from the tread all the way to the stream. From here on the river, though in earshot, is out of sight. A little bridge crosses a creek at 8.4; this stretch suffers badly from the churning of horses' hooves.

Contour to the junction with Elbow Creek Trail No. 248 at 8.8; turn left at the junction and start climbing up the ridge to the east. Beyond the small creek at 8.9, the Trail switchbacks several times over the next mile. Trees completely obstruct any view at the crest of Elbow Pass, at 10.2. Descending on good treadway at a steady, easy, grade, step over headwaters of Elbow Creek at 10.5 and 10.6. There are a couple of switchbacks in forest at 11.1 and a couple more on the sloping meadow at 11.4.

Reach the bank of Straight Creek at 11.6. The flat grassy area here is a very good place to camp. Straight Creek, like the South Fork, is about ten yards wide; but the water seems to be a bit shallower and the current not quite so strong.

After crossing Straight Creek, immediately turn right at the junction with Straight Creek Trail No. 212 and continue as described for the recommended route. (Pass junctions with Petty-Crown Creek Trail No. 232 at 13.3 and with Cigarette Creek Trail No. 247 at 13.9.) The Section ends at 14.5, at the junction with Green Fork Trail No. 228.

Distances and elevations are:

0.0	Road junction (5291)	5300
0.1	Benchmark Administrative Site	5300
0.4	Trailhead	5250
0.5	Straight Creek	5250
0.6		5300
0.9	South Fork, Sun River	5250
1.0	South Fork Trail (202) Junction	5300
2.2		5450
2.3	Meadow	5400
3.4		5500
3.6	Hoadley Creek Trail (226) Junction	5450
4.2		5700
4.6	Streambank	5600
5.6	Ellis Creek Trail (227) Junction	5700
5.8		5750
6.6		5650
7.7	Meadow	5750
8.8	Elbow Creek Trail (248) Junction	5900
9.7	Enter Wood Lake Quadrangle	6400
10.2	Elbow Pass	6550
10.6	Elbow Creek	6300
11.6	Straight Creek	5750
11.6	Straight Creek Trail (212) Junction	5750
13.3	Petty-Crown Creek Trail (232) Junction	5900
13.9	Cigarette Creek Trail (247) Junction	5950
14.0	Enter Scapegoat Mountain Quadrangle	6000
14.5	Green Fork Trail (228) Junction	6050

SCAPEGOAT WILDERNESS SEGMENT
Section 2
GREEN FORK TO WHITETAIL CREEK
12.6 Miles

The devastating Canyon Creek fire of 1988 burned forest and grazing lands within a perimeter of 240,000 acres, including a broad swath east and northeast of Scapegoat Mountain. The effects of the fire, along with revegetation in coming years, give the Section its special interest.

The designated route, which is recommended, is almost as straight as an arrow. From the junction with Green Fork Trail No. 228, it ascends the valley of Straight Creek. The burned area commences at 1.7. Straight Creek Pass, at 3.8, offers very fine views down the valley of the Dearborn River. The Trail descends nearly 1000 feet to Welcome Creek Guard Station at 6.3. Some patches of forest have survived near the easy ford of the Dearborn River at 8.4. The burn continues on and off, though, for another couple of miles. The Section concludes with a stretch of undamaged forest in the narrow, steep-sided Dearborn valley, ending at the junction with Whitetail Creek Trail No. 218 at 12.6.

The Canyon Creek fire was ignited by lightning on June 25, 1988, but did not spread until late July. It still covered less than 40,000 acres when it jumped to the Atlantic side of the Continental Divide on August 9. Some of the damage along the Dearborn River resulted from controlled burns set deliberately in an unsuccessful effort to create a barrier, but strong winds pushed the blaze many miles beyond. The fire continued until mid-September when, after unprecedented drought, rain and cooler weather enabled it to be contained.

Water is readily available along the route. There are a few attractive campsites, but none in the first five miles of the Section. All of the designated route is situated in the Rocky Mountain Ranger District of the Lewis and Clark National Forest, as well as the Scapegoat Wilderness.

A more scenic alternate route was described in the first edition of this guidebook. However, in the absence of post-fire reconnaissance reports, particularly with reference to its cross-country patches, it can only be recommended with some hesitation. It involves the ascent of Green Fork to 2.8, followed by a climb over a low saddle to Halfmoon Park at 4.1; the towering cliffs all along the way make for very enjoyable travel. Established footways skirt to the northeast of Scapegoat Mountain, rather circuitously, to the Continental Divide at 9.7. Travel is largely cross-country—or at least not on maintained trail—for the next three miles along the Divide and then down to Tobacco Valley (along the North Blackfoot) at 13.7. Picking up established tread once again, the route crosses over the Divide at 14.8 before descending Whitetail Creek to its confluence with the Dearborn River, just before the designated route at 21.4. The Canyon Creek Fire has left scars all the way from Halfmoon Park to the headwaters of Whitetail Creek—that is, from about 3.8 to 14.8. Water sources and campsites are adequate; before the 1988 fire, Halfmoon Park would have been hard to beat. The maps are the same as the ones specified for the designated route.

U.S.G.S. Maps: **Scapegoat Mountain** and **Jakie Creek**. Also: our Map **15**.

Detailed Trail data are:

Begin the Section at the junction with Green Fork Trail No. 228, which forks to the right. Continue up the valley of Straight Creek, climbing gradually along the hillside above the right (north) bank. Pass a small side creek, with a bridge of cross-logs, at 0.3.

The scenery of the next half mile, opposite the Green Fork valley, is notable for the cliff bands that form steep walls along that valley's sides. Morning shadows outline a man's face, with the darkness of an overhung cave entrance forming the hair behind his left ear; it is a couple of miles up the Green Fork, about halfway up above its left bank.

After contouring around a gully, pause at the overlook at 1.2 to enjoy the view down Straight Creek and far off toward the northwest. Water can be obtained from a spring on the uphill side of the Trail at 1.4, high up a draw. The dainty Arctic rockjasmine was noted a bit farther on.

The Canyon Creek burn starts at 1.7. The blackened lodgepoles will eventually fall, and in the meantime grasses, forbs, and shrubs will flourish in the sunlight. One beneficial effect of the fire is the splendid clear view, at 2.2, up the valley of

PATTI JOHNSTON

Scapegoat Mountain.

Halfmoon Creek to Scapegoat Mountain—a summit that is otherwise visible only at much longer distances.

A side trail joins from the right at 2.4. (It connects with a route up Halfmoon Creek and, apparently, an earlier location of the Straight Creek Trail as well.) Boulderhop the creek at 2.5 and back again to the right (north) bank at 2.6. Although the area will be unattractive until the scarred ground heals, it would be feasible to camp here or at various places as far as 2.8, where a good spring sits off a couple of feet to the right of the Trail. The final two crossings, at 2.9 and 3.2, are likely to be dry gullies.

Climb, with a long switchback, to reach Straight Creek Pass; pause on the far side of the pass, at 3.8, with the excellent view southeast to Caribou Peak. Descending, walk along little

Welcome Creek from 4.0, stepping to its left bank at 4.1. After sloping down the hillside at a steady and easy grade, return to the narrow valley floor at 4.8. Watch for dippers flying along the stream. Boulderhop to the right bank at 5.0 and back to the left bank at 5.1.

The first satisfactory campsite is along the creek at 5.3, where a patch of pines has survived at the edge of a meadow. To the east, a hill juts up, Gibraltar-like, with cliffs of tilted rock layers.

The Trail swings around to the right at a junction, at 5.4, in the middle of the meadow. (The Jakie Creek Trail continues up to the left, soon crossing Welcome Pass.) At one time the route apparently followed the valley of Welcome Creek, but it now climbs the hillside well above the left bank, reaching a high point at 5.6. The subsequent descent, with occasional switchbacks, returns to the bottom, where the old route joins from the right, at 6.0.

Boulderhop Welcome Creek at 6.2, followed by a ford of calf-deep Dearborn River within the next 50 yards. Welcome Creek Guard Station is to the right, across the river at 6.3, easy to pass by without notice.

Make a sharp turn to the left at the junction at 6.4. (For the remainder of the Section, follow Dearborn River Trail No. 206.) After rising a bit, contour along through blackened forest. The next mile remained devastated in 1989, with little more than patches of beargrass in the mostly bare soil (though by 1991 wildflowers were found in profusion). Cross several gullies along the way, most or all of them waterless. Return to living forest around 7.6, as the Trail drops down to the valley floor; although it might be nice to camp here, restrictions have been placed in effect so as to enable the wilderness to recover from past overuse.

The Lost Cabin Creek Trail forks right at 8.1—once again in burned ground. Boulderhop or ford shallow Lost Cabin Creek at 8.2. There is a good, authorized, campsite at 8.4, just before the ford of the Dearborn River (five yards wide, calf-deep).

The country is mostly green beyond the Dearborn River, except for a patch past the culvert at 8.7. Keep straight at the junction at 8.9, where Elk Pass Trail No. 205 turns left and ascends. Continuing the level path in the valley, boulderhop a small side creek at 9.1. (You could camp nearby, close to the river, beneath the cottonwoods and Douglas firs.) At 9.3, opposite the mouth of Bald Bear Creek, there are nice views upstream to Crown Mountain.

Step over Lookout Creek at 9.4. Make a hairpin bend, at contour, to cross a gully at 10.1; it might be nice to rest just beyond, overlooking the stream. The Trail rises a few feet, directly above the water's edge, at 10.7 and then follows a course well back from the river. Continuing in wilderness unaffected by the 1988 fire, enjoy pleasant views of Caribou Peak from openings along the way. Step over a small creek, at the edge of a wide gully, at 11.4.

The Section ends at the junction with Whitetail Creek Trail No. 218, in a meadow, at 12.6. (It is 500 feet to the right, down that trail, to the Dearborn River. The grassy area by the river would be a splendid place to camp, but it may be unavailable— either for wilderness restoration purposes or because reserved for use by a commercial outfitter.)

Distances and elevations are:

0.0	Green Fork Trail (228) Junction	6050
1.7	Enter Canyon Creek Fire perimeter	6350
2.4	Trail (216) junction	6350
3.8	Straight Creek Pass	6750
4.0	Enter Jakie Creek Quadrangle	6600
5.4	Jakie Creek Trail (214) Junction	6000
5.6		6100
6.2	Dearborn River	5850
6.4	Dearborn River Trail (206) Junction	5900
6.5		5950
8.1	Lost Cabin Creek Trail (254) Junction	5750
8.4	Dearborn River	5700
9.4	Lookout Creek	5600
10.7	Leave Canyon Creek Fire perimeter	5500
11.4	Creek	5450
12.6	Whitetail Creek Trail (218) Junction	5350

SCAPEGOAT WILDERNESS SEGMENT
Section 3
WHITETAIL CREEK TO SCAPEGOAT BOUNDARY
13.0 Miles

Although the Trail in this strenuous Section starts in a valley, most of it is a hike along the crest or high slopes of the Continental Divide. The scenery, from many grand viewpoints, will continue to reflect the consequences of the 1988 fire.

The Trail descends the Dearborn River only to 1.4, then climbs along Blacktail Creek to reach the Continental Divide at 3.8. Walking cross-country along the crest is delightful—and even though the next five-mile portion is within the fire perimeter, the former tree cover was so sparse that deadfall is only occasionally a problem.

From 9.7 to 11.6, the Trail dips into the Valley of the Moon—a pretty basin on the slopes of Caribou Peak—before returning to the Divide near the wilderness boundary, where the Section ends, at 13.0.

The described route is largely the same as the designated route. However, in order to follow established tread (suitable for horse travel), the designated route makes a long and unrewarding detour. (See detailed data below, at 3.8, for further description. As noted there, the official route is about 8.4 miles longer and will add several hours to your trip.)

All of the Section is in, or along the boundary of, the Scapegoat Wilderness—still in the Rocky Mountain Ranger District of the Lewis and Clark National Forest on the eastern slope, but in the Lincoln Ranger District of the Helena National Forest on the western slope. There are campsites and water sources as far as the head of Blacktail Creek. Thereafter, the most reliable water, and best campsite, is at the Valley of the Moon; but on occasion the springs there may go completely dry.

U.S.G.S. Maps: **Jakie Creek**, **Steamboat Mountain**, **Caribou Peak**, and **Heart Lake**.

Also: our Map **16**.

Detailed Trail data are:

The Section begins in the meadow where Whitetail Creek Trail No. 218 intersects Dearborn River Trail No. 206. Continue down the Dearborn valley, with small rises and dips, through dry country. Cross Pear Creek at 0.2. At 0.8, just after a trail converges from the flatland on the right, reach and again cross the Dearborn River. After moving off to the right, approach the stream once more as it winds through wide gravel beds. There are good campsites here, at about 1.4.

The Trail leaves the Dearborn River at an unmarked junction at 1.4. (*Caution:* see note at the end of this paragraph.) Veer off to the right, climbing into a clearing at 1.5 where outfitters have erected the framework for a shelter (though this may subsequently have been removed). Cross the small West Fork of Blacktail Creek at the clearing. Contour southeast, intersecting a good blazed trail (Blacktail Creek Trail No. 207) at 1.6. (*Note:* the route from 1.4 to 1.6, used by the author and described here, seems to be a shortcut developed by informal use. The designated route most likely would continue a little farther down the Dearborn River to a signed junction, beyond Blacktail Creek. From there you would climb on Trail 207. You would intersect the shortcut immediately after having returned to the west side of Blacktail Creek proper. A further possible complication is that, according to some topographic maps, an entirely different, unnumbered, outfitters' trail leaves the Dearborn valley around 1.4 and proceeds westward up the West Fork of Blacktail; however, its starting point was not observed. The large Forest Service map has the route remaining on the left bank of the river all the way to the mouth of Blacktail Creek—possibly a relocation, but more likely an error. In short, things may be confusing from the start of the Section to 1.6.)

Turning right at 1.6, follow Trail No. 207 as it climbs steeply, well above the left (west) bank of Blacktail Creek. At 2.9, another good but unblazed trail (presumably the outfitters' trail up the West Fork) joins from the right, also ascending.

Reach the Continental Divide and the boundary of the Helena National Forest at 3.8, having gained 1700 feet of elevation. Immediately to the north of the Divide is a trickle, one of the headwaters of Blacktail Creek. White bog-orchid, fringed parnassia, elephantshead and others crowd close to the water, while just a few feet away on the dry slopes are stonecrop, gaillardia, umbrella plant and many more besides. Although sheltered flat ground is limited, the site is a good place to pitch camp. By climbing a few feet eastward, you can look out to the austere mountains north of the Dearborn River. (A second possible campsite can be found about 200 yards along the trail into the Helena, where there is another small creek.)

Although the designated route follows the established treadway and descends to the south, it is much better for hikers to turn left at the Continental Divide and head cross-country in the direction of the prominent open ridge. Carry plenty of water, as none may be available for many miles to come. Enjoy good views on both sides of the Divide including, to the south, 9400-foot snow-patched Red Mountain. The route from here to Caribou Peak lies within the perimeter of the 1988 Canyon Creek Fire; and although the terrain at these elevations is open for the most part, patches of trees occur and no doubt suffered greatly.

The designated route (which is not recommended) continues across the Continental Divide. After descending 1.2 miles to Landers Fork, it turns left and climbs a ridge before dropping to Bighorn Creek (6.1 miles from start). It then proceeds up the narrow valley of Bighorn, still on Forest trail. It converges with the recommended route after a total of 10.7 miles and 1550 feet of climbing (as compared with 2.3 miles and 700 feet for the recommended route). Fire damage is reported to be extensive along the way.

After dipping to a lower saddle on the Continental Divide at 4.0, ascend the ridge to the southeast. A path that has been used by horses can usually be followed without difficulty. Scapegoat Mountain comes into view as the prominent peak to the northwest.

Reaching a minor summit at 4.8, avoid the wooded ridge that leads off to the right; instead, stay left and descend the established path eastward through the woods to the grassy saddle seen below. Make a way through the saddle (at 5.0) until you reach a prominent grassy gully at 5.2. Turn right here and leave the Divide. Descend on the left of the gully,

Caribou Peak, from the spur ridge above the Valley of the Moon.

with a used track providing a way down to the meadow seen below. (Any route down to the meadow is likely to be difficult, because of deadfall from the 1988 fire.)

You may sometimes find water at places along the creekbed on the right side of the meadow, at 5.6; if so, it would be the last place to do so for several miles. Continue southeast along this dry watercourse, following a horse track, to the flat grassy bottomland at 6.1. Here intersect the circuitous designated route once again. Turn left, soon starting to climb toward the Continental Divide; walk, on recognizable trail, along the right (north) bank of the dry creek.

Reach the Continental Divide at 6.7. Turn right at an unmarked junction and ascend along the crest of the Divide. Climb fairly steeply, passing through a stretch of spruce-fir forest from 6.9 to 7.2. Emerging into open country again, stay slightly to the right of the ridge and above the wooded areas along the slope.

Rejoin the Divide at 7.8, just past minor summit 8096, with good views of Caribou Peak ahead. Drop slightly through a grassy area toward the saddle on the Divide at 8.0. Follow the established trail as it ascends on the right of the ridge; from the high point, at 8.5, there is a precipitous drop to the northwest down the headwall of Bighorn Creek. Prairie falcons may on occasion be observed nearby.

Leaving the established tread at its high point, proceed cross-country in a counter-clockwise direction; contour in this manner around summit 8655, perhaps gaining a few feet of elevation along the way. (According to reports, there are now trail markers.) Along this traverse you can enjoy fine views of Bighorn Lake in the cirque almost a thousand feet below. Continue in this way to the spur ridge, at 9.1, that extends south from summit 8655; from this vantage point you can look out not only toward Bighorn Lake on the west, but also to the Valley of the Moon on the east below Caribou Peak.

Swing off to the right and follow the spur ridge, keeping to the right of a small rise (hill 8416) at 9.3. Then descend the open gravelly crest southeast to 9.7, where a clearly visible path cuts back acutely to the left. Take this path and descend steeply. Although the track disappears near the valley, it can be followed for the steeper and longer part of the descent.

Pause at 10.0, in the northwest corner of the Valley of the Moon. The small waterhole and creek here, visible from the ridge a mile back, will be welcome. As there is plenty of flat land, a fine camp can be located in the shelter of the scrubby pine and fir, amidst gardens of wildflowers. (But in September of 1990, an especially dry year, no water could be found.)

Leaving the waterhole, proceed in an easterly direction, pretty much at contour (remaining above the valleys that descend to the right). Be sure to take an ample supply of water when setting out from the campsite.

There is a little park at 10.7, quite near the base of the cliffs directly below the summit of Caribou Peak, from which summit 8655 (mentioned above) bears 312°; begin a long gradual ascent from here.

The Trail, climbing south southeast, crosses a dry gully at 11.1. The remainder of the Section reportedly has been marked more clearly in recent years, but when visited by the author its location was obscure at places. Eventually climb above treeline and head for the ridge.

Reach the Divide itself at about 11.6, just to the southeast of a minor hump on the Caribou ridge. The route ahead along the Divide is obvious, as it follows a grassy crest between valleys on both sides; a footpath exists close to the crest.

After descending a bit, walk along the Divide from 12.0 to 12.6 at a fairly constant elevation. Then climb easily once again on open slopes covered with small rocks. The Section ends at 13.0, as the track contours to the north of the next summit, the easternmost point of the Scapegoat Wilderness.

Distances and elevations are:

0.0	Whitetail Creek Trail (218) Junction	5350
0.8	Dearborn River (5278)	5300
1.1	Enter Steamboat Mountain Quadrangle	5300
1.4	Trail junction	5250
1.6	Blacktail Creek Trail (107) Junction	5300
2.1	Enter Caribou Peak Quadrangle	5550
2.3	Enter Heart Lake Quadrangle	5750
2.9	Trail junction	6350
3.8	Continental Divide	6950
4.0	Saddle	6850
4.8	Minor summit	7550
5.1	Enter Caribou Peak Quadrangle	7400
5.6	Meadow	7050
6.1	Intersect designated route	6850
6.7	Continental Divide	7150
7.8	Continental Divide	8050
8.0	Saddle	8000
8.5	Leave trail	8300
9.1	Ridge	8350
9.7	Leave ridge	8050
10.0	Valley of the Moon	7700
10.7	Park	7600
11.1	Gully	7900
11.6	Continental Divide	8250
12.3		7950
13.0	Leave Scapegoat Wilderness	8150

SCAPEGOAT WILDERNESS SEGMENT
Section 4
SCAPEGOAT BOUNDARY TO ROGERS PASS
16.5 Miles

The Section is of special historical interest, for here Meriwether Lewis crossed the Continental Divide on the return leg of his epic expedition to the Pacific. The country is rather dry and sparsely timbered, with gentle grades that allow travel along the crest.

Having left the Scapegoat Wilderness, follow the Divide eastward, crossing minor summits along the way, to the head of an old road at 2.8. Walk down the roadway to the valley of Alice Creek at 7.7. (This is an interim route: the Forest Service intends to locate new trail along the Divide, bypassing the roadwalk down to Alice Creek. Backpackers have reported being able to make their way cross-country along the crest, without particular difficulty, so that is an option that should be considered.) Cars can ordinarily drive to the Trail at 7.7, by ascending the valley on County Road 456 and Forest Road 293.

The Trail climbs along road to Lewis and Clark Pass at 9.5 before continuing on obscure path and cross-country to the top of Green Mountain. Minor summits are passed before and after Cadotte Pass at 14.1. (However, as Cadotte Pass lies outside the national forest, new construction is planned to detour around it.) The Section ends with a steep descent to Montana Route 200, the first highway in about 160 miles, at 16.5. Lincoln, some 20 miles to the west, provides a full range of services, including a register notebook (at the post office) for the use of travelers on the Continental Divide Trail.

Nearly all of the Section falls within the Lincoln Ranger District of the Helena National Forest. (The first 2.8 mile stretch is along the boundary with the Rocky Mountain Ranger District of the Lewis and Clark National Forest; some damage from the 1988 fires may be encountered along the Lewis and Clark side, but the Alice Creek drainage escaped injury.)

It is necessary to leave the Continental Divide to obtain water. Accordingly, a good supply should be carried when setting out from Valley of the Moon in Section 3 and, again, from Alice Creek. Camping opportunities are limited because of the lack of water sources.

U.S.G.S. Maps: **Caribou Peak**, **Blowout Mountain**, **Cadotte Creek**, and **Rogers Pass**.

Also: our Map **17**.

Detailed Trail data are:

The Section begins at the boundary of the Scapegoat Wilderness, as the trail contours around a hundred yards or so to the north of a minor summit. (Avoid the spur ridge that heads south from that summit.) Descend northeast along the Continental Divide, through forest.

Reach a pretty sheltered grove of pine and fir at a saddle at 0.5. Remain on the crest of the Divide at the junction here, avoiding the Caribou Trail, to the left, that returns to the Dearborn basin. (The description for the next couple of miles reflects unmarked, cross-country travel; because of recent improvements, the current route may not correspond exactly to the following account.) Proceed eastward, crossing grassy open terrain past a minor rise and dropping slightly to another saddle at 1.4. Blowout Mountain is the flat-topped mountain to the northeast.

Climb somewhat more steeply to a higher summit, with fair tree coverage near the top. Be careful here. Be sure to climb to the highest point, at 2.0, leaving the worn track that leads off to the right. (That route appears to continue southward to the lookout tower on Silver King Mountain, about four miles down the ridge of the Alice Mountains.)

The correct route is to the east. From the Trail at 2.0, it can be observed that a mile ahead the Continental Divide leaves the ridge line, drops off to the south, and then continues along the top of a prominent cliff face. (The main ridge goes east another mile out Burned Point before dropping off.) Descend from 2.0, remaining as close as possible to the crest.

Come to a disturbed area on the Divide at 2.8. The designated route includes a trail that is to be constructed along the Continental Divide to Lewis and Clark Pass. Even now it is said to be feasible to continue along the Divide, sometimes along lightly-traveled paths and sometimes cross-country; but

107

note that water may not be available on the way. For more details, see the Blowout Mountain Quadrangle.

From the disturbed area, descend to the right on a gravel restricted-travel road. Around 3.5, there are good views of the cliffs of the Continental Divide, and Lewis and Clark Pass and Green Mountain. Continue with several long switchbacks. Water may be found at an intermittent creek as the road makes its third sharp bend—a hairpin to the right—at 4.4.

Reach the confluence of two branches of Alice Creek at 5.8. Although these may be dry, Alice Creek (to the right) will shortly provide a reliable supply. After a more gradual descent, come to a road intersection at 7.3. Continue by taking the left fork. (About 100 yards on the fork to the right is a good campsite on Alice Creek.) Only the foundations of the former Alice Creek Ranger Station remain, at 7.6; a camp can be made slightly upstream, across the road, near the creek.

The road at 7.7 is marked by a historical sign: "Alice Creek. This valley was a major camp spot on the historic 'road to the buffalo.' Generations of Indians passed along this trail to their buffalo hunting grounds east of the Continental Divide....Captain Lewis and nine men passed here on July 7, 1806. They stopped for lunch about four miles downstream. Lewis wrote: 'halted to dine at a large beaver dam...deer are remarkably plenty and in good order. Reuben Fields wounded a moos deer this morning near our camp, my dog much worried.'" The sign also records the crossing of Lewis and Clark Pass by F. W. Lander, engineer with the 1853 Stevens railway survey.

Turn left at the intersection and follow the dirt road toward Lewis and Clark Pass. (To the right, it is eleven miles down the Alice Creek valley to Montana Highway 200; with care, you can drive this far by passenger car.) Ascend slowly through open sagebrush country used as cattle range. The creek to the right may be dry near the valley, but will probably have water from 8.4 to 9.0.

The road switchbacks to the right at 9.0, just below a spring. Obtain water before proceeding, as the remainder of the Section is dry. At 9.3, pass a jeep track to the right and continue climbing to Lewis and Clark Pass on the Continental Divide, with appropriate historical signs, at 9.5.

Turn southward, following the west side of the Divide through scrub growth to intercept the jeep track (the same one that was bypassed at 9.3). Follow the jeep track, which disintegrates into a pack trail. *Note:* although the remainder of this Section is described as a cross-country hike, posts, cairns, and other marks may now identify a slightly different, improved, location.

Ahead on the right is a grassy-topped ridge. At 10.2, turn away from this ridge and climb directly up to the Divide. There is a short flat stretch at 10.6 and then more climbing to the summit of Green Mountain at 11.0. (Along the way, cross several short segments of scree at around 10.8.) Green Mountain, at 7453 feet, is the highest named summit on the route of the Trail within the limits of this book. To the east and southeast are plains stretching to ranges on the far side of the Missouri River. Well-named Red Mountain, snow-capped, is almost due west. From the top of Green Mountain, the general route to Rogers Pass can be made out. Note the several ridges to the west of the Divide that must be avoided.

Descend Green Mountain toward the saddle and toward the hill beyond it that is scarred with obvious road tracks. The descent, through rather open woods, is quite easy. Reach a road at about 11.7 and follow it to the left, dropping directly into the saddle at 12.2. There may be some water in the creeks not far off the Trail to the west, but it would be preferable to carry a more certain supply from the Alice Creek headwaters.

Beyond the saddle, take the more steeply ascending road, crossing over the top of the hill at 12.8, and then descend eastward on the other side. (The designated route apparently follows the lower road, somewhat longer than our recommendation, but with 200 less feet of climb. Be sure, if you go that way, to cut back to the left at the spur ridge and contour half a mile back to the Divide, at 13.2 on the described route.)

Passing the head of Bartlett Creek, follow the jeep road as it forks left at 13.3. (*Caution:* watch for new trail construction from this point, as the Continental Divide is located outside the forest boundary for a mile, and the CDT may therefore be routed down to Cadotte Creek, at elevation 5400, before returning to the main ridge once again.) After the jeep road peters out, at 13.6, descend in the open along the crest.

The long narrow ridge in Cadotte Pass would be a place of inspiring beauty were it not for the major power transmission line at its low point, at 14.1. (When explorations for a railroad to the Pacific were carried out in the 1850's, Cadotte Pass and Lewis and Clark Pass were prime candidates for the northern route until a different crossing—at Mullan Pass, on the Trail in Southern Montana—was found to be more practicable; three decades later, surveys by Maj. A. B. Rogers for the Great Northern revealed, perhaps for the first time, the low passage at the end of the Section.)

Proceed southeast up the next obvious hill, at 14.7, without particular difficulty. From the south end of its flat top, observe the route toward Rogers Pass. Make a short descent eastward (not along the spur ridge to the southwest) to a saddle at 15.0. The minor rise ahead can be avoided by remaining to its right. Stay on the ridge, heading for a small outcrop at 15.4. Traffic on the highway is visible below.

(Do not attempt to descend directly to Rogers Pass from this outcrop. The slope is nothing but alder thicket and dense forest, eventually ending at the top of a steep roadcut that can't be negotiated safely.)

From the outcrop, follow the ridge to the top of the first bump (where there is a large cairn), at 15.8. Leave the ridge, which continues south; instead, follow the poorly-defined Continental Divide as it abruptly turns east. The descent, though still quite steep, is in the open, not in wooded thickets.

The Section terminates in Rogers Pass, at 16.5. There are no structures of any kind in the vicinity. Montana Highway 200 is the main route between Great Falls and Missoula. It is about 20 miles west to Lincoln, where there are motels, cafes, post office (with CDT register), and the ranger station for the Lincoln Ranger District. (You can find good water and a place to camp by dropping down 0.2 mile toward Lincoln and walking a short way up the jeep road to the east of the highway.)

Distances and elevations are:

0.0	Boundary of Scapegoat Wilderness	8150
0.5	Trail (266) junction	7700
1.0	(7961)	7950
1.4	Saddle	7800
2.0	Minor summit (8135)	8150
2.2	Enter Blowout Mountain Quadrangle	8100
2.4	Narrow defile	7950

2.8	Roadhead	7900
4.4	Creek	6750
5.8	Confluence	6000
7.3	Road intersection	5600
7.7	Road intersection (5574)	5550
9.0	Switchback	6150
9.3	Jeep track cutoff (6341)	6350
9.5	Lewis and Clark Pass (6421)	6400
11.0	Green Mountain (7453)	7450
11.2	Enter Cadotte Creek Quadrangle	7250
11.7	Road	6750
12.2	Saddle	6450
12.8	Minor summit (6973)	6950
13.2	Head of Bartlett Creek	6550
14.1	Cadotte Pass	6050
14.7	Hill (6499)	6500
15.3		6100
15.4	Outcrop	6150
15.8	Leave ridge	6350
16.0	Enter Rogers Pass Quadrangle	6150
16.5	Rogers Pass (Montana Highway 200)	5600

Trail Description

South-to-North

The slopes of the north side of Rogers Pass.

SCAPEGOAT WILDERNESS SEGMENT
Section 4
ROGERS PASS TO SCAPEGOAT BOUNDARY
16.5 Miles

The Section is of special historical interest, for here Meriwether Lewis crossed the Continental Divide in 1806 on the return leg of his epic expedition to the Pacific. The country is rather dry and sparsely timbered, with gentle grades that allow travel along the crest. But this also results in a lot of climbing—mile for mile, it is as strenuous as you will find anywhere along the Trail.

The route leaves Montana Highway 200—the last paved road for about 160 miles—at Rogers Pass. The initial stretch is a steep climb to the skyline. The hike then follows the crest, crossing minor summits both before and after Cadotte Pass, at 2.4. (However, as Cadotte Pass lies outside the national forest, new construction is planned to detour around it.) Beyond the summit of Green Mountain, at 5.5, descend on obscure ways to Lewis and Clark Pass at 7.0.

Following roads, the route drops down from Lewis and Clark Pass to the valley of Alice Creek, at 8.8, and then back up to the main ridge at 13.7. (This is an interim route: the Forest Service intends to locate new trail along the Divide, bypassing the roadwalk down to Alice Creek. Backpackers have reported being able to make their way cross-country along the crest, without particular difficulty, so that is an option that should be considered.) Proceed westward, crossing some minor summits, to the boundary of the Scapegoat Wilderness at 16.5.

Nearly all of the Section falls within the Lincoln Ranger District of the Helena National Forest. (The final 2.8 mile stretch is along the boundary with the Rocky Mountain Ranger District of the Lewis and Clark National Forest; some damage from fires in 1988 may be encountered along the Lewis and Clark side, but the Alice Creek drainage escaped injury.)

It is necessary to leave the Continental Divide to obtain water. Accordingly, a good supply should be carried when setting out from Rogers Pass and, again, from Alice Creek. Camping opportunities are limited because of the lack of water sources. Lincoln, about 20 miles to the west of Rogers Pass, provides a full range of services.

U.S.G.S. Maps: **Rogers Pass**, **Cadotte Creek**, **Blowout Mountain**, and **Caribou Peak**.

Also: our Map **17**.

Detailed Trail data are:

The start of the Section is Rogers Pass (on the Continental Divide), on Montana Highway 200, the main route between Great Falls and Missoula. There are no structures of any kind in the vicinity. However, Lincoln, to the west, offers the traveler all conveniences, including motels, cafes, post office (with CDT register), and the ranger station for the Lincoln Ranger District. Be sure to obtain water before setting out. (You can find good water and a place to camp by dropping down 0.2 mile toward Lincoln and walking a short way up the jeep road to the east of the highway.)

Begin by climbing around the steep roadcut. Ascend steeply, on the grassy slope directly above Rogers Pass. Reach a large cairn at the top at 0.7. Once at the crest, turn right and descend gradually along the ridgeline. Traffic on the highway is still visible from the small outcrop at 1.1. Circle to the left of a minor rise so as to reach a saddle at 1.5. (*Caution:* watch for new trail construction from this point, as the Continental Divide is located outside the forest boundary for a mile, and the CDT may therefore be routed down to Cadotte Creek, at elevation 5400, before returning to the main ridge once again.)

Climb to the summit bench of a flat-topped knoll at 1.7. Swing around to the right, crossing over the high point (elevation 6499) at 1.8, and then descending the open ridge to Cadotte Pass at 2.4. The long narrow ridge would be a place of inspiring beauty were it not for the major power transmission line at its low point. (When explorations for a railroad to the Pacific were carried out in the 1850's, Cadotte Pass and Lewis and Clark Pass were prime candidates for the northern route until a crossing at Mullan Pass, on the Trail in Southern Montana, was found to be more practicable; three decades later, surveys by Maj. A. B. Rogers for the Great Northern revealed, perhaps for the first time, the low passage at the start of the Section.)

Cadotte Pass.

Hike up the open crest. There are jeep trails to follow beyond 2.9. The road improves somewhat at 3.3 at the head of Bartlett Creek. From there, climb the steep route, straight up to the top of hill 6973 at 3.7. (If you fork off to the left on the lower road, follow it for half a mile to a spur ridge, and then bend sharp right, descending along the jeep road back to the Divide; though longer, this alternate—which is apparently the designated route—would involve some 200 less feet of climb.) Descend steeply, passing the intersection with the lower road on the way to a saddle at 4.3.

Although it would be better to carry water from Rogers Pass, you might be able to locate something to drink from the head of Bear Creek, which is a short way off to the west of the Trail. Begin the ascent of Green Mountain on the road, which makes an abrupt swing to the left away from the Divide at 4.7. Follow the road for about 100 yards more and then turn right to ascend Green Mountain. Remain as close to the Divide as is convenient, heading pretty much due north. The slopes are

117

mostly rather open woods and there should be no difficulty. (As in other stretches that are described here as cross-country, you may find a more recently established treadway, marked by blazes and cairns.)

The summit of Green Mountain is at 5.5. Green Mountain, at 7453 feet, is the highest named summit on the described route of the Continental Divide Trail within the limits of this book. To the east and southeast are plains stretching to ranges on the far side of the Missouri River. Well-named Red Mountain, snow-capped, is almost due west. One can also study the route of the Divide as it swings around the basin of Alice Creek and proceeds north and then west.

Descend Green Mountain by continuing north along the Divide. Cross several short segments of scree at around 5.7. Avoid the spur ridge that heads due west at 6.3; instead, turn sharply to the right, perhaps soon intersecting a pack trail which then improves and becomes a jeep track. Continue northward either cross-country or (not quite so directly) along the jeep route so as to reach the flat saddle on the Divide at 7.0.

This saddle is Lewis and Clark Pass, where Meriwether Lewis left Pacific waters for the last time, on July 7, 1806. (From Lewis and Clark Pass, it is said to be feasible to continue along the Divide, sometimes along lightly-traveled paths and sometimes cross-country; but note that water may not be available on the way. For more details, see the Blowout Mountain Quadrangle. If you choose to try the higher route, obtain water from the spring mentioned in the next paragraph.)

Take the jeep road descending westward from Lewis and Clark Pass. As the road bends to the right, at 7.2, the jeep track from Green Mountain comes in from the left. Continue dropping down to one of the upper forks of Alice Creek. The road switchbacks to the left at 7.5, just below a spring. Descend gradually through open sagebrush country used as cattle range. The creek to the left will probably have water between 7.5 and 8.1, though it may be dry farther down the valley.

Reach a road intersection at 8.8. Here a historical sign reads: "Alice Creek. This valley was a major camp spot on the historic 'road to the buffalo.' Generations of Indians passed along this trail to their buffalo hunting grounds east of the Continental Divide....Captain Lewis and nine men passed here on July 7, 1806. They stopped for lunch about four miles downstream. Lewis wrote: 'halted to dine at a large beaver dam ... deer are remarkably plenty and in good order. Reuben Fields wounded a moos deer this morning near our camp, my dog much worried.'" The sign also records the crossing of Lewis and Clark Pass by F.W. Lander, engineer with the 1853 Stevens railway survey.

Turn right at this intersection. (Straight ahead on the road, which is passable with care by passenger car, it is eleven miles down the Alice Creek valley to Montana Highway 200.) The foundations of the former Alice Creek Ranger Station are to the right of the road at 8.9. A camp can be made slightly upstream, across the road, near to Alice Creek. Curve right at the road intersection at 9.2. (To the left it is about 100 yards to a good campsite on Alice Creek.) The Trail continues northwest up the Alice Creek valley, climbing very gradually. Obtain water at a convenient point in this vicinity, as there is no assurance of a supply at higher elevations.

Come to the confluence of two branches of Alice Creek (which may be dry) at 10.7. Vehicle traffic is barred at a gate at 10.8. Ascend more steeply on the mining road, which makes several long switchbacks. Water may be found as the road approaches an intermittent creek, at 12.1, at the end of one of these switchbacks. Around 13.0, there are good views of the cliffs of the Continental Divide to the east.

The gravel restricted-travel road terminates in a disturbed area on the Divide at 13.7. Head westward on the Divide, on newly improved, well-marked, trail. Ascend close to the crest to the summit at 14.5. There are good views ahead toward Caribou Peak in the west. Another ridge, heading south from here, is known as the Alice Mountains; take care to avoid a worn track that appears to follow this ridge for about four miles to the lookout tower on Silver King Mountain.

Continue along the Divide. After a short stretch of fairly steep descent down a slope with moderate tree cover, the Trail continues through grassy open terrain past a broad saddle at 15.1. After a minor rise, reach another saddle—in a pretty sheltered grove of pine and fir—at 16.0. Here the Caribou pack trail (No. 266) reaches the Divide.

Climb through forest toward the next minor summit, at 16.5, at the easternmost point of the Scapegoat Wilderness.

The Section ends here as the Trail contours around this rise, a hundred yards or so to the north of its high point.

Distances and elevations are:

0.0	Rogers Pass (Montana Highway 200)	5600
0.5	Enter Cadotte Creek Quadrangle	6150
0.7	Crest	6350
1.1	Outcrop	6150
1.2		6100
1.8	Knoll (6499)	6500
2.4	Cadotte Pass	6050
3.3	Head of Bartlett Creek	6550
3.7	Minor summit (6973)	6950
4.3	Saddle	6450
4.8	Leave road	6750
5.3	Enter Blowout Mountain Quadrangle	7250
5.5	Green Mountain (7453)	7450
7.0	Lewis and Clark Pass (6421)	6400
7.2	Jeep track cutoff (6341)	6350
7.5	Switchback	6150
8.8	Road intersection (5574)	5550
9.2	Road intersection	5600
10.7	Confluence	6000
12.1	Creek	6750
13.7	Road ends	7900
14.1	Narrow defile	7950
14.3	Enter Caribou Peak Quadrangle	8100
14.5	Minor summit (8135)	8150
15.1	Saddle	7800
15.5	(7961)	7950
16.0	Trail (266) junction	7700
16.5	Boundary of Scapegoat Wilderness	8150

SCAPEGOAT WILDERNESS SEGMENT
Section 3
SCAPEGOAT BOUNDARY TO WHITETAIL CREEK
13.0 Miles

For most of this Section, the Trail follows the crest or high slopes of the Continental Divide. There are many excellent viewpoints, but the scenery reflects the consequences of the great Canyon Creek Fire of 1988.

Entering the Scapegoat Wilderness, the route avoids the summit of Caribou Peak by dropping to the Valley of the Moon—a pretty basin on its south slopes—at 3.3. The route returns to the high country, proceeding in large part cross-country along the Continental Divide. Several miles are within the fire perimeter, but the former tree cover was so sparse that deadfall is only occasionally a problem. The route leaves the Divide at 9.2 and descends to the Dearborn River at 11.6. The Section concludes with a walk up the valley to a trail junction, near the mouth of Whitetail Creek, at 13.0.

The described route is largely the same as the designated route. However, in order to follow established tread (suitable for horse travel), the designated route makes a long and unrewarding detour. See the detailed data below, at 6.9, for a further description.

All of the Section is in, or along the boundary of, the Scapegoat Wilderness—in the Rocky Mountain Ranger District of the Lewis and Clark National Forest on the eastern slope, but in the Lincoln Ranger District of the Helena National Forest on the western slope. The first good campsite is in the Valley of the Moon, but the springs there may on occasion dry up. The head of Blacktail Creek and the Dearborn valley are other fine places to stop.

The Canyon Creek fire—which impacted the route in this Section between 5.0 and 9.2 as well as most of the next Section—was ignited by lightning on June 25, 1988, but did not spread until late July. It still covered less than 40,000 acres when it jumped to the Atlantic side of the Continental Divide on August 9. Some of the damage along the Dearborn River (in Section 2) resulted from controlled burns set deliberately in an unsuccessful effort to create a barrier, but strong winds pushed the blaze many miles beyond. The fire continued until mid-September when, after unprecedented drought, rain and cooler weather enabled it to be contained.

U.S.G.S. Maps: **Caribou Peak, Heart Lake, Steamboat Mountain**, and **Jakie Creek**.

Also: our Map **16**.

Detailed Trail data are:

The Section begins on the north side of summit 8271, the easternmost point of the Scapegoat Wilderness. Descend easily on open slopes covered with small rocks. Follow the Divide at a fairly constant elevation from 0.4 to 1.0 and then begin climbing directly toward Caribou Peak.

The maintained trail down to the Valley of the Moon, which lies at the base of the steep southern slopes of Caribou Peak, is easy to follow, but it may be difficult to locate. The author found the track along the grassy ridge to be quite obscure—though recently the marking reportedly has been improved—so one might end up bushwhacking down the steep hillside through fairly dense forest. Leave the Divide at 1.4 just to the southeast of a minor hump on the Caribou ridge. Contour around to the left and then start down in a northwesterly direction. After passing treeline, swing a bit to the right, descending north northwest gradually. Cross a dry gully at 1.9. Go by a little park, quite near the base of the cliffs directly below the principal summit of Caribou Peak, at 2.3. This is the northeast corner of the Valley of the Moon; from here the western summit of Caribou (8655 on the 7.5-minute map) bears 312°.

Proceed west northwest, through sparse forest. The route is roughly parallel to the slopes of Caribou Peak, pretty much at contour or climbing slightly, remaining above the valleys which descend to the left.

This route will lead to an amphitheater formed by the Continental Divide and a high spur ridge leading south from the Divide. Nestled below, in the northwest corner of the Valley of the Moon, at 3.0, is a clearing and a small waterhole—quite a good campsite, with plenty of flat land, the shelter of scrubby pine and fir, and gardens of wildflowers.

(But in September of 1990, an especially dry year, no water could be found.)

Carry an ample supply of water when setting out, as there may be nothing to drink for the next six miles. Climb to the spur ridge, heading generally south and ascending the slope diagonally. A formerly obscure path has been cleared and marked here (as Trail No. 440).

Having attained the open ridge at 3.3, follow it northward toward the west summit of Caribou Peak (hill 8655). From the depression at 3.9, enjoy the view overlooking the deep cirque of Bighorn Lake (to the west) and Valley of the Moon (to the east); keep to the left and traverse, close to contour, well below summit 8655. Intersect a pack trail at 4.5 and follow it northward, reaching the Continental Divide at a saddle at 5.0. (The pack trail, in the opposite direction, connects with Bighorn Lake.)

From the saddle, the Trail rises a bit through a grassy area. Continue in open country, hiking slightly to the left of the Divide and above the wooded areas along the slope. Pass through a stretch of spruce-fir forest from about 5.8 to 6.1, descending fairly steeply. The Trail then proceeds down the crest of the Divide on untimbered slope.

Leave the Divide at the pass at 6.3, taking the good footway to the left at the trail junction. Proceed west, soon following the right bank of a dry creek. Enter a flat grassy bottomland. The main valley swings to the left at 6.9.

(From here, the designated route descends the main valley, on established trail. After about 4.6 miles, it leaves Bighorn Creek and crosses a ridge on the way to Landers Fork at 9.5. It then climbs back to the Divide, intersecting the recommended route at the head of Blacktail Creek. The designated route is 10.7 miles long, with 1650 feet of climbing—as compared with 2.3 miles and 800 feet for the recommended route. Fire damage is extensive along the way.)

Instead of following the designated route, bear right at 6.9 and climb gradually, following another dry creek northwest in the direction of the Continental Divide. This route opens up into a small meadow; at some points, the creek on the left side of this meadow may have a little water.

Climb cross-country from the meadow to the Continental Divide to the north. (Deadfall from the 1988 fire makes this difficult.) Reaching the Continental Divide at 7.8, turn left (west). Climb on a path that has been cut through the woods. After reaching a high point at 8.2, descend the narrow ridge toward Scapegoat Mountain, which is about ten miles to the northwest. Avoid the wooded ridge that leads off to the left at 8.2; the descent along the Divide stays more to the right, just above the steep dropoff to the drainage of Blacktail Creek.

The Trail proceeds for the most part through open country, but with some patches of trees. It is not difficult, and often it is convenient to follow a track made by horses. Enjoy good views on both sides including, to the south, 9400-foot snow-patched Red Mountain.

Follow the Divide past a low saddle, at 9.0, until a major transmountain trail is intersected at 9.2. Here turn right, leaving the Helena National Forest for the last time. (The circuitous detour of the designated route, which comes up from the left, ends at this point.)

A trickle, part of the headwaters of Blacktail Creek, lies immediately north of the Divide. White bog-orchid, fringed parnassia, elephantshead and others crowd close to the water, while just a few feet away on the dry slopes are stonecrop, gaillardia, umbrella plant and many more besides. Although sheltered flat ground is limited, the site is a good place to pitch camp. By climbing a few feet eastward, you can look out to the austere mountains north of the Dearborn River. (Another possible campsite can be found about 200 yards along the trail into the Helena, where there is another small creek.)

The descent to the Dearborn River is on Blacktail Creek Trail No. 207; it is quite steep, following Blacktail Creek and losing 1700 feet in two miles. (The route indicated on the 7.5-minute topographic maps starts out the same way, but then swings west to the West Fork of Blacktail Creek. The junction of these two routes is at 10.1; at this point, take the blazed path that turns right and descends through forest.) The Trail is well above the left bank of Blacktail Creek until it finally drops down steeply to a stream crossing at 11.4. (*Note:* the next 0.2 mile is an unmarked shortcut developed by informal use; the designated route is presumed to cross Black-tail Creek and continue on for a quarter of a mile to an intersection with Dearborn River Trail No. 206, but farther downstream than is necessary.) Contour to the left, not cross-

The open crest of the Continental Divide as it approaches the pass at the head of Blacktail Creek.

ing Blacktail Creek; the track soon leads across the West Fork of Blacktail Creek to a clearing where outfitters have erected the framework for a shelter (though this may subsequently have been removed). Continue by path to the flats along the Dearborn River, at 11.6, where Dearborn River Trail No. 206 is intersected.

From the unmarked junction at 11.6, turn left and follow Trail 206 west. (The footpath may be overgrown and difficult to make out for the next mile.) The ground is flat and open and there are good campsites. The Dearborn River is accessible just to the right as it winds its way through wide gravel beds. After moving away from the river, once again approach it and cross to its left (north) bank at 12.2. Though it is a small stream, fording may be required. Take the right fork at the unsigned trail junction just past the crossing. Continue up, parallel to the riverside, through dry and open terrain. Cross Pear Creek at 12.8.

After some small rises and dips, reach a junction in a meadow close to the Dearborn River. The Section ends here, at 13.0, as Whitetail Creek Trail No. 218 turns off to the left.

Distances and elevations are:

0.0	Enter Scapegoat Wilderness	8150
0.7		7950
1.4	Leave Continental Divide	8250
1.9	Gully	7900
2.3	Park	7600
3.0	Valley of the Moon	7700
3.3	Ridge	8050
3.9		8350
4.5	Trail	8300
5.0	Saddle	8000
5.2		8050
6.3	Trail junction	7150
6.9	Leave designated route	6850
7.4	Meadow	7050
7.9	Enter Heart Lake Quadrangle	7400
8.2	Minor summit	7550
9.0	Saddle	6850
9.2	Blacktail Creek Trail (207) Junction	6950
10.1	Trail junction	6350
10.7	Enter Caribou Peak Quadrangle	5750
10.9	Enter Steamboat Mountain Quadrangle	5550
11.4		5300
11.6	Dearborn River Trail (206) Junction	5250
11.9	Enter Jakie Creek Quadrangle	5300
12.2	Dearborn River (5278)	5300
13.0	Whitetail Creek Trail (218) Junction	5350

SCAPEGOAT WILDERNESS SEGMENT
Section 2
WHITETAIL CREEK TO GREEN FORK
12.6 Miles

The devastating Canyon Creek fire of 1988 burned forest and grazing lands within a perimeter of 240,000 acres, including a broad swath east and northeast of Scapegoat Mountain. The effects of the fire, along with revegetation in coming years, give the Section its special interest.

The route here is almost as straight as an arrow. It heads up the narrow, steep-sided Dearborn valley. After a couple of miles, it runs through patches of burned forest. Some trees have survived near the easy ford of the Dearborn River at 4.2. There is severe damage en route to Welcome Creek Guard Station at 6.3. The Trail then climbs nearly 1000 feet to Straight Creek Pass, at 8.8, from which there is a fine prospect backward over the route. The burn continues on the descent above Straight Creek. Finally leaving the fire perimeter at 10.9, the Section ends with a pretty walk—with nice views up Green Fork—to the junction with Green Fork Trail No. 228 at 12.6.

Water is readily available along the route. There are a few attractive campsites, but none in the last five miles of the Section. All of the designated route is situated in the Rocky Mountain Ranger District of the Lewis and Clark National Forest, as well as the Scapegoat Wilderness.

The guidebook's first edition included a more scenic route that traversed the sides of Scapegoat Mountain and visited the cliff-encircled amphitheater of Halfmoon Park. Much of the way, including a cross-country stretch east of Scapegoat was forested, and the fire damage was no doubt severe. In the absence of post-fire reconnaissance reports, that route can now be recommended only to the venturesome. (The alternate route starts out by ascending Whitetail Creek. After crossing the Continental Divide, it drops down into the Tobacco Valley, along the North Blackfoot River. Next comes the cross-country hike, up to the Divide again and then along the crest for three miles. The route then circles around Scapegoat, on trails, to Halfmoon Park. A descent of Green Fork completes the circuit, rejoining the designated route at the end of the Section. Overall, the alternate is about nine miles longer, with nearly 3000 feet additional climb. Except for the Whitetail and Green Fork drainages, all of it lies within the burned area.)

U.S.G.S. Maps: **Jakie Creek** and **Scapegoat Mountain**. Also: our Map **15**.

Detailed Trail data are:

The Section begins in a meadow at the junction of Dearborn River Trail No. 206 and Whitetail Creek Trail No. 218. (It is 500 feet to the left, down Trail 218, to the Dearborn River. The grassy area by the river would be a splendid place to camp, but it may be unavailable—either for wilderness restoration purposes or because reserved for use by a commercial outfitter.)

Hike along the left (north) bank of the river, well up from its bank. Step over a small creek, at the edge of a wide gully, at 1.2. Enjoy pleasant views, especially looking downstream, from openings along the trail. Entering the perimeter of the Canyon Creek fire, approach the river closely; it might be nice to rest just before the gully at 2.5, which the Trail crosses by way of a hairpin bend at contour.

Step over Lookout Creek at 3.2. There are nice views upstream to Crown Mountain from the route at 3.3, opposite the mouth of Bald Bear Creek. Boulderhop a small side creek at 3.5. (You could camp nearby, close to the river, beneath the cottonwoods and Douglas firs.) Continuing along level path in the valley, pass Elk Pass Trail No. 205 (which turns right and ascends from the junction at 3.7).

Ford the Dearborn River at 4.2; in summer, it is five yards wide and calf-deep. A wooded, authorized, campsite on the far bank would be a good place to spend the night. The terrain is soon badly scarred, starting before Lost Cabin Creek (to be boulderhopped or forded) at 4.4.

Pass the junction with the Lost Cabin Creek Trail (which goes off to the left) at 4.5. It might be nice to camp along the river over the next half mile, which has retained its tree cover, but restrictions have been placed in effect so as to enable the wilderness to recover from past overuse.

Leaving the valley, make your way for a mile through a blackened area—in 1989 little more than patches of beargrass grew in the bare earth (though by 1991 wildflowers were found in profusion). Cross several gullies, most or all of them waterless, hiking pretty much at contour.

After descending a bit, make a sharp turn to the right at the junction at 6.2. The Trail once again parallels the Dearborn River; Welcome Creek Guard Station is to the left, across the river at 6.3, easy to pass by without notice. Soon ford the calf-deep river and, after another 50 yards, boulderhop Welcome Creek at 6.4.

The next stretch is a walk up the Welcome Creek drainage, sometimes on overgrown footway. But instead of following the former trail close to the stream (it is the left fork at 6.6), take the high route up the left (east) bank. There are some switchbacks before the path reaches a high point, well above the water, at 7.0.

Turn left at the trail junction in the middle of the meadow at 7.2. (The Jakie Creek Trail turns off to the right, soon crossing Welcome Pass.) A patch of pines has survived at the far edge of the meadow, along Welcome Creek; until the fire scars have healed somewhat, this must be considered the last satisfactory campsite in the Section.

Climbing, boulderhop to the right bank of the creek at 7.5 and back to the left (east) bank at 7.6. Watch for dippers flying along the stream. Leave the narrow valley floor at 7.8 and ascend at a steady moderate grade. Step over to the right bank at 8.5 and back to the left at 8.6.

Stop to enjoy the backward view from Straight Creek Pass at 8.8; the fine scenery extends southeast all the way to Caribou Peak. Continue across the pass and then descend, with a long switchback, to the headwaters of Straight Creek. The first couple of crossings of the main gully, at 9.4 and 9.7, are likely to be dry. There is a good spring a couple of feet off to the left of the Trail, though, at 9.8. There, or at various places a little farther down, it might be feasible to camp—but the scarred ground is not inviting. Boulderhop to the left bank at 10.0 and back to the right at 10.1.

Remain on the newer, higher, path at a junction at 10.2. (A side trail going off to the left connects with a route up Halfmoon Creek and, apparently, an earlier location of the

Straight Creek Trail as well.) At 10.4, enjoy the splendid, fire-cleared, view up the valley of Halfmoon Creek to Scapegoat Mountain—a summit that is otherwise visible only at much longer distances.

Leave the Canyon Creek burn, at last, at 10.9. Water can be obtained from a spring on the uphill side of the Trail at 11.2, high up a draw. The dainty Arctic rockjasmine might be noted a bit before it. Another fine vantage point is at 11.4, with a view looking down Straight Creek and far off to the northwest. Just beyond, contour around a gully.

The scenery from 11.8 to 12.3—opposite the valley of Green Fork—is notable for the cliff bands that form steep walls along its sides. Morning shadows outline a man's face, with the darkness of an overhung cave entrance forming the hair behind his left ear; it is a couple of miles up the Green Fork, about halfway up above its left bank.

Pass a small side creek, with a bridge of cross-logs, at 12.3. Descend gradually along the hillside. The Section ends at the junction at 12.6, where Green Fork Trail No. 228 joins from the left.

Distances and elevations are:

0.0	Whitetail Creek Trail (218) Junction	5350
1.2	Creek	5450
1.9	Canyon Creek Fire perimeter	5500
3.2	Lookout Creek	5600
4.2	Dearborn River	5700
4.5	Lost Cabin Creek Trail (254) Junction	5750
6.1		5950
6.2	Trail junction	5900
6.4	Dearborn River	5850
7.0		6100
7.2	Jakie Creek Trail (214) Junction	6000
8.6	Enter Scapegoat Mountain Quadrangle	6600
8.8	Straight Creek Pass	6750
10.2	Trail (216) junction	6350
10.9	Leave Canyon Creek Fire perimeter	6350
12.6	Green Fork Trail (228) Junction	6050

SCAPEGOAT WILDERNESS SEGMENT
Section 1
GREEN FORK TO BENCHMARK
Recommended (Straight Creek) Route: 10.0 Miles
Designated (South Fork) Route: 14.5 Miles

Each of the two alternate routes involves a hike, largely in forest, down a valley. There is an occasional view, but not the magnificent vistas of the high country.

The recommended route is clearly superior with respect to both scenery and ease of travel. The only reasons to consider the designated route—other than the fact that it is the official one—are, first, proximity to the Continental Divide and, second, convenience for people who wish to bypass Benchmark and continue north over the Hoadley-Ahorn Divide.

From start to finish, the Trail in this Section travels along the banks of Straight Creek. There is plenty of water, but desirable campsites are few—the best is at 6.1. The recommended and designated routes are identical to 2.9.

The Section is in the Rocky Mountain Ranger District of the Lewis and Clark National Forest, with all but the last three miles in the Scapegoat Wilderness as well. Benchmark, at the end of the Section, is an important resupply point. (Refer to the introductory text to the next Section for details.)

U.S.G.S. Maps: **Scapegoat Mountain, Wood Lake**, and **Benchmark**.

Also: our Map **14**.

Detailed Trail data are:

The Section commences at the junction of Green Fork Trail No. 228 and Straight Creek Trail No. 212. Walk north on the latter, along the right bank of Straight Creek.

Pass the junction with Cigarette Creek Trail No. 247, which crosses Straight Creek, at 0.6. At the next junction, at 1.2, Petty-Crown Creek Trail No. 232 turns off, to the right, toward Petty and Ford Creeks. Crown Creek, just past the junction, is sometimes dry. Pass another creek at 1.8. Straight Creek is much divided as it runs through gravel beds at 2.3.

131

There is an unsigned junction at 2.9, soon after you traverse a landslide. (The designated route, Elbow Creek Trail No. 248, forks off to the left and crosses the stream.) Continuing ahead, follow the bank of Straight Creek closely to 3.1. The route is in lodgepole pine forest, with occasional openings. The small side creeks, including Park Creek at 3.8, have bridges or culverts. The best place to camp in the Section is on the dry grassy flats that line Straight Creek from roughly 5.9 to 6.2—as, for example, near the register box at 6.1.

After passing several creeks and seeps, leave the Scapegoat Wilderness at a sign at 6.9. The Patrol Mountain Lookout Trail joins from the left at 7.2. Enjoy excellent views of Patrol Mountain and picturesque bends of Straight Creek at 8.8 and 9.2.

Reach a service road (accessible by passenger vehicle) at the trailhead at 9.5. From the parking area here, walk along the road, past the entrance to Benchmark Campground and past Wood Creek. Intersect the high-standard Benchmark-Augusta road, Forest Road 235, at 9.8 and turn left. (To the right, it is two miles to the Benchmark Wilderness Ranch, where supplies can be mailed in advance. See the introductory text for the next Section for details.) The Section ends at the next junction, at 10.0, where a side road turns left to the Benchmark administrative site.

Distances and elevations are:

0.0	Green Fork Trail (228) Junction	6050
0.5	Enter Wood Lake Quadrangle	6000
0.6	Cigarette Creek Trail (247) Junction	5950
1.2	Petty-Crown Creek Trail (232) Junction	5900
2.9	Elbow Creek Trail (248) Junction	5750
6.1	Register box	5550
6.9	Leave Scapegoat Wilderness	5600
7.2	Patrol Mountain Lookout Trail (213) Junction	5500
8.1	Enter Benchmark Quadrangle	5450
9.5	Trailhead	5300
9.8	Road junction	5300
10.0	Benchmark-Augusta road (5291)	5300

Designated (South Fork) Route

If you hike this way, you will have a longer trip, quite often with mucky spots, with more up-and-down and fords. Why bother (unless you are bypassing Benchmark and going over the Ahorn-Hoadley Divide)?

The designated route follows Straight Creek Trail No. 212—the same as the recommended route—as far as 2.9. It then fords Straight Creek and climbs over a low ridge before descending to the valley of the South Fork of the Sun River at 5.7. After heading downstream for several miles, the route fords the South Fork at 10.9. (If bypassing Benchmark, see text for the next Section from here.) Keep level to a second ford of the river at 13.6 and Straight Creek shortly thereafter. The route then passes by the Benchmark administrative site to 14.4, where it intersects the high-standard route between Benchmark and Augusta. (The formally designated route, Trail No. 202, avoids the last two stream crossings; but we assume that anyone who comes this close to Benchmark will detour to the road in order to resupply.)

Water and campsites are available as needed. There is one nice view—up Ellis Creek to Sugarloaf Mountain—but most of the way is densely forested, with only occasional meadows.

U.S.G.S. Maps: **Scapegoat Mountain, Wood Lake,** and **Benchmark.**

Also: our Map 14.

Detailed Trail data are:

The Section begins in the same way as the recommended route—down Straight Creek Trail No. 212, passing junctions with Cigarette Creek Trail No. 247 at 0.6 and Petty-Crown Creek Trail No. 232 at 1.2.

Turn left at the unsigned junction at 2.9, on Elbow Creek Trail No. 248. Ford Straight Creek, which is about ten yards wide, right away. The flat grassy area on the far bank is a very good place to camp. Climb the ridge to the west. There are switchbacks on the sloping meadow at 3.1 and higher up, in forest, at 3.4. Step over headwaters of Elbow Creek at 3.9 and 4.0. The tread is good and the grade is a steady and moderate one. Trees completely obstruct any view at the crest of Elbow Pass, at 4.3. Descend with switchbacks, and cross a small creek at 5.6.

Turn right at the junction with South Fork Trail No. 202 at 5.7. Proceeding downstream, use a little bridge to cross a creek at 5.9, in a stretch that has been torn up by the hooves of horses. Although the river cannot be seen, it can sometimes be heard off to the left.

A broad meadow at 6.8 extends from the tread down the slope all the way to the side of the stream. This is perhaps the best place in the South Fork valley for camping, but there is access to the river farther on and no doubt you could find somewhere to stop. The route is at water level, for example, at 7.9, after which it again moves up the bank. Although it lies mostly in forest, there are occasional openings. Great stands of cow parsnip sometimes crowd the tread, which is mucky at spots.

Ellis Creek Trail No. 227 joins from the left at 8.9, about 100 feet past a large dry gully. Continue along the hillside, well above the river, passing a couple of small but vigorous side creeks.

The scenic highlight of the Section is the view south southwest at 9.2, up Ellis Creek, toward flat-topped Sugarloaf Mountain, a cliff-sided summit on the Continental Divide. Step over a willow-lined creek at 9.5. Walk carefully along the narrow ledge directly above the river's edge at 9.7. Dip to the streambank at 9.9; there is room for a little camp a few feet to the left, by the water. Return to the slope and proceed with small ups and downs to 10.5. Descend into the valley again, crossing a little creek at 10.7.

Ford the South Fork of the Sun River, which is about 10 yards wide, at 10.9. (Though about the same width as Straight Creek, this stream is a bit deeper and its current is somewhat stronger.) There are places to camp on both sides of the river.

Turn right at the trail junction just past the ford. (Hoadley Creek Trail No. 226, to the left, is the recommended route between Benchmark and Indian Point.) Hike from here with only minor elevation changes. Much of the forest of lodgepole pines dates from a 1910 fire. Pass a small meadow at 12.2, close to river level.

Leave the Scapegoat Wilderness at a sign at about 12.7. Boulderhop a wide but shallow creek at 13.0. The next half mile is delightful—flat and with frequent overlooks of the bending and rushing stream.

South Fork Cutoff Trail No. 255 bears off to the right at a junction at 13.5, near a register box. (This description takes Trail

No. 255, but the officially designated route, Trail No. 202, continues north along the left bank of the river.) Ford the South Fork once again at 13.6. Make a clockwise swing around a ridge into the valley of Straight Creek. (The prominent peak to the north is Prairie Reef.) Ford Straight Creek—about ten yards wide and, in midsummer, still only calf-deep—at 14.0.

The pack trail ends at 14.1, as it comes to the end of a gravel road (passable by passenger car). Follow the road past outfitters' large corrals and curve around to the left. Pass the entrance to the Benchmark administrative site at 14.4. The Section ends at 14.5, at the intersection with the road to Augusta.

Distances and elevations are:

0.0	Green Fork Trail (228) Junction	6050
0.5	Enter Wood Lake Quadrangle	6000
0.6	Cigarette Creek Trail (247) Junction	5950
1.2	Petty-Crown Creek Trail (232) Junction	5900
2.9	Elbow Creek Trail (248) Junction	5750
2.9	Straight Creek	5750
3.9	Elbow Creek	6300
4.3	Elbow Pass	6550
4.8	Enter Benchmark Quadrangle	6400
5.7	South Fork Trail (202) Junction	5900
6.8	Meadow	5750
7.9		5650
8.7		5750
8.9	Ellis Creek Trail (227) Junction	5700
9.9	Streambank	5600
10.3		5700
10.9	Hoadley Creek Trail (226) Junction	5450
11.1		5500
12.2	Meadow	5400
12.3		5450
13.5	South Fork Cutoff Trail (255) Junction	5300
13.6	South Fork, Sun River	5250
13.9		5300
14.0	Straight Creek	5250
14.1	Trailhead	5250
14.4	Benchmark Administrative Site	5300
14.5	Benchmark-Augusta road (5291)	5300

BENCHMARK TO INDIAN POINT GUARD STATION
Recommended (Hoadley Reef) Route: 17.0 Miles
Designated (Sun River) Route: 11.2 Miles

This Section offers a choice—either an up-and-down hike to the cliffs below the Continental Divide or a water level walk in the valleys of the Sun River. The high route is recommended, because of the views; but the shorter riverside alternative would save some time.

The recommended route begins on the side road that passes the Benchmark administrative site. From the end of the road, at 0.4, it soon fords Straight Creek and the South Fork of the Sun River. The route heads up the South Fork to 3.6, after which it climbs the valley of Hoadley Creek to the high country.

The Trail leaves the Scapegoat Wilderness and enters the Bob Marshall Wilderness at a saddle at 9.3. The backward view—toward Scapegoat and other ridges and peaks near and far—is splendid. A short steep descent leads to a lovely subalpine meadow, encircled by an amphitheater of high cliffs, at 9.9. The route then descends through forest along Ahorn Creek. The Section ends at 17.0, at the trail junction just past the ford of the West Fork of the Sun.

The Section is located in the Rocky Mountain Ranger District of the Lewis and Clark National Forest, with all but the first three miles lying in one of the wilderness areas as well as the Sun River Game Preserve. Water is generally available at short intervals in this Section, but good sites for camping are scarce. River crossings might be difficult during spring runoff, when the designated route would be more practical. (The fords of Straight Creek and the South Fork can be avoided, however, by using the South Fork bridge near Benchmark, as described for the designated route, and then backtracking south on South Fork Trail No. 202.)

Forest Road 235, a high-standard gravel road maintained for use by passenger cars, connects Benchmark to Augusta, Montana. Augusta is an hour away, so it is more convenient to make arrangements to resupply at Benchmark Wilderness

Ranch, which is located at the far end of the airstrip, about 2 miles from the Trail. (For a reasonable fee, the Ranch will hold parcels for arriving hikers. Cabins and showers are also available. To obtain current information, contact Beverly Heckman, Benchmark Wilderness Ranch, Box 190, Augusta MT 59410. You can also try calling 406-562-3336, a phone in Augusta. The assistance of outfitters along the Trail is greatly appreciated, so CDT users are urged to keep their requests as simple and straightforward as possible.)

U.S.G.S. Maps: **Benchmark**, **Trap Mountain**, and **Prairie Reef**.

Also: our Map **13**.

Detailed Trail data are:

From the Benchmark-Augusta road, turn left, passing the entrance to the Benchmark administrative site at 0.1. Bend around to the right to the end of the road, at 0.4, by outfitters' large corrals.

Pick up South Fork Cutoff Trail No. 255. Ford Straight Creek, which in midsummer is about 10 yards wide and calf-deep, at 0.5. Make a counterclockwise swing around a ridge into the valley of the South Fork of the Sun River. Follow the river briefly before fording it at 0.9; it is about the same width and depth as Straight Creek, though perhaps with a stronger current.

Intersect South Fork Trail No. 202 at 1.0 and follow it upstream, immediately passing a register box. The next half mile is excellent—flat and with frequent overlooks of the bending and rushing river. Boulderhop a wide but shallow creek at 1.5. Enter the Scapegoat Wilderness at a sign about 1.8. Continue, with slight rises and dips, through lodgepole forest dating from a fire in 1910. Pass a small meadow at 2.3, close to river level.

Leave the valley at 3.6, at the trail junction. (A camp can be made along the river, on a gravel bank.) Keep to the right, on Hoadley Creek Trail No. 226. Approaching the mouth of Hoadley Creek, bend around to the right and head up the side valley. From 3.9 to 4.1, Hoadley Creek runs through a small but pretty gorge that is headed by a narrow chute of falling water. Hiking above the left (north) bank of Hoadley Creek, pass several tributaries that are likely to be dry; a small side stream at 6.1 might, however, provide some water. There is room for a single tent near the crossing of Hoadley Creek at 6.4; forested creek bottoms such as this are good places to find winter wrens, golden-crowned kinglets, and other small birds.

Keep to the right at the trail junction at 6.5. (The trail ascending to the left is a popular route of access from Benchmark to the southern part of the Bob Marshall Wilderness.) At switchbacks at 7.5, cross two branches of Hoadley Creek just above their confluence.

The terrain soon opens up. As you climb in open country, blazes and cairns may be obscure and hard to locate; if you lose the marks, keep going up the slope on a course parallel to Hoadley Reef and a couple of hundred yards from the base of its sheer cliffs. Cross a small headwater of Hoadley Creek at 8.4. Reach the divide between Grizzly Basin on the right and the Hoadley drainage on the left at 8.7; turn to the left and follow the narrow ridge uphill.

The Hoadley-Ahorn Divide, at 9.3, marks the boundary between the Scapegoat Wilderness and the Bob Marshall Wilderness. The superlative view of the island-like mass of Scapegoat Mountain to the south and of the mountains to the southeast, along the Continental Divide as far back as Caribou Peak, rewards you for climbing here instead of following the designated route in the valleys.

Descend a talus-filled gully to 9.5. The route (now East Fork Ahorn Trail No. 225) continues to drop very steeply; take it slow, enjoying the scenery and wildlife, including perhaps some mountain goats.

Although there may be some bugs, camping should be excellent in the beautiful meadow—50 yards or so off the main tread—at 9.9. Water is available from the meandering source of the East Fork of Ahorn Creek. A western extension of Hoadley Reef forms a magnificent backdrop. Look out over the Ahorn valley, toward Red Butte, as you descend. Pass side creeks at 10.8, 11.7, and 12.1.

Come to the junction with Ahorn Creek Trail No. 209 at 13.4. Follow Trail No. 209 from here, keeping straight. (To the left, Trail No. 209 crosses the East Fork in 100 feet and then heads for Camp Creek Pass.) Just past the junction, a short unmarked path to the left leads to a campsite by the creek.

Looking south from Hoadley-Ahorn Divide.

Pass some more side streams, characteristically with brook saxifrage and arrowleaf groundsel nearby; and queencup's white flower dots the forest floor early in the year. A fallen log may be available to get over to the left bank of Ahorn Creek at 14.7. Continuing on in the spruce-fir forest, cross Blind Fork easily at 15.4.

The ford of the West Fork of the South Fork of the Sun River, at 16.8, might be difficult (or even impassable) during spring runoff, but ordinarily should present no problem. There are good campsites nearby. The Section ends at a trail junction, at 17.0, in the meadows on the far side of the river. Here intersect the designated route, West Fork Trail No. 203.

Distances and elevations are:

0.0	Road junction	5300
0.1	Benchmark Administrative Site	5300
0.4	Trailhead	5250
0.5	Straight Creek	5250
0.6		5300
0.9	South Fork, Sun River	5250
1.0	South Fork Trail (202) Junction	5300

2.2		5450
2.3	Meadow	5400
3.4		5500
3.6	Hoadley Creek Trail (226) Junction	5450
4.7		5750
4.9		5700
6.4	Hoadley Creek	5950
6.5	Trail junction	6000
7.5	Hoadley Creek	6500
7.6	Enter Trap Mountain Quadrangle	6550
8.4	Headwater	7150
9.3	Hoadley-Ahorn Divide	7800
9.9	Meadow	7250
10.3	Enter Prairie Reef Quadrangle	7050
12.1	Creek (6400)	6400
13.4	Ahorn Creek Trail (209) Junction (5635)	5650
14.7	Ahorn Creek	5450
14.9		5500
15.4	Blind Fork (5438)	5450
16.8	West Fork of South Fork, Sun River	5300
17.0	West Fork Trail (203) Junction	5300

Designated (Sun River) Route

The designated route is the primary travelway from the roadhead at Benchmark to the Chinese Wall. It is very direct and uncomplicated. The first part is a walk up the South Fork of the Sun River, through forest well above the level of the stream. The route then turns west, crossing the West Fork on a sturdy bridge at 5.3 and ascending its valley. This is a pretty stretch, with a number of nice open spots, to the junction with the recommended route at 11.2. (See introduction to the recommended route for resupply and other information for Benchmark.)

Camping is not permitted near the West Fork bridge. There are some possibilities for overnight stays along the West Fork, but the best campsites are at the very end of the Section. There is a dry stretch from Deer Creek at 2.3 to the West Fork at 5.3, but elsewhere drinking water is available at frequent intervals.

U.S.G.S. Maps: Benchmark, Pretty Prairie, and Prairie Reef.

Also: our Map 13.

Detailed Trail data are:

From the turnoff to the Benchmark administrative site, proceed north on the main gravel road. After climbing to 0.2, drop down to the trailhead, near the Forest Service's South Fork Campground, at 0.7.

Take the well-worn wide trail, following the valley downstream. Cross the horse bridge over the South Fork at 1.0. Intersect South Fork Trail No. 202 on the far side of the bridge. (To the left, Trail No. 202 is the formally designated route; but here we have assumed that anyone coming this close to Benchmark will want to detour to the road and pick up supplies.)

Follow Trail No. 202 north, rising a bit in the forest back from the river itself. (An unmarked trail—presumably the route of Trail No. 202 before the construction of the bridge—comes in from the left at 1.3.) Boulderhop small Burned Creek at 1.5. The trees open up to provide a view over the bending river at 1.6.

Ford ankle-deep Deer Creek in a sunny patch at 2.3; this is the last water for three miles. Hike well back from the river, in forest, with minor elevation changes. Bighead Trail No. 242 descends to the right from the junction at 3.3. Take the left fork, after a register box, at 4.4; the right fork (the low water branch of Trail No. 202) is roundabout and inconvenient (because it requires fording of the West Fork). Beyond the long meadow at 4.8, converge with the river.

Walk over the West Fork of the South Fork of the Sun River on the sturdy horse bridge at 5.3. (Camping is not permitted along the trail within 1/4 mile of the bridge.) Turn left at the junction, at 5.4, on the far side of the stream. Continuing on West Fork Trail No. 203, cross Wapiti Creek at 5.6. Break out of forest at 5.8.

Ascend the valley of the West Fork. This is open country, with fine scenery, and very enjoyable. An especially nice spot is the high point at 6.5, with a view up the meandering stream toward the mountains. Hike along well above the level of the river, occasionally crossing small creeks, including one at the rise at 7.9.

Walking now in lodgepole pine forest, drop down to the riverside, where there is good ground for camping, at 8.1. Continue up the valley, as it bends around to the right, in pine forest interrupted occasionally by aspen clumps; pass several more small creeks along the way.

Boulderhop Reef Creek at 9.7; nearby, the sunflower-like balsamroot is conspicuous on the grassy south-facing slope. At 10.0, a side trail (No. 224) goes off to the right to climb over 3000 feet to Prairie Reef Lookout. Cross White Bear Creek at 11.1.

The Section ends at 11.2, in a meadow, at the signed junction with Ahorn Creek Trail No. 209. There are good places to camp over by the river.

Distances and elevations are:

0.0	Road junction	5300
0.3		5350
0.5	Enter Pretty Prairie Quadrangle	5300
0.7	Trailhead	5250
1.0	South Fork, Sun River (5208)	5200
1.4	Trail junction	5200
1.5	Burned Creek (5219)	5200
2.3	Deer Creek	5200
3.3	Bighead Trail (242) Junction	5250
3.7	(5278)	5300
4.4	Trail junction	5150
5.3	West Fork of South Fork, Sun River	5050
5.4	West Fork Trail (203) Junction	5050
5.6	Wapiti (Elk) Creek	5100
6.5		5150
6.8		5100
7.9	Creek	5250
8.1	Enter Prairie Reef Quadrangle	5150
9.7	Reef Creek	5350
10.0	Trail (224) junction	5400
11.2	Ahorn Creek Trail (209) Junction	5300

BOB MARSHALL WILDERNESS SEGMENT
Section 4
INDIAN POINT GUARD STATION TO SPOTTED BEAR PASS
17.6 Miles

The Chinese Wall, a sheer limestone reef marking the Continental Divide, is the central feature of this Section. This best-known attraction of the Bob Marshall Wilderness, a full 20 miles or more from roads of any description, preserves a sense of solitude despite its deserved renown. In addition to the scenic quality of vast open country below the Chinese Wall, the hiker can enjoy the flowers and wildlife.

The Trail starts out by climbing through lodgepole forest along the West Fork of the South Fork of the Sun River. The terrain becomes more open, at higher elevations, as the route continues up through the side valley of Burnt Creek to the base of the Chinese Wall at 7.8. From here on, mighty cliffs—sometimes a thousand feet high—form a backdrop to the west, while graceful glacial valleys complete the unobstructed view eastward. The Trail traverses along beneath the Chinese Wall to Larch Hill Pass, at 14.2. It then contours around to the south of Larch Hill; this stretch, including My Lake at 16.4, is notable for its stands of alpine larch, a distinctive lacy conifer that sheds its bunches of needles each winter. The end of the Section is on the Continental Divide, at Spotted Bear Pass, at 17.6.

There are ample water sources, including springs at the base of the Chinese Wall. But unfortunately, owing to overuse in past years, severe camping restrictions (such as closure of the Moose Creek drainage) may be in effect. (Efforts are being made to permit one-night stops for small backpacking parties.) For current status, contact the Rocky Mountain Ranger District (of the Lewis and Clark National Forest), which encompasses the entire Section. The area is also the heart of the Sun River Game Preserve, an important elk range, closed to hunting since 1913.

U.S.G.S. Maps: **Prairie Reef**, **Slategoat Mountain**, and **Amphitheatre Mountain**.

Also: our Maps **11** and **12**.

Detailed Trail data are:

The flat meadows near the West Fork are full of flowers—among them meadow deathcamas, Columbia puccoon, nineleaf biscuitroot, and Baker's mariposa. Good campsites are available near the river.

Starting at the signed junction with Ahorn Creek Trail No. 209, proceed upstream on West Fork Trail No. 203, in lodgepole pine forest. Cross a small creek at 0.2; a path to the right rises 100 yards to the Indian Point Guard Station (which is not visible from the Trail). Another side trail, from the cabin, joins from the right at 0.4.

Come to the junction with Indian Creek Trail No. 211, close to the gorge of the river, at 1.1. This would be a very good small campsite, with a rivulet as a convenient water source; other places are available, however, farther north at various points near the West Fork.

Cross Black Bear Creek, at 1.6, beneath the bare western slopes of Prairie Reef. The cliffs of Red Butte are visible, high to the west, at 2.7. Continue at contour, some distance from the main stream. Pass a small tributary from No Name Gulch at 3.4.

At 3.9, the much-reduced West Fork (here only about 10 feet wide) may have to be forded. Walk on up the west bank; look back over the river, from a viewpoint at 4.5, toward the burned slopes of Prairie Reef.

Return to the left (east) bank at 5.0, a short way below a prominent foot-high ledge in the stream; and then, for the last time, cross back to the west bank by boulderhopping at 6.1.

Proceed westward, climbing up the valley of Burnt Creek and crossing to its left (north) bank at 6.6. Pass a small side creek at 7.3 and a spring, just to the right of the Trail, at 7.4.

Approaching the base of the Chinese Wall, bend to the right at 7.8. Scars remain from a fire long ago, leaving a break in the forest. A side trail joins from the right at 8.7. (It comes from a large campsite about 100 yards off the Trail.)

Enjoy the magnificent view from the crest, near the base of Cliff Mountain, at 9.0. The Chinese Wall commands the scene on your left, with the high country of the Wilderness sweeping around to your right. Bend around to the north and commence the grandest part of the hike. (From here the route is Wall Trail No. 175 rather than West Fork Trail No. 203.)

Descend to a shallow, algae-covered, pond—the source of Moose Creek—at 9.6; a campsite formerly used by large parties shows severe damage. Continue along the base of the Wall, with the rounded valley of Moose Creek to the right. This is extraordinarily scenic open terrain, beneath the cliffs, with numerous tiny creeks. Golden eagles may soar above; and rosy finches, mountain chickadees, and red-breasted nuthatches may be found close at hand. Enjoy the many wildflowers—elephantshead, Sitka valerian, Siberian chive, veronica, subalpine daisy, globeflower, elk thistle, yellow columbine, red-stemmed saxifrage, and willowherb among them. Keep going north at the junction at 10.6, where Moose Creek Trail No. 131 turns right and descends to the North Fork of the Sun River.

The divide between Moose Creek and Rock Creek, at the base of Salt Mountain, is at 11.0. There are excellent photo opportunities here, as at almost any place along the Wall. After dipping to cross the headwaters of Rock Creek at 11.6, climb back to the cliffs and resume the walk along their base. If camping is allowed, one fine place would be in the fairly sheltered area, shortly beyond an obvious small rise, at 13.2.

You have a choice at the junction at 14.2. The designated route goes to the right, to My Lake. If the weather is bad then take this option and go directly to My Lake, but otherwise a slightly longer and more scenic option may be preferred. (This alternate route, the one used by the author, goes through Larch Hill Pass and swings around the north side of Larch Hill. It offers some outstanding views—to snow-dotted Silvertop Mountain to the northwest; far-distant peaks to the north, perhaps even Mount St. Nicholas and other mountains in Glacier National Park; the Three Sisters to the northeast; and the Chinese Wall to the south. And, according to some hikers' reports, the panorama becomes still more spectacular if you detour to the summit of Larch Hill.) Following the designated route, hike around the south side of Larch Hill, going over a spur ridge at 15.6.

Besides the larches, there are some pretty flowering shrubs—notably swamp laurel and purple mountain heath—at My Lake, at 16.4. (Camping restrictions may be in effect here, too.) After rising a little bit, intersect the alternate route at the junction at 16.7. Turn right and descend quite steeply, with a few switchbacks, through firs and pines. You can look out occasionally through clearings toward Three Sisters, to the north, and the Rock Creek valley to the south. The Section ends at Spotted Bear Pass, on the Divide, at 17.6.

Distances and elevations are:

0.0	Ahorn Creek Trail (209) Junction	5300
0.2	Indian Point Guard Station	5400
0.8		5450
1.1	Indian Creek Trail (211) Junction	5400
1.6	Black Bear Creek	5500
2.7		5750
3.9	West Fork of South Fork, Sun River (5662)	5650
4.2	Enter Slategoat Mountain Quadrangle	5700
5.0	West Fork (5797)	5800
6.1	West Fork	6050
6.6	Burnt Creek	6200
7.8	Chinese Wall (6924)	6900
9.1	Enter Amphitheatre Mountain Quadrangle	7600
9.6	Moose Creek	7150
9.8		7200
10.3		7100
10.6	Moose Creek Trail (131) Junction	7200
11.0	Moose Creek/Rock Creek Divide	7350
11.6	Rock Creek	6950
12.8	Spur	7250
13.2		7050
14.2	Trail junction	7500
15.0		7300
15.6	(7596)	7600
15.9		7400
16.2		7450
16.4	My Lake	7350
16.7	Trail junction	7450
17.1	Enter Slategoat Mountain Quadrangle	7200
17.6	Spotted Bear Pass	6700

BOB MARSHALL WILDERNESS SEGMENT
Section 3
SPOTTED BEAR PASS TO KEVAN MOUNTAIN
Recommended (Pentagon) Route: 19.2 Miles
Designated (Gates Park) Route: 26.1 Miles

A massive limestone ridge—a northern extension of the Chinese Wall—lies at the heart of this Section. Although the designated route does incorporate a fine stretch below this cliff face, it is so circuitous and fire-scarred that it cannot be recommended. The alternate route described below—along the valleys to the west—offers some rewarding, if less spectacular, scenery.

The recommended route, west of the Continental Divide, begins with a long hike down the narrow, forested, valley of the Spotted Bear River. The descent ends at the Pentagon Guard Station, at 10.4. The Trail then turns north, climbing nearly 3000 feet and passing timberline along the way, to Switchback Pass at 16.8. The final portion of the Section is outstanding, with extraordinary vistas in the vicinity of Switchback Pass and from the crest of the Continental Divide (looking south along the cliffs) at 17.5. (The designated route, east of the Divide, is discussed below. According to some reports, it is also possible to make an exceptional cross-country skyline trek, of approximately 18.1 miles, but this has some very steep, often rocky, parts; it is also exposed, snow-covered at places in early summer, and requires about 2300 feet more elevation gain than the recommended route. Anyone attempting to hike cross-country should carry topographic maps and observe grizzly bear precautions scrupulously.)

Water is available at frequent intervals except near the end of the Section. (The last 6.3 miles may be completely dry.) Locating a campsite with water is often difficult because of the slopes and dense vegetation; the best place is near the confluence of the Spotted Bear River and Pentagon Creek, not far from the Pentagon Guard Station. Although streams must be forded at several places, the only one that is likely to prove to be tricky is Pentagon Creek, just above this confluence.

The Trail is in the Spotted Bear Ranger District of the Flathead National Forest except for the final 1.7 miles, east of the Divide, in the Rocky Mountain Ranger District of the Lewis and Clark National Forest. There is no road access within ten miles of any part of the Section.

U.S.G.S. Maps: **Slategoat Mountain, Three Sisters, Bungalow Mountain, Trilobite Peak**, and **Pentagon Mountain**.

Also: our Maps **9, 10**, and **11**.

Detailed Trail data are:

Take Spotted Bear River Trail No. 83 north from Spotted Bear Pass. Although the route is heavily forested for most of the Section, you will at first have occasional views down the valley. Despite the presence of numerous small creeks and seeps, the steepness of the terrain and the fallen timber make the area unattractive for camping. Pass a major feeder creek (with the aid of fallen logs, most likely) at 1.7, just below a pretty little waterfall. After a muddy seep, followed shortly thereafter by a small side stream at 2.3, drop down to the Spotted Bear River at 2.6. The Trail from Spotted Bear Pass to this point needs maintenance; it is often overgrown or very wet.

Cross the river; a logjam a short distance upstream may provide a ready means to get over to the left bank. Large spruces and firs make up the forest as you hike on down the valley. At 3.1, where the Trail is close to the river, an obscure track comes in from the right, between two large spruces, from a possible campsite; a small party could spend the night there, in dry weather, on some gravel patches. Pass another small seep at 3.8.

From about 4.1—and continuing on past Christopher Creek at 4.8—thousand-foot cliffs crowd the left side of the Trail. Christopher Creek is sometimes dry, and so too are the even smaller tributaries at 5.3, 5.8, and 6.2. Continue an easy gradual descent through the forest parallel to the left bank of the Spotted Bear River, but well back from it.

The Spotted Bear River becomes a much greater stream after it is joined, at 5.8, by Three Sisters Creek. Ford the river, which is normally about five yards wide and calf-deep, at 6.3. (The Bob Marshall Wilderness map erroneously indicates that the trail cuts across the river and Three Sisters Creek above their confluence.) Pass a landslide and small creek at 6.9, and boulderhop or use a logjam to get by another side stream at 7.2.

Although the Trail is generally screened by forest, there are occasional views upstream toward the peaks of the Three Sisters. Step over a small creek, possibly with strawberries in fruit, at 8.7; there is room to camp nearby, close to the river.

The Wall Creek Trail comes in from the left, from across the river, at 8.9. (The Lime Divide Trail, which may no longer be maintained, also crosses the river, intersecting the route at 9.2.) Continuing down the right bank in lodgepole forest, boulderhop Hart Creek at 9.7. Pass a wilderness restoration area—perhaps some day once more open to camping—at 9.9. Keep straight again at the junction at 10.3, where Trail No. 92 goes off to the right to Hart Lake.

Pentagon Creek, at 10.4, must be forded, with caution; it could well prove to be the most challenging stream crossing on the Trail in Montana.

Turn right at the junction just past the ford, and continue on Trail No. 173. (The Pentagon Guard Station is to the left, on the riverbank; it is a well-constructed wooden cabin, with privy and corral nearby.) Just after making this turn, look for a good established campsite on the right, on Pentagon Creek.

Hike up the forested valley of Pentagon Creek, well up from the bank, on excellent treadway. A side trail at 10.6 turns off to the left and ascends to Pot Mountain. Pentagon Mountain is prominent upstream as you approach the next ford.

Cross Pentagon Creek at 11.9, perhaps getting over it on a logjam a little way above the route. The trail splits at a junction at 12.1; instead of continuing up Pentagon Creek proper on Trail No. 173, take the right fork and proceed up the East Fork on Basin Creek-Pentagon Cabin Trail No. 177.

Use the moss-covered rocks to get across a good side creek at 12.9. Pick up a good supply of water, as there may be nothing else to drink for the remainder of the Section. (There is a campsite just north of the creek.) Soon leave the valley and begin the long climb, with numerous switchbacks, to timberline. Pass a talus slide at 14.4. With the rapid elevation change, the transition from Douglas fir to spruce-fir forest is clearly marked.

Looking southeast along the Continental Divide from the pass on Kevan Mountain.

Pause at the junction in Switchback Pass, at 16.8. It is especially worthwhile walking the short distance to the dropoff to the left; from there you can enjoy a fine view overlooking the hanging valley and headwalls at the upper end of Basin Creek.

Turn right at the junction in Switchback Pass. (But you could shorten the trip slightly by turning left and hiking past Dean Lake down Clack Creek to Gooseberry Park, rejoining the designated route near the mouth of Bowl Creek. That alternate has been described to be very satisfactory; its principal drawback is that it bypasses the very fine views in the remainder of this Section. Another possibility is to drop steeply down the headwall to Basin Creek; the Pentagon Mountain Quadrangle indicates a series of switchbacks, but a clear travelway does not actually exist.)

Ascend on Open Creek Trail No. 116 (though in the Flathead, it may be No. 732). The route is sometimes faint. However, the objective is clear—namely, the obvious pass on the Continental Divide to the southeast. Reach a high point on the west flank of Kevan Mountain and then drop slightly to reach the crest of the Divide at 17.5.

The views from this thin, exposed ridge are outstanding. Near at hand, just half a mile to the north, the summit of Kevan Mountain rises an additional 400 feet. Far to the west you can make out the Swan Range, including snow-covered 9255-foot Swan Peak. To the southwest and south, to the left of nearby Table Mountain, are Silvertip Mountain, Bungalow Mountain, and familiar Larch Hill. Beyond the sheer cliffs of the Divide and Lake Levale to the southeast, it is about 15 miles to 9392-foot Rocky Mountain on the eastern edge of the Bob Marshall (and the highest point in the Wilderness). To the east is the wide glacial valley of Open Creek, with a backdrop of Porphyry Reef, Wrong Ridge, and a string of summits beyond (probably including Mt. Patrick Gass, Mt. Wright, and Mt. Lockhart). The Continental Divide here is the type locality for the Pentagon shale formation, with its abundant trilobite fossils. White dryads and other alpine flowers abound.

The route descends to the flat bench at the head of Open Creek. Although it is possible to take a steep shortcut down the open slope, you should follow the somewhat longer route marked by cairns. After the steep descent, continue close to the edge of an escarpment, with views over Open Creek and toward the reefs and peaks to the east; Lake Levale remains visible, ahead, to the southeast.

A beautiful little basin, carpeted with buttercups, lies at the foot of cliffs at 18.1. The ground is spongy and wet, but there is no obvious source of drinking water. Weave through some long-lasting snowpatches at 18.4. Although the path is sometimes obscure in this open country, the route to Open Creek should not be difficult to find.

Open Creek, at 19.2, is the first reliable source of water since the valley of Pentagon Creek. Cross to the right bank. The Section ends just beyond the creek, at the junction with Wall Trail No. 175, the designated route, which forks off to the right.

Distances and elevations are:

0.0	Spotted Bear Pass	6700
0.8	Enter Three Sisters Quadrangle	6350

1.7	Creek	6100
2.6	Spotted Bear River	5650
3.1	River access	5550
4.8	Christopher Creek	5400
5.3	Streambed	5350
5.7		5300
5.8	Streambed	5350
6.3	Spotted Bear River	5200
6.9	Creek	5250
7.2	Creek	5200
7.6		5250
8.2	Enter Bungalow Mountain Quadrangle	5100
8.9	Wall Creek Trail Junction	5000
9.2	Lime Divide Trail (349) Junction	4950
9.7	Hart Creek	4900
10.4	Pentagon Guard Station	4850
10.6	Trail (359) junction	5000
10.8		5100
10.9	Enter Trilobite Peak Quadrangle	5050
11.9	Pentagon Creek	5150
12.1	Basin Creek-Pentagon Creek Trail (177) Jct.	5150
12.9	Creek	5400
14.5	Enter Pentagon Mountain Quadrangle	6350
16.8	Switchback Pass	7750
17.2	Flank of Kevan Mountain	8050
17.5	Continental Divide	7950
18.1		7450
18.4	Snowpatches	7250
19.2	Wall Trail (175) Junction	6750

Designated (Gates Park) Route

The last several miles of this route, on Wall Trail No. 175, are exceptional. The terrain is grassy, the views magnificent, and water supplies are frequent. The problem is that before you can get to that fine high country, you must make a long detour far down to Gates Park; and much of the way is severely scarred by the Gates Park Fire of 1988. In addition, unless you were to take a short side trip for the view, you would miss some of the scenery near Switchback Pass, at the end of the recommended route.

Note: the following sketchy report is based exclusively on topographic maps, not field investigations.

U.S.G.S. Maps: **Slategoat Mountain, Gates Park, Three Sisters,** and **Pentagon Mountain.**

Also: our Maps **9, 10,** and **11.**

Detailed Trail data are:

From Spotted Bear Pass, turn right and descend the eastern slope on Rock Creek Trail No. 111. Drop down a narrow side ravine, which then joins the main valley of Rock Creek. The valley is constricted in the vicinity of the Rock Creek Guard Station, at 2.8. Cliff-lined ridges also close in above Baldy Bear Creek, at 5.5. (While the topographic maps suggest that there might be a more direct cross-country route from here to the high country—at 17.2 on the route described below—it would be roundabout, perhaps with bushwhacking along Baldy Bear, and would require extra climbs of 900 and 500 feet. It would certainly not save any time and is not recommended.)

Continue the gentle walk down the left bank of Rock Creek to 6.9. Then swing left, rising a bit to get over a low ridge, in order to proceed more directly to Gates Park. Pass Miners Creek, along the way, at 7.5 and Horsey Creek at 8.1. Switchback down into the ravine of Red Shale Creek—perhaps a problematic ford in June—at 10.1. Rise a bit on the far side, crossing a minor ridge at 10.3.

Reach a trail junction in Gates Park, just to the south of the dirt landing strip, at 10.8. Here the characteristic dense forest is broken by wide open grassy flats. Turn left at the junction, heading up Red Shale Creek, on Trail No. 130. Remain on this trail at 11.2, ignoring Trail No. 161 that turns off to the right.

Hike well above Red Shale Creek as it cuts through a narrow ravine. The side creek at 13.1 is a source of drinking water. Keep climbing, in burned forest, crossing to the right (south) bank of Red Shale Creek at 16.2 and back to the left (north) bank at 17.2.

The splendid high country traverse beneath the cliffs of the Continental Divide finally begins. (This is Trail No. 175, no longer Trail No. 130.) After passing a spur ridge at 17.8, drop to the head of the South Fork of Lick Creek at 18.8. Complete the circuit of this basin by climbing the ridge at 20.6. Cross the North Fork of Lick Creek at 21.2.

Keep following Trail No. 175 at the junction at 21.6. (Trail No. 151 turns right to go down the North Fork of Lick Creek.) Continuing along the base of the cliffs, go over a rise at 22.0 and dip to a tarn at 22.2.

Climb to another spur ridge at 22.8, where side trail No. 132 turns right and heads for the nearby minor summit known as Moonlight Peak. Remain on Trail No. 175 and circle around the head of the South Fork of Open Creek, crossing it at 23.2. Ascend one last time, over yet another ridge at 24.6.

Pass the outlet of Lake Levale at 25.1. (It is 0.2 mile up the little valley to the lake, with places to camp, beneath a backdrop of cliffs.) Descend to the junction with Open Creek Trail No. 116, at 26.1, where the designated route for the Section ends.

Distances and elevations are:

0.0	Spotted Bear Pass	6700
2.8	Rock Creek Guard Station	5800
3.2	Creek	5850
5.5	Baldy Bear Creek (5561)	5550
6.0	Enter Three Sisters Quadrangle	5500
6.7	Enter Gates Park Quadrangle	5550
7.5	Miners Creek	5750
8.1	Horsey Creek	5650
8.4	(5618)	5600
8.7		5650
10.1	Red Shale Creek	5350
10.3	Ridge (5443)	5450
10.8	Trail (111) junction (Gates Park)	5350
11.2	Trail (161) junction (5398)	5400
13.1	Creek	5700
14.1	Enter Three Sisters Quadrangle	5900
16.2	Red Shale Creek	6600
17.2	Red Shale Creek	7000
17.8	Spur ridge (7220)	7200
18.8	South Fork, Lick Creek	6450
20.1		7100
20.2		7000
20.6	Spur ridge	7100
21.2	North Fork, Lick Creek	6650
21.6	Trail (151) junction	6450

22.0	(6700)	6700
22.2	Tarn	6650
22.8	Trail (132) junction	7100
23.2	Enter Pentagon Mountain Quadrangle	6850
24.6	Spur ridge (7535)	7550
25.1	Lake Levale (0.2 mile)	7100
25.9		6750
26.1	Open Creek Trail (116) Junction	6800

BOB MARSHALL WILDERNESS SEGMENT
Section 2
KEVAN MOUNTAIN TO BADGER PASS
25.3 Miles

Leaving the lofty cliffs behind, the Trail proceeds along watercourses, through forest and parks, in the uncrowded northern portion of the Bob Marshall Wilderness.

The start of the Section is a descent of the Open Creek valley, moderately steep for the first mile but then very easy. At 6.0, a little way past Round Park, the Trail turns north, rising a bit to get over viewless Sun River Pass (on the Continental Divide) at 9.1. The route then descends Bowl Creek to its mouth at 14.3. The remainder of the Section is a long, gradual climb along Strawberry Creek.

Only one travelway is described for this Section—it is both the designated Continental Divide Trail and the route described in the first edition of the guidebook. However, as was mentioned in the text of the preceding Section, you could turn off before Kevan Mountain, descending past alpine Dean Lake on Clack Creek Trail No. 160 to Gooseberry Park. This has been reported to be a very fine walk and a desirable choice if you have hiked by way of Pentagon Creek instead of Gates Park. The alternative ends at the junction at 14.3 of the described route.

Water supplies are good throughout the Section. Starting at Round Park, at 5.7, camping sites are available at convenient intervals. Heavy pack use has damaged the treadway, all too often making it a quagmire. Since it is about ten miles or more from any point within the Section to the nearest vehicle access, resupply here is not practical.

All of the Section lies within the Bob Marshall Wilderness—in the Rocky Mountain Ranger District of the Lewis and Clark National Forest as far as Sun River Pass, the Spotted Bear Ranger District of the Flathead National Forest thereafter.

U.S.G.S. Maps: **Pentagon Mountain**, **Porphyry Reef**, **Gooseberry Park**, and **Morningstar Mountain**.

Also: our Maps **8** and **9**.

Detailed Trail data are:

The Section begins at the junction of Open Creek Trail No. 116 and Wall Trail No. 175. Descend along the right bank of Open Creek, through open subalpine forests; wildflowers are abundant—paintbrush, yellow columbine, gentian, valerian, mariposa, stonecrop, American vetch, and many more, along with the beargrass and cow parsnip. Cross to the left bank at 0.2 and pass a good side creek at 0.7.

The Trail flattens out. In order to avoid two fords of Open Creek, leave the obvious pack route at 1.1 and angle left across a small meadow (a possible campsite). Remain in the flat bottomland until a bend of Open Creek, on the north edge of the valley, is reached at 1.3. Make a way through light woods, possibly finding an obscure path, very shortly intersecting the pack trail again.

For the next two miles, the Trail crosses a number of small tributary creeks as it descends very gradually through spruce-fir forest. For the most part, the Trail to Round Park remains well back from Open Creek, but there is an occasional view of Signal Mountain on the other side of the valley. From time to time there may be more than one treadway, as new paths have been put in place to avoid eroded spots; look for recent axe blazes to point the right way.

The large meadow on the Trail is Round Park. Cross the meadow, heading northeast, to a sheltered camping area at its edge, adjacent to Fool Creek, at 5.7. After boulderhopping the creek, come to a trail junction in a clearing at 6.0. Turn left, heading north. (The trail continuing ahead leads to a roadhead at West Fork Guard Station, but it requires a 2000-foot climb over Washboard Reef to get there.)

Cross a small creek at 7.6. This isn't the best part of the Trail—there are several short climbs and descents, the treadway suffers from heavy stock traffic, and the moist forest may seem unusually buggy.

Sun River Pass, at 9.1, is completely forested and offers no view. Cross the Continental Divide and once again enter the Flathead National Forest. Descend, passing through an area burned some time ago, to a trail junction at 9.9. To the west are cliffs and steep slopes below the Continental Divide, with Pentagon Mountain prominent at the head of the Basin Creek valley. Stay to the right at the trail junction. (To the left is the Basin Creek Trail, which crosses Basin Creek about 100 yards from the junction.)

After crossing to the right bank of Bowl Creek at 10.2, swing to the left and proceed downstream. There are good grassy campsites near this crossing. (It may be possible to boulderhop a few yards upstream.) At 10.3, intersect Bowl Creek Trail No. 324, which comes in from the right. A camp can be made along the Trail, close to Bowl Creek, at 10.5.

Enter the wet meadows of Grizzly Park. Shortly before leaving Grizzly Park at 11.0, a side trail leads up the slope to the right, to Grimsley Park.

Pass a stretch of scree overlooking Bowl Creek at 11.5 and descend short switchbacks at 11.8. Cross a small creek at 12.1. The abandoned Basin Creek Cutoff Trail may be noted taking off to the left at 12.5; remain to the right there, and also at the junction with Scalp Creek Trail No. 315 at 13.0.

Reach Bowl Creek at 13.3. Fast water such as occurs here is typical habitat for the ouzel, a gray chunky bird that dips to the stream bottom for tasty morsels. At one time it was necessary to ford across the stream and back (cautiously), but new treadway allows you to remain on the right bank.

The Trail climbs a bit, to a junction at 13.7 where the Mt. May Trail turns off sharply to the right, leading 1.9 mile to a lookout. Ford Strawberry Creek at 14.1—though about ten yards wide, it is only a few inches deep.

Turn sharp right on Strawberry Creek Trail No. 161 at the junction at 14.3. (If you elect to hike the Clack Creek alternative described in the introductory text, you would rejoin the described route here.) Heavy pack use formerly made quite a mess of the trail up Strawberry Creek, but some minor relocations of the route have corrected the problem in this area, at least temporarily.

Bypass Trail Creek Trail No. 216, which forks off to the right at 15.4. Walk over Grimsley Creek on a relatively high bridge at 15.8. (There are good places to camp nearby, along Strawberry Creek,) Disregard an unmarked path that crosses the route after another 50 yards; this presumably leads, to the right, to the Trail Creek Trail.

After passing more side creeks with small bridges, cross Strawberry Creek without difficulty at 17.1. Soon there is a fine campsite by the creek, with grassy flat ground and an unobstructed view up the valley.

Turn left at the marked trail junction at 17.4. (Gateway Trail No. 322 climbs straight ahead; after a couple of miles, it passes through the Gateway Gorge, a marvelously tight passage between 1000-foot cliffs.) Continue through mixed forest, parallel to the left (east) bank of Strawberry Creek, passing some small side streams on bridges made of short cross-logs.

Reach the boulder-strewn channel of the East Fork of Strawberry Creek at 19.8. Cross the East Fork and come to a small clearing at 20.2, where the minor East Fork Trail (No. 371) turns off sharply to the right. The Trail proceeds up the main valley, moving to the west bank of Strawberry Creek by easy boulderhop at 21.6. The route ascends gradually, mostly in forest, usually a considerable distance from the stream. There are a number of small tributaries and an occasional mucky spot. Where the path divides from time to time, keep to the uphill route. Cross Strawberry Creek, here only three feet wide and a couple of inches deep, for the last time at 23.9.

Approaching Badger Pass, the terrain is flat open meadow and the precise location of the Continental Divide (at 25.2) is not obvious. Pass a little open water, to the right of the Trail.

Leaving the Bob Marshall Wilderness, the Trail reaches a junction at the end of the Section, at 25.3. (The Trail continues by turning left on North Fork of Birch Creek Trail No. 121, coming immediately to a little creek where you can make a small camp.)

Distances and elevations are:

0.0	Wall Trail (175) Junction	6750
0.2	Open Creek	6600
0.7	Creek	6250
1.1	Open Creek bypass	6150
4.3	Enter Porphyry Reef Quadrangle	5850
5.7	Round Park	5800
6.0	Trail junction	5800
7.6	Creek	6150
8.7		6300
9.1	Sun River Pass (6251)	6250
9.9	Basin Creek Trail Junction (5813)	5800

10.3	Bowl Creek Trail (324) Junction	5800
10.7	Enter Pentagon Mountain Quadrangle	5750
11.0	Grizzly Park	5800
13.0	Scalp Creek Trail (315) Junction	5450
13.3	Bowl Creek	5400
13.7	Mt. May Trail (256) Junction	5550
14.1	Strawberry Creek	5350
14.2	Enter Gooseberry Park Quadrangle	5350
14.3	Strawberry Creek Trail (161) Junction	5400
15.4	Trail Creek Trail (216) Junction	5450
15.8	Grimsley Creek	5500
16.8		5600
17.1	Strawberry Creek	5500
17.4	Gateway Trail (322) Junction	5550
18.9	(5647)	5650
19.2		5600
19.8	East Fork, Strawberry Creek	5700
20.2	East Fork Trail (371) Junction	5750
21.3		5900
21.6	Strawberry Creek	5850
23.9	Strawberry Creek	6100
24.6	Enter Morningstar Mountain Quadrangle	6250
25.2	Badger Pass	6300
25.3	Trail junction	6250

BOB MARSHALL WILDERNESS SEGMENT
Section 1-B
BADGER PASS TO NORTH BADGER CREEK
10.2 Miles

The Trail in this Section, largely in wooded valleys, includes a final brief excursion into the Bob Marshall Wilderness.

The route crisscrosses the Divide a couple of times near the start of the Section, so that from 0.9 to Muskrat Pass, at 2.1, one travels once again in the Bob Marshall. The route then descends easily to Elbow Creek, at 5.9. There is a climb to the minor ridge, at 8.3, that separates the South Badger drainage from that of North Badger Creek. The final stretch is a descent to North Badger, and then down along it, to the junction of two alternate routes to Marias Pass.

Convenient water sources are infrequent before Elbow Creek. Campsites are available at several location, including Badger Pass and Lost Horse Camp (5.9).

Most of the Section lies in the Rocky Mountain Ranger District of the Lewis and Clark National Forest; but the mile west of the Divide, in the Bob Marshall Wilderness, is in the Spotted Bear Ranger District of the Flathead National Forest.

U.S.G.S. Maps: **Morningstar Mountain** and **Crescent Cliff**.

Also: our Map **8**.

Detailed Trail data are:

The Section begins at a trail junction just north of Badger Pass. Arriving at this T-intersection from Section 2, make a 90° turn to the left and immediately cross one of the headwaters of South Badger Creek. This is a good place to camp.

After a small dip and then a rise, come once again to the Continental Divide at 0.9. Return briefly to the Bob Marshall Wilderness. There is some confusion about the proper course to take from the crest. The shorter way, which is recommended (with reservations) even though it may be overgrown, continues ahead and remains well north of Beaver Lake (which, from higher elevations, is visible to the south). Reportedly, how-

161

ever, the official route as indicated by signs angles off to the left and descends to the lake; after circling around the south shore, it intersects the recommended route as indicated below.

So, following the recommended unofficial route, descend to a flat basin and pass a corral, shortly thereafter coming to a trail junction at 1.4. Here make a bend to the right around a large lonesome spruce tree. (To the left, Cox Creek Trail No. 175 crosses a small stream in meadow in about 50 yards and then continues around the east side of Beaver Lake and descends Cox Creek.) Pass a small pond on the left. At 1.7, take the right fork. (The left fork, which leads around the west shore of Beaver Lake, marks the end of the alternate, presumably official, route from 0.9.)

Reach Muskrat Pass at 2.1. Cross the Continental Divide once again, in a flat meadow with scattered spruces and firs. At the carved sign, leave the Flathead National Forest and the Bob Marshall Wilderness.

Bypass an obscure unmarked trail that forks off to the right at 2.4. One of the headwaters of Muskrat Creek, crossed at 2.6, may have a little water. If you step a few feet off the Trail to the left at 3.0, you can look out over Blue Lake some 100 feet below. It is a pretty spot, with the Continental Divide as a backdrop; but because of the steep slope and probable insect problems, it is not recommended for camping.

Descend for a ways and then climb slightly to a junction at 3.8. Turn sharply to the left, continuing on Muskrat Creek Trail No. 147. Cross a muddy spot on a low horse bridge. The Trail continues through forest without much scenic interest; it descends gradually, well up the flank of Elbow Mountain and above Muskrat Creek, occasionally circuiting small slides.

Cross Muskrat Creek and Elbow Creek, just above their confluence, at 5.9. This should be a simple boulderhop. Lost Horse Camp, just across these streams, once featured a wide flat grassy bench suitable for camping, with wild strawberries as an extra bonus; there are reports, though, that it has been flooded out within the past few years, and rock and timber debris may still be scattered about. There is a nice view down the open valley of Elbow Creek toward Curly Bear Mountain.

Intersect Elbow Creek Trail No. 145 at the marked junction at Lost Horse Camp. Take Trail No. 145 to the left and ascend. (To the right, it descends two miles to the South Fork of Badger

Creek. According to the U.S.G.S. topographic map, the trail junction is farther on, at 6.2; but that doesn't square with our observations.) Climb through mixed forest and meadow. There are clear views backward up the Muskrat valley to the Continental Divide. From 6.9, the Trail is screened by forest. Pass a saddle, just to the south of the almost bare Bruin Peaks, at 8.3. Descend by switchbacks.

Cross North Badger Creek at 9.0 and pass a campsite on the left of the Trail. Cross a meadow and reach a junction at 9.2. Here turn right on North Badger Trail No. 103. (To the left, Trail No. 103 climbs to the Continental Divide at Big Lodge Mountain.) Pass small creeks at 9.6.

Cross Kip Creek at 10.2 and bend back to the right. The summit on the Continental Divide, up Kip Creek and beyond Running Owl Mountain, is Bullshoe Mountain. Fifty yards beyond Kip Creek, come to the junction of the two alternate trails to Marias Pass.

Distances and elevations are:

0.0	Trail junction	6250
0.9	Continental Divide	6300
1.4	Cox Creek Trail (175) Junction	5950
1.7	Trail junction	5950
2.1	Muskrat Pass (Continental Divide)	6000
3.0	Blue Lake overlook (5940)	5950
3.4		5850
3.8	Trail junction (5943)	5950
4.4		5900
4.6		5950
4.8		5900
4.9		5950
5.5	Enter Crescent Cliff Quadrangle	5600
5.9	Lost Horse Camp	5500
8.3	Saddle	6250
9.0	North Badger Creek	5750
9.2	North Badger Creek Trail (103) Junction (5797)	5800
10.2	Kip Creek Trail (142) Junction	5700

NORTH BADGER CREEK TO MARIAS PASS (U.S. 2)
Interim (Valley) Route: 17.1 Miles
Designated (Divide) Route: 15.1 Miles

When the designated route is actually located and marked, this Section will prove to be an excellent skyline hike, with fine panoramas. In the interim, though, the Trail descends quite pleasantly down the wooded valley of a rushing mountain stream.

After continuing down the valley of North Badger Creek for another couple of miles, the interim route crosses a rise on the way to the Badger Guard Station at 4.3. Leaving the Badger drainage at 5.6, the Trail begins its long descent of the South Fork of the Two Medicine River. Whiterock Creek Camp, at 6.1, is a good place to spend the night. The travelway includes fords that might be difficult in spring, when the snow is melting. The last ford is at Sawmill Flats, at 14.6. The Trail then crosses over a minor ridge to reach Marias Pass, on the Continental Divide, at 17.1. As there are no good campsites with water in the next several miles, plan to stop at the campground here or else hitch a ride to East Glacier.

The Section is closed to vehicles (except for a bit near Sawmill Flats). It receives little backpacking use, because of the distance between U.S. 2 and the popular parts of the Bob Marshall Wilderness. There does seem to be a fair amount of horse travel, though, on the valley trails, which are in good condition.

The interim route is situated in the Rocky Mountain Ranger District of the Lewis and Clark National Forest. Water is in good supply, and it should not be difficult to find a satisfactory place to camp. (But no camping is permitted in the immediate vicinity of the Badger Guard Station.) An important paved highway (U.S. 2) runs through Marias Pass, on the Continental Divide; unfortunately, however, public transportation is not currently available.

U.S.G.S. Maps: **Crescent Cliff**, **Hyde Creek**, and **Summit**.

Also: our Map **7**.

Detailed Trail data are:

To follow the interim route, continue down the valley from the junction with Kip Creek Trail No. 142. Approach North Badger Creek closely at a rocky overlook at 1.3, below the cliffs of Running Owl Mountain. This is a pleasant rest stop, and just about the only good view up and down North Badger Creek. The scramble down to the creek to get water is quite steep, so caution should be exercised. With luck, a golden eagle may be seen soaring along the cliffs above the Trail.

The Trail continues along old jeep road. Pass a pole fence. For a short distance, at 2.5, follow an axe-blazed path to avoid a wet spot in the road. Across the creek, note the talus slopes of rugged Goat Mountain.

Leave the valley and ascend on the jeep road. Cross Lee Creek at 3.3 and swing back to the right. The signed Lee Creek Trail No. 141 is an obscure footpath that takes off to the left at 3.7. Descend through a field and come to a junction at 4.1. Here follow the road as it curves around to the left. In this area there are pleasant views overlooking the Badger valley to the southeast.

Cross a small creek and go through a barbed wire fence at the Badger Guard Station, the locked cabin just to the right at 4.3. Camping is not permitted near the cabin.

Trail No. 103 terminates. Continue ahead on Trail No. 101, the Two Medicine Trail. (To the right, Trail No. 101 passes through the grounds of the guard station.)

Reach a signed jeep road intersection at 4.9. Continue on Trail No. 101. (To the right is Trail No. 102, the Little Badger Creek Trail, which goes to Palookaville by way of Whiterock Creek.) Pass a wet area (off to the left of the Trail). Reach the high point on the divide between the Badger and Two Medicine drainages at 5.6.

Continue through mixed fields and woods, crossing Whiterock Creek at 6.1. Nearby Whiterock Creek Camp is a good campsite, with room for several parties. The route descends the valley of the South Fork of Two Medicine River. (The jeep trail to the right goes up Whiterock Creek.) There are small ponds in a marshy area to the left of the Trail at 6.6. At 7.5, a brief crossing to the left bank of the river can be avoided by following the foot path on the right bank. Pass a creek (actually, the East Fork of the river) at 8.3.

Elk Calf Mountain Trail No. 137 turns left, fording the river, at a junction at 8.7. (It is a viewless up and down slog that, contrary to the maps, does not climb Elkcalf Mountain; avoid it at all costs.) Continue down the valley, still on onetime jeep road. Go through the fence gate 50 yards past the trail junction. Pass a small side creek at 9.8. (At 10.3, Trail No. 136 should turn left, heading west toward Elkcalf Mountain, but the junction was not observed.)

Although the author's route continues down the valley, there is said to be an improved trail that contours, for the next couple of miles, along the hillside above the right bank of the river. (Because the river is bounded by steep slopes, a hike down the valley requires several fords that can be avoided if you use the improved trail.) The valley shows signs of former jeep use, but a distinct travelway is sometimes lacking; but this makes no difference, as you can't lose your way if you just follow the course of the water.

The improved route converges with the valley at about 12.6. Fords at 12.9 and 13.1 are probably unavoidable; the river in July is likely to be about a foot deep and up to 15 feet wide, but earlier in the season a strong current may be encountered. A pipe barrier formerly gated the road at 14.0. There are some pretty viewpoints between 14.1 and 14.5, a stretch in which Pike Creek cascades down a narrow gorge and tumbles into the South Fork.

Leave Two Medicine Trail No. 101 at the junction at 14.5; fork left and cross the broad open bottom (Sawmill Flats) to reach the South Fork at 14.6. Continue straight on pack trail at a signed junction in meadow at 15.1; avoid Elk Calf Mountain Trail No. 137, which forks off to the left. Climb a bit; a side trail (a shortcut to U.S. 2) is supposed to take off to the right near the small meadow at 15.7, but it was not observed.

The route follows a former logging road, dipping a couple of times at small drainages; it splits at 16.2, but comes back together at 16.3. Cross a cleared pipeline swath at 16.4. The trail picks up again on the far side, after perhaps 100 feet along the pipeline, but the location may not be immediately apparent. Descend in forest. A side trail joins from the right at 16.7.

Reach the Summit Campground at 16.8. (There is a little creek about 200 feet before the fence.) Enter the campground at a hairpin bend in the service road. Follow the road to the right until you reach the campground entrance, on U.S. 2. Marias Pass, a historic landmark on the Continental Divide, is just to the left, at 17.1. This is the end of the Section and the Bob Marshall Wilderness Segment.

Distances and elevations are:

0.0	Kip Creek Trail (142) Junction	5700
1.3	Overlook	5500
2.7	Leave North Badger valley	5350
3.2	Enter Hyde Creek Quadrangle	5500
3.7	Lee Creek Trail (141) Junction	5600
4.3	Badger Guard Station	5500
4.9	Little Badger Creek Trail (102) Junction (5689)	5700
5.6	Badger-Two Medicine Divide	5800
6.1	Whiterock Creek Camp (5749)	5750
7.5	Bypass ford	5600
8.3	East Fork, Two Medicine River	5550
8.7	Elk Calf Mountain Trail (137) Junction	5500
10.5	Enter Summit Quadrangle	5350
12.9	South Fork, Two Medicine River (5184)	5200
14.6	Sawmill Flats (South Fork, Two Medicine R.)	5050
15.1	Elk Calf Mountain Trail (137) Junction	5300
15.7	Meadow	5500
16.4	Pipeline	5450
16.8	Summit Campground	5250
17.1	Marias Pass (U.S. 2)	5250

Designated (Divide) Route

This should be a very fine Section, especially along the skyline south of Elkcalf Mountain. The description is based upon detailed planning maps prepared by the Lewis and Clark National Forest (not personal observation). Although the designated route is more direct than the interim route, don't expect to save any time by following it. (There is some question whether—in view of concerns recently expressed by members of the Blackfeet Nation—the designated route will ever be constructed.)

The route will leave North Badger Creek and rise over a low spur to the headwaters of Lee Creek at 3.7. Pick up a good water supply here, as the next convenient drinking sources may be as much as nine miles off. Climb up to the Continental Divide, at 5.0, and follow it northward past Running Crane Mountain and Elkcalf Mountain. The route will often lie directly on the high crest. Leaving the Divide at 12.2, skirt a little pond (probably the best campsite) at 12.9. The Section ends by descending to Marias Pass at 15.1.

As the Section tracks the Continental Divide over much of its length, portions lie in both the Hungry Horse Ranger District of the Flathead National Forest (west slope) and the Rocky Mountain Ranger District of the Lewis and Clark National Forest (east slope).

U.S.G.S. Maps: **Crescent Cliff, Hyde Creek,** and **Summit.**
Also: our Map 7.

Detailed Trail data are:

The designated route, leaving the deep valley of North Badger Creek, turns off to the left on Kip Creek Trail No. 142. The Trail climbs, at a moderate grade at first and then more steeply, crossing feeder creeks at 0.6, 1.1, and 2.6.

Reach the saddle between Bullshoe Mountain and Running Owl Mountain at 3.0. The route (now Trail No. 141) dips to a junction at 3.3; turn left at the junction and rise to little Lee Creek at 3.7. Pick up water when crossing Lee Creek, as there may be no more springs or creeks in the next nine miles.

Angle gradually uphill to the crest of the Continental Divide, at the head of Sidney Creek, at 5.0. Contour around the west side of Running Crane Mountain to 5.8, and contour (again to the left) around the summit beyond to the narrow gap at 7.5.

Climb to a high point, with switchbacks before and then after it, at 8.4. Enjoy a pleasant hike, with easy grades, mostly just to the west of the crest. Follow the Divide from the gap at 9.6 to 10.4 (at the head of the Townsend Creek basin). At Elkcalf Mountain, contour around the Flathead (west) side of the summit and then descend the well-defined ridgeline to a saddle at 11.7. Remain to the right of the next knoll, returning to the Divide at 12.2.

There are two options—either continuing along the Divide over Flattop Mountain or veering off to the left and traversing below

168

the summit; the CDT goes off to the left so as to skirt a pond (campsite) at 12.9. The two options reunite at a junction at 13.2.

Descend fairly steeply beyond this junction; disregard the road that intersects the route at 13.8 and descend a bit farther to a small creek at 13.9. Proceed with little elevation change, along a bench, to 14.3. Then drop off, fairly steeply at places, reaching the dirt Pike Creek Road at 14.8. Crossing Pike Creek Road, continue north, descending to Marias Pass, on U.S. 2, at 15.1.

Distances and elevations are:

0.0	Kip Creek Trail (142) Junction	5700
0.6	Creek	5950
1.1	Creek	6100
2.6	Creek	6850
3.0	Saddle	7200
3.3	Trail junction	7050
3.5		7000
3.7	Lee Creek	7150
5.0	Continental Divide	7300
5.8	Enter Hyde Creek Quadrangle	7150
6.1	Enter Summit Quadrangle	7200
6.8		7300
7.5	Gap	7050
8.4	High point (summit 7370)	7300
9.6	Gap	6900
10.6	Elkcalf Mountain (summit 7607)	7250
11.7	Saddle	6450
12.0		6550
12.2	Trail junction	6450
12.6	Flattop Mountain (summit 6650)	6550
12.9	Pond	6250
13.0		6300
13.2	Trail junction	6250
13.8	Road	5700
14.8	Pike Creek Road	5300
15.1	Marias Pass (U.S. 2)	5250

GLACIER NATIONAL PARK SEGMENT
Section 6
MARIAS PASS (U.S. 2) TO EAST GLACIER PARK
14.4 Miles

This Section has none of the grandeur of the more northern portions of Glacier National Park. The Trail gets relatively little use and in parts is badly overgrown. Still, it provides a serviceable connection between Marias Pass and the townsite of East Glacier Park.

Leaving U.S. Highway 2, the route soon contours in forest along the flanks of Summit Mountain and Calf Robe Mountain, on the Autumn Creek Trail. Beyond the cutoff of the Firebrand Pass Trail, at 7.7, rank vegetation in the mountain meadows sometimes obscures the tread. (Generally the route is marked by fluorescent orange metal markers, but they are not always visible in the open sections.) Returning to more consistently wooded terrain, the path climbs to a high point, at 10.6, where a side trail leads off to the open upper slopes of Squaw Mountain. The route descends to the boundary of Glacier National Park at 12.4, continuing on unused jeep roads to Midvale Creek—in East Glacier Park, just behind and below Glacier Park Lodge.

As it is reasonably short and involves little climbing, the Section requires less than a day to complete. There are no authorized campsites, and for that matter it would be hard to find any place that one would like to pitch a tent. If traveling north, consider hitch-hiking to East Glacier, with the idea of returning on the morrow to walk this Section as a day hike. Water should be readily available for the first half of the Section. The last reliable source is Railroad Creek (at 9.1 and 9.2), so check your water bottle before continuing on from there.

See the introduction to Section 5 for information concerning services and transportation at East Glacier. (Refer also to the Background Information for additional notes on the history of Marias Pass.)

U.S.G.S. Maps: **Summit**, **Squaw Mountain**, and **East Glacier Park**.

Also: our Map **6**.

Detailed Trail data are:

The Section begins in Marias Pass, at the crest of the Continental Divide, near the granite obelisk erected in honor of Theodore Roosevelt and the statue of John Stevens, the engineer who firmly established the suitability of the gap for transcontinental rail travel.

Cross the railroad tracks—formerly the Great Northern, but now the Burlington Northern—to the boundary of Glacier National Park, where an orange metal blaze on a tree marks the way. Turn left and follow the tracks for 200 feet to the signed trailhead, at 0.1.

Turning right, set out on the Summit Trail. The route is a wide abandoned road at 0.4, where a snowmobile trail crosses it an angle. The low dike at the west end of Three Bears Lake, at 0.8, separates the Atlantic-bound lake waters from a creek, just a few feet away, that flows to the South Seas. Follow the Divide northwest, rising a bit through stands of beargrass.

Keep walking straight, on the Autumn Creek Trail, at the junction at 1.2. (The route to the left is the continuation of the Autumn Creek Trail.) From here the Continental Divide rises to high ridges, but the Trail is content to contour east along their slopes. The walk leads through occasional meadows, with some small creeks.

Cross a creek at 2.7, directly below Summit Mountain (which is visible to the north). Bend left and ascend along its course to 2.9, where the Trail switchbacks right. The route continues its gentle rise, generally in forest, with frequent rivulets draining from the Continental Divide above. You may recognize one of these creeks, at 3.8, where the path dips to cross and then parallels it up for a few feet before continuing the traverse; you might watch for green bog-orchid and blue camas in the wet spots a little bit before the creek.

Top out in a meadow, at the confluence of two forks of another small creek, at 4.4. Off to the right lies the long valley of the South Two Medicine River. Gradually lose elevation. There is little of special note; but one landmark is at 5.1, where the Trail (again in meadow) crosses a creek just below a miniature waterfall. Pass Coonsa Creek, at 6.6, and a number of other small creeks as well. Despite the occasional meadow, the route is mostly in forest, and frequent metal blazes mark the way.

Turn left at the junction at 6.9. (The Firebrand Pass Trail descends to the right, reaching U.S. 2 in 1.6 miles.) Walk for the next mile on the merged Autumn Creek and Firebrand Pass Trails. Turn right at the junction in the meadows at 7.7, continuing on the Autumn Creek Trail. (Here the Firebrand Pass Trail turns left, crossing over Firebrand Pass after 2.4 miles.)

The next three miles may be hard going. Dense patches of cow parsnip, as well as other tall growth, may cover the tread and require some effort to negotiate. The Trail may be completely obscured for short stretches, and blazes or posts to point the way may be few and far between. One consideration to be kept in mind is that there is little elevation change, so it would be a mistake to wander far uphill or downhill at any time.

Drop down, after a short switchback, to the south fork of Railroad Creek at 9.1. Not far beyond, at 9.2, cross the north fork. Railroad Creek (here, just above the confluence of its two forks) is the last reliable water supply in the Section, so pick up something to drink before proceeding.

The Trail climbs to a high point at 10.6; a well-worn side trail makes a right-angle bend to the left toward the open slopes of Squaw Mountain, from which good vistas can be obtained. Continue straight ahead, on much improved travelway. Descend somewhat steeply to 11.1, where you come to the end of a wide path—a fire road or former logging road. Descend on this road. In about a mile or so a side road turns left through the lodgepole forest, but continue straight ahead.

Leave Glacier National Park at 12.4. A beaver pond is on the left of the route at 13.1. Proceed on the unused road, descending slightly. There are extensive flat meadows as the Trail approaches East Glacier. A dirt road joins from the left at 13.9. Emerge on a maintained dirt road, passable by car, at 14.3; this is the trailhead for the Autumn Creek Trail, and so identified by an orange blaze tacked to a tree.

Turn left and drop down to the end of the Section, where the road crosses a bridge over Midvale Creek, at 14.4. This is just below, and behind, Glacier Park Lodge. It would be possible to spend the night in the area (in the meadows at 14.1

172

or at the trailhead at 14.3), but it would be prudent to secure water from a safe source—not Midvale Creek.

Distances and elevations are:

0.0	Marias Pass (U.S. 2)	5250
0.8	Three Bears Lake	5300
1.2	Autumn Creek Trail Junction	5400
2.7	Creek	5500
4.4	Creeks	5950
5.1	Creek	5750
6.4	Enter Squaw Mountain Quadrangle	5550
6.6	Coonsa Creek	5500
6.9	Firebrand Pass Trail Junction	5500
7.1		5550
7.4		5450
7.7	Firebrand Pass Trail Junction	5500
8.5		5550
8.9		5500
9.0		5550
9.1	Railroad Creek, south fork	5450
9.2	Railroad Creek, north fork	5450
10.6	Squaw Mountain side trail	5750
11.1	Road end	5450
12.4	Glacier National Park boundary	5150
12.9	Enter East Glacier Park Quadrangle	5050
13.1	Beaver pond	5000
13.9	Trail junction	4850
14.3	Trailhead	4800
14.4	Midvale Creek	4750

GLACIER NATIONAL PARK SEGMENT
Section 5
EAST GLACIER PARK TO TWO MEDICINE
10.4 Miles

The Trail from East Glacier to Two Medicine is an easy one-day hike. After a long climb to Scenic Point, the hiker is rewarded with views of the distant high peaks along the Continental Divide and beyond.

The Section starts at the bridge crossing Midvale Creek just to the west and below Glacier Park Lodge. The Trail skirts the golf course behind the Lodge and leaves the populated portion of East Glacier on a dirt road heading west from the East Glacier Ranger Station.

From 0.7 to 3.0, the route follows a mixture of jeep tracks, dirt roads, and some trail. Although fluorescent metal strips have been nailed to trees along the way, this portion is outside the national park and the markers, when lost, may not be replaced for some time.

Enter Glacier National Park at 3.5 and swing around to the north of Bison Mountain. From 5.2, the route climbs along the open top of a prominent curving ridge. Shortly after passing Scenic Point at 6.6, Two Medicine Lake and the mountains to the west come into view. Make a long descent, losing 2200 feet of elevation, to Two Medicine Road at 10.1. Follow the road west to the ranger station at 10.4, at the end of the Section.

Although camping is not restricted outside the Park boundary, most parties cross the entire Section without any overnight stop. In any event, the absence of water between Fortymile Creek (4.9) and Two Medicine makes most of the Section unsuitable for camping. East Glacier is on the main Amtrak line between Chicago and Seattle, with daily train service in each direction. During the summer, scenic tour buses connect East Glacier with Two Medicine and other points in the Park as well as Waterton Townsite in Canada.

A wide range of tourist services is available in East Glacier. The elegant Glacier Park Lodge provides the most convenient lodging; more simple accommodations are available in the center of town. Other facilities in the village are groceries, laundry, shower (at trailer campground), post office, and various shops. As mentioned above, there is a ranger station (on State Route 49) half a mile north of the Lodge and center of town. (It is not always staffed, so travelers may have to wait until they reach Two Medicine before they can obtain permits for northbound travel through the park.)

Although through hikers are allowed to spend the night at the Two Medicine Campground, it would be advisable—especially in the crowded part of the season—to confirm the availability of space before you arrive. The store at Two Medicine has a line of trail foods and limited counter service.

U.S.G.S. Maps: **East Glacier Park** and **Squaw Mountain**.

Also: our Map **5**.

Detailed Trail data are:

The Section begins at the vehicular bridge across Midvale Creek. Follow the dirt road northward, ascending with the Glacier Park Lodge golf course to the right. (At 0.1, you might walk up along the edge of the golf course to the lodge; from there it is 300 yards to East Glacier Park, using the Highway 49 underpass under the Burlington Northern tracks.)

Take the left fork at the junction at the top of the hill, at 0.2. (To get to the ranger station, take the right fork and then turn right again to reach Highway 49.) Follow Clarke Drive, past private residences. Squaw Mountain, to the left, is named for the Old Squaw rock formation on the talus slopes below the summit; from this perspective you might imagine her, with a papoose on her back, to be scanning the scene to the south. Turn left on First Street (a graded dirt road) at the next intersection, at 0.4. Follow First Street westward along a fenced field.

Leave the road at the signed trailhead at 0.7; bear right, taking the well-used path in the direction of Scenic Point and Two Medicine. Unless metal markers indicate otherwise, choose the left fork at an unsigned junction at 1.4 and continue straight at 1.5 where another trail joins from the right. (*Note:* author's route was to follow the right fork at 1.4; this soon meets another trail and, turning left at this junction, one will come to another intersection in a couple of hundred yards. The intersecting trail is presumably the principal route, at 1.5.)

Continue ascending, through pleasant aspen-lodgepole woods, with a small stream off to the left. Crossing an open field with a lone aspen, reach an ungraded dirt road at 1.9 and turn left. This deteriorates into a jeep track that climbs Bald Hill. At 2.6, near the base of Bald Hill, take the right fork. Reach the edge of Bald Hill at 3.0 near its open top. An obscure path from the left joins the Trail here. (This path is the trail that forks left at 2.6.) A beaver pond is to the left at 3.2.

Leave the Blackfeet Indian Reservation and enter Glacier National Park at the well-marked boundary at 3.5. Continue through aspen, lodgepole, and spruce woods to Fortyone Mile Creek at 3.7. Cross the creek on a log bridge. From about 3.9, the Trail—sometimes a badly-eroded gully—climbs through open country.

Pass a high point under The Head (the northeast buttress of Bison Mountain) at 4.5. Descend slightly and cross thicket-lined Fortymile Creek on a log bridge at 4.9. This is the last good water supply directly on the route before Two Medicine, so fill a canteen before proceeding. The Trail is close to a headwater stream at 5.2 and 5.4.

Ascend the prominent shoulder, heading first northward and then curving to the west, passing treeline about 5.8. From a sign at 6.7, Scenic Point is about 300 yards up the hill to the right; from its summit you can enjoy a panoramic view of the Glacier high country to the west and the plains to the east.

Continuing on the worn path, reach a crest at 7.0. From here on, Two Medicine Lake and the mountains are a scenic delight. Contour to the north of a minor summit, the highest elevation on the Section, at 7.2. Follow an open ridge at 7.4, with the aid of some cairns, remaining just a few yards to the left of the crest. Much of the route in Section 4, including Dawson Pass on the Continental Divide, is visible to the west.

Descend gradually, with long switchbacks, passing gnarled limber pine and low mats of common juniper. At 9.3, pass an overlook over the narrow gorge of Appistoki Creek. A short side trail to Appistoki Falls turns off to the left, at a sharp angle, at 9.6. Continue down in forest to a service road at 10.1. Turn right for a few feet to paved Two Medicine Road. Turn left on Two Medicine Road, following it to the ranger station at the road intersection at 10.4, at the end of the Section.

Scenic Point, from Fortymile Creek.

Distances and elevations are:

0.0	Midvale Creek	4750
0.2	Clarke Drive	4850
0.4	First Street	4850
0.7	Trailhead (4865)	4850
1.5	Enter Squaw Mountain Quadrangle	5100
1.9	Dirt road	5200
3.0	Bald Hill	5500
3.5	Glacier National Park boundary	5700
3.7	Fortyone Mile Creek	5750
4.5		6150
4.9	Fortymile Creek	6000
6.6	Scenic Point (summit 7522)	7400
7.2	High point of Section	7450
9.6	Appistoki Falls Trail Junction	5450
10.1	Trailhead	5250
10.4	Two Medicine Ranger Station (5199)	5200

GLACIER NATIONAL PARK SEGMENT
Section 4
TWO MEDICINE TO PITAMAKAN PASS
Recommended (Dawson Pass) Route: 10.6 Miles
Designated (Dry Fork) Route: 8.5 Miles

This is the Continental Divide Trail as we like to imagine it—a thin line at the very crest of the continent, with breathtaking vistas from a perch just below the clouds. This magnificent route is not the official one, though, as it is always closed to horses; and, when snow conditions or bad weather are a factor it is not good for hikers either. (The alternate route, described below, is the officially-designated location of the Trail.)

After following paved roads through Two Medicine Campground, the route crosses Two Medicine Creek to the junction with the alternate route at 0.6. It next skirts the north shore of Two Medicine Lake and then climbs steeply to Dawson Pass, on the Continental Divide, at 7.1. The final part of the Section gives it its distinction—along the rocky west slopes of Flinsch Peak and Mt. Morgan and the narrow hogback between them.

The one backcountry campground in the Section is at No Name Lake (on a short spur from the Trail at 5.1). In addition, however, through hikers can arrange an overnight stop at the Two Medicine Campground (though it might be best to make arrangements for this in advance). Apart from snowmelt, which is not always available, there may be no water past the side creek at 4.9.

Tour buses run twice a day, in each direction, between Two Medicine and East Glacier. There are no lodgings at Two Medicine—but you will find, in addition to the ranger station and campground, a general store (with snack bar). The store, which looks out over Two Medicine Lake, commands a splendid view over the water and on up the valley to the Continental Divide.

U.S.G.S. Maps: **Squaw Mountain, Mount Rockwell,** and **Cut Bank Pass.**

Also: our Map **5**.

Detailed Trail data are:

The Section begins at the Two Medicine Ranger Station. Follow the road northward past the picnic area through the enormous Two Medicine Campground. A horse ford is off to the left at 0.2. Continue through the campground around Pray Lake.

Leaving the road, cross a concrete and wood bridge over Two Medicine Creek at 0.6. Turn left at the junction immediately beyond the bridge. (*Caution:* in bad weather, turn right and follow the Pitamakan Pass Trail, which is the designated route.) After completing the circuit of Pray Lake, come to a trail junction at 0.8. (The trail joining from the left is a shortcut from the campground by way of the shallow horse ford.)

The Trail parallels the north shore of Two Medicine Lake. Cross a small creek at 2.9 and continue through forest with minor rises and dips. Turn right at the trail junction at 3.7. (The trail to the left, which follows the south shore of Two Medicine Lake, is a somewhat longer alternate route from Two Medicine.)

Pass Pumpelly Pillar, which rises just to the left of the Trail, and enter the Bighorn Basin. From about 4.6 to 4.9, cross several small creeks. Obtain water here, as there are no other reliable sources for the next seven miles. At 5.1, a trail leads 0.1 mile to the left to No Name Lake, where there is a camping area. (Permits must be obtained, in advance, as at all sites in Glacier National Park). The Trail continues to climb, becoming rather steep at the higher elevations.

From Dawson Pass, on the Continental Divide at 7.1, the view encompasses the Two Medicine and Nyack valleys to the east and west, respectively. The rugged pinnacle of Mt. Saint Nicholas and its surrounding peaks are especially impressive to the south. Turning north, the Trail ascends by switchbacks.

Leaving the crest at 7.7, the Trail continues around the west slope of Flinsch Peak, following narrow rocky footing and gradually descending. In the exceptional stretch from 8.7 to 9.1, the path lies on or close to the Continental Divide in the saddle separating Flinsch Peak and Mt. Morgan. The route then contours around to the west spur of Mt. Morgan at 9.6, the last point overlooking the Nyack drainage and the Mt. Saint Nicholas group.

Nyack Valley, from west ridge of Mt. Morgan.

The Trail abruptly changes direction, heading northeast toward Pitamakan Overlook. As it contours along the north-west slope of Mt. Morgan, there may be a chance to observe the fleet prairie falcon. Pitamakan Overlook, at 10.1, is the highest point in Glacier Park on our route. It is another outstanding vantage point. Triple Divide Peak (adjacent to the Trail in the next Section) is clearly visible to the north, partially obscuring Mt. Siyeh. Beyond Tinkham Mountain in the foreground, the spectacle to the west includes Blackfoot Mountain, Mt. Thompson, 10,142-foot Mt. Stimson (second highest in the Park), and flat-topped Mt. Pinchot.

The route next bends eastward and starts to descend away from the Divide. At 10.4, the Trail is joined from the left by a track from Cut Bank Pass. (The latter drops to the Nyack valley by way of steep scree-covered slopes; though little used these days, the path was once the Indians' principal way across the mountains.)

Reach Pitamakan Pass, on a saddle between Mt. Morgan and a small summit, at 10.6. This is the junction with the designated route and marks the end of the Section. There are fine views of the Cut Bank valley to the north and the Dry Fork valley and distant plains to the east. Enjoy the varied flower display as you rest.

Distances and elevations are:

0.0	Two Medicine Ranger Station	5200
0.6	Pitamakan Pass Trail Junction	5150
1.2	Enter Mount Rockwell Quadrangle	5200
2.4		5250
2.6		5200
2.9	Creek	5250
3.4		5200
3.7	Trail junction	5250
4.9	Creeks	5900
5.1	No Name Lake Trail Junction	6000
7.1	Dawson Pass (7598)	7600
7.7	Continental Divide	7950
8.4	Enter Cut Bank Pass Quadrangle	7800
8.6		7900
8.7	Continental Divide	7850
9.1	Continental Divide	7950
9.6	Contour Mt. Morgan	8000
10.1	Pitamakan Overlook	8100
10.4	Trail junction	7700
10.6	Pitamakan Pass	7600

Designated (Dry Fork) Route

This designated route involves a nice walk up the narrow Dry Fork valley. It is well sheltered and usable in June and into the fall, when the exposed Dawson Pass route may be hazardous.

The Section is identical with the recommended route to a trail junction at 0.6. It then rises over a low ridge to enter the valley of Dry Fork. After crossing that stream at 2.8, it ascends the valley, much of it burned in a 1929 fire, through alternating patches of forest and meadow. From the cirque at the head of Dry Fork, the route climbs the last two miles to Pitamakan Pass at 8.5.

There is a scenic backcountry campsite, at Oldman Lake (a detour from the Trail at 6.3). See the introductory text for the recommended route for additional information concerning Two Medicine.

U.S.G.S. Maps: **Squaw Mountain, Kiowa,** and **Cut Bank Pass.**

Also: our Map **5**.

Detailed Trail data are:

The Section begins at the Two Medicine Ranger Station. Follow the road northward past the picnic area through the vast Two Medicine Campground. A horse ford is on the left at 0.2. Continue through the campground around Pray Lake.

Leaving the road, cross a concrete and wood bridge over Two Medicine Creek at 0.6. Turn right at the junction immediately beyond the bridge. (The recommended route, described above, turns off to the left.) There is a little up and down first, before the Trail starts the climb over a ridge into Dry Fork. Cascading Two Medicine Creek, and Lower Two Medicine Lake, are on the right as the Trail swings counter-clockwise at 1.5.

Pause at the small creek at 1.9; its source is the narrow waterfall that drops several hundred feet, in several grand leaps, from hidden Sky Lake far above. Descend a bit from the bench here to the bottomlands along Dry Fork at 2.2.

Cross Dry Fork on a narrow bridge, with handrail, at 2.8. The cottonwoods, winding stream, and pyramidal mountains make a pleasant prospect upstream. In the gravel along the creek you can find both whiteleaf and silky phacelia, showy Jacob's-ladder, yarrow, field chickweed, stonecrop, woolly groundsel, sandwort, and sticky cinquefoil.

Turn left at the signed junction on the left (north) bank of Dry Fork. There are several side creeks along the way up the valley; the largest, at 2.9, is fed by some waterfalls off to the right. The climb is an easy grade through alternating bands of young lodgepole and meadow.

Enjoy the fine views ahead toward Flinsch Peak and Mt. Morgan as you gain elevation, well up the hillside above the left bank. Use a short plank bridge, at 4.0, to cross a side creek that rushes down a slickrock chute. The 25-foot falls of Dry Fork are

Dry Fork.

clearly in view at 4.2. The gully at 5.6, a tumble down contorted layers of red shale, is a curiosity; likely to be dry in the morning, it turns into a graceful cascade as the midday sun melts the snow in the basin above it.

Ascending excellent footpath, among firs and whitebark pines, come to a trail junction at 6.3. The through route keeps to the right. The side trail to the left leads (in 1000 yards) to the campsite on Oldman Lake; it is worth a detour to visit, even if you do not plan to camp there, for the lakeside view of towering Flinsch Peak. From Oldman Lake, the side trail continues around to rejoin the through route (after another 500 yards) at a junction at 6.9.

From the head of Dry Fork, leave the cirque at 7.2 and climb to Pitamakan Pass. There are long switchbacks along the way. The Section ends at 8.5, at the pass, at the junction with the recommended route via Dawson Pass.

Distances and elevations are:

0.0	Two Medicine Ranger Station	5200
0.6	Pitamakan Pass Trail Junction	5150
0.7		5200
0.8		5150
1.2	Enter Kiowa Quadrangle	5300
1.9	Bench	5550
2.2		5450
2.6	Enter Cut Bank Pass Quadrangle	5500
2.8	Dry Fork	5500
4.0	Creek	5700
6.3	Trail junction (Oldman Lake 0.6)	6500
6.9	Trail junction (Oldman Lake 0.3)	6800
8.5	Pitamakan Pass	7600

GLACIER NATIONAL PARK SEGMENT
Section 3
PITAMAKAN PASS TO GOING-TO-THE-SUN ROAD
31.2 Miles

The Triple Divide—where the watersheds of the Atlantic and the Pacific abut that of Hudson Bay—is the major landmark of this rugged Section. The terrain is so difficult, in fact, that the route must deviate from the Continental Divide, descending far down into the Cut Bank and St. Mary valleys. Although there are few spectacular vistas, the scenic lakes and waterfalls, flowers, and wildlife make this Section a rewarding hiking experience.

The Section begins with a descent of the Cut Bank valley to 6.1, losing over 2000 feet of elevation and passing some small lakes on the way. Nearly all of the height is regained with the climb up Atlantic Creek to Triple Divide Pass at 9.3. Once again there is a great loss of elevation as the route descends the Hudson Bay Creek valley. The Trail skirts scenic Red Eagle Lake from 16.5 to 17.4 and proceeds down Red Eagle Creek to 19.8. Having detoured to the east to avoid some high ridges, the route crosses over to St. Mary Lake. From 21.6 onward, it parallels the south shore of the lake for several miles before passing beneath Virginia Falls at 27.8 and St. Mary Falls at 28.5. A final climb leads up to the Going-to-the-Sun Road (a highway across the heart of Glacier National Park) at the Jackson Glacier Overlook at 31.2.

Camping permits will need to have been obtained at Two Medicine Ranger Station (or East Glacier, if the ranger station is open) before setting out. Established campgrounds are at Morning Star Lake (3.4), Atlantic Creek (6.4), and Red Eagle Lake (head of lake at 16.5, foot of lake at 17.4). Through hikers proceeding on to Many Glacier may obtain special authorization to camp along Reynolds Creek, near the end of the Section, at 29.9.

The closest developed facilities are the motel and cabins at Rising Sun (on Going-to-the-Sun Highway). Also at Rising Sun are a campground, restaurant, and general store. If space is available, the morning tour bus from Rising Sun will drop you off at the end of the Section to resume the hike north.

U.S.G.S. Maps: **Cut Bank Pass**, **Mount Stimson**, **Saint Mary**, **Rising Sun**, and **Logan Pass**.

Also, our Maps **3** and **4**.

Detailed Trail data are:

From scenic Pitamakan Pass, descend northward by switchbacks and pass timberline. Lake of the Seven Winds lies about 200 feet to the left of the Trail at 1.0, but it is not directly accessible. Cross the North Fork of Cut Bank Creek, at the outlet of Pitamakan Lake, at 1.4. Lying in the shadow of treeless Mt. Morgan on the Continental Divide, this is a splendid tarn with green meadow and patches of pine and subalpine fir. Camping is not permitted at this beautiful and fragile spot.

Cross the outlet for Katoya Lake at 2.3. The North Fork, to the left of the Trail, drops over several ledges and then a waterfall at 2.5. The route, continuing its descent, circles around the east shore of Morning Star Lake, where there is an authorized camping area, in a lovely setting beneath steep slopes.

Leaving the lake, cross the North Fork of Cut Bank Creek at 3.5. After a small rise, hike down to a flat meadow at 4.9, passing small creeks there as well as at 4.3 along the way. Climb briefly again, with the meadow to the right of the Trail, before descending through forest to cross Atlantic Creek by bridge at 5.8. Atlantic Falls is immediately upstream.

Turn left at the junction with the Triple Divide Pass Trail at 6.1. (To the right, it is about four miles to the Cut Bank ranger station and campground.) The route now begins the ascent of Atlantic Creek, passing a campground along the stream at 6.4. Medicine Grizzly Trail forks off to the left at 6.7. (The side trail leads 1.4 mile to Medicine Grizzly Lake, which was formerly the site of an authorized campground; the campground has been closed since 1986 because of bear feeding in the area.)

There are a number of steep gullies along the long and gradual climb, but most (or all) of them may be dry; one of the more likely water sources is a spring at 9.1. The treadway on the open slopes of Mt. James is frequently quite narrow at

Razoredge Mountain and e Continental Divide, looking south from Triple Divide Pass

higher elevations Medicine Grizzly Lake appears on the floor of the valley be w.

The Trail r ches Triple Divide Pass at 9.3. Mountain goats haunt this r ged open terrain. To the left, Triple Divide Peak rises anot r 600 feet; from its slopes Hudson Bay Creek, Atlantic reek, and Pacific Creek start their journeys to far-separat d waters by way of the Nelson, Mississippi, and Columbi Rivers. To the south, the Continental Divide follows the vel top of a long straight cliff which has the fitting name of Razoredge Mountain.

Descend fairly steeply to Hudson Bay Creek at 10.9. This is a delightful spot, with several waterfalls dropping into the green basin from the shelf below Norris Mountain. Cross the creek by way of a straightforward boulderhop and continue down the valley. A side creek at 12.4 is fed from a cascade that drops perhaps a thousand feet down the sheer eastern wall of Split Mountain. Flowers sparkle in the meadows all about.

Turn right at the junction at 14.7. (The Red Eagle Pass Trail, leading upstream to the left, is no longer maintained.) Just past this junction, cross Red Eagle Creek by bridge. Then, after going over a rise of land, there's another bridge over the creek at 15.4. Ignore an unmarked path that bears to the right at 15.7. Some falls are visible off to the left on Red Eagle Creek.

There is an authorized campsite at the head of Red Eagle Lake at 16.5. Continue around the east shore to another camping area, at the foot of the lake, at 17.4. The precipitous mountain backdrop makes this an exceptional place to stop. Descend to the east on the Red Eagle Trail, through alternating stretches of forest and meadow, with occasional minor side creeks.

Cross Red Eagle Creek on a wide bridge and reach a trail junction at 19.8. Leave the Red Eagle Trail, which continues downstream. Instead, go left and ascend by switchbacks to a high bluff overlooking the creek at 20.1. The Trail, sometimes obscure, drops slightly to 20.5, where it makes a sharp turn to the right. (A former trail drops off, to the left, to the valley.) Climb and cross a divide out of the Red Eagle Creek drainage.

Descend to the shore of St. Mary Lake at Red Eagle Landing at 21.6. The remains of a dock are still evident a few feet out in the lake. (Before construction of the St. Mary Lake Trail, hikers would arrive here by launch to begin a hike to Red Eagle Lake.) Ducks seen during the summer from this point are probably Barrow's goldeneyes. Although the beach consists of rounded stones rather than sand, the view westward and the pleasant cottonwood shade make this a good lunch stop.

The Trail parallels the south shore of St. Mary Lake for the next several miles. Stretches of Douglas fir alternate with open patches overgrown with cow parsnip, stinging nettle, and other rank vegetation. There are occasional bare scree slopes, as at 21.9 and 22.1. The Trail is generally well back from the lake.

At 23.1, pass a long spit known as Silver Dollar Beach that extends out into the lake. Although there is no obvious access to the spit, a switchback trail that cuts down the scree at 23.4 may follow the shore and end up there. This area, called the Narrows of St. Mary Lake, offers good views, with Going-to-the-Sun Mountain an especially prominent feature to the west.

Continue with only minor elevation changes. Two creeks are reliable sources of water. (The first is at 24.8, where a small shaded island between two forks of the stream makes an inviting spot for a rest; the second, at 26.1, is opposite Going-to-the-Sun Point, which juts out from the north shore.)

Take a break as the Trail crosses Virginia Creek on the sturdy bridge at 27.8. Virginia Falls, with a principal drop of about 80 feet, is directly above. Having hiked at least from Red Eagle Lake, you will probably find the scene to be too shaded for ideal photography. Descend along Virginia Creek, passing a series of pretty cascading drops.

Cross the St. Mary River on a solid wooden bridge at 28.5. Just upstream, St. Mary Falls shoots through a red mudstone bed in two powerful fifteen-foot leaps. Early morning would be best for pictures here, too. Turn left at the trail junction at 28.8. (The path to the right is a spur that leads to a parking area on the Going-to-the-Sun Road.)

Keep going straight at the junction at 29.9, where the Gunsight Pass Trail turns left and promptly crosses Reynolds Creek. (There is a campsite, just past the bridge, that is reserved for through hikers. It is the only campsite between Red Eagle Lake and Many Glacier; keep it clean and observe all regulations scrupulously, so as to help ensure its continued availability.)

The route from here is part of the Gunsight Pass Trail. There is a fine rest stop at 30.0, close to Deadwood Falls, where Reynolds Creek cuts a narrow channel through a resistant band of the Grinnell Formation. Climb in damp forest to the end of the Section, where the trail comes to Going-to-the-Sun Road. This is at 31.2, at the lower end of the Jackson Glacier Overlook parking area.

Distances and elevations are:

0.0	Pitamakan Pass	7600
1.0	Lake of the Seven Winds	7000
1.4	Pitamakan Lake	6800
2.3	Katoya Creek	6350
3.4	Morning Star Lake	5750
3.5	North Fork, Cut Bank Creek	5750
3.6		5800
4.9	Meadow	5450
5.1		5500
5.8	Atlantic Creek	5350

6.1	Triple Divide Pass Trail Junction	5350
6.4	Atlantic Creek Campground	5450
6.7	Medicine Grizzly Trail Junction	5450
8.7	Enter Mount Stimson Quadrangle	6900
9.3	Triple Divide Pass (7397)	7400
10.9	Hudson Bay Creek	5900
12.4	Creek	5300
13.7	Enter Rising Sun Quadrangle	5100
14.7	Red Eagle Creek (Red Eagle Pass Trail Jct.)	4850
14.9	Rise	4900
15.4	Red Eagle Creek	4800
16.5	Red Eagle Lake (head)	4750
17.4	Red Eagle Lake (foot)	4750
17.5	Enter Saint Mary Quadrangle	4800
18.8	(4673)	4650
19.1		4700
19.8	Red Eagle Trail Jct. (Red Eagle Creek)	4600
20.1		4750
20.5	Sharp turn	4700
20.9		4800
21.6	Red Eagle Landing (Rising Sun Quadrangle)	4500
22.6	(4690)	4700
24.0	(4552)	4550
24.8	Creek	4750
		4800
26.1	Creek	4650
		4850
		4750
27.8	Virginia Creek (Virginia Falls)	4800
28.5	Saint Mary River (Saint Mary Falls)	4500
28.8	Trail junction	4550
29.4	Enter Logan Pass Quadrangle	4600
29.9	Gunsight Pass Trail Junction	4650
30.0	Deadwood Falls	4650
31.2	Jackson Glacier Overlook	5250

GLACIER NATIONAL PARK SEGMENT
Section 2
GOING-TO-THE-SUN ROAD TO MANY GLACIER
13.3 Miles

A rewarding full-day hike awaits the traveler in this Section. The layout is simple—from the Saint Mary drainage the Trail climbs a high spur ridge and then drops, past several waterfalls and lakes, to beautiful Many Glacier. There are opportunities aplenty to enjoy the scenery, wildlife and flowers, but the absence of authorized campsites dictates a steady pace.

The Section starts out with a steady ascent in forest to Preston Park, a lovely subalpine oasis with fine views, at 2.9. The Trail continues to its high point at Piegan Pass, at 4.7. The descent includes numerous switchbacks, some of them back and forth across long-lasting snowbanks. The valley of Cataract Creek, featuring vigorous Morning Eagle Falls at 8.0 and lacy Feather Plume Falls at 8.9, comes next. The Trail then levels out as it skirts Lake Josephine and Swiftcurrent Lake to the Grinnell Glacier trailhead between Many Glacier Hotel and Swiftcurrent village.

Campsites are unavailable in the Section. You could spend the night before the trip at Reynolds Creek (or at Rising Sun, from which the morning tour bus could drop you off at the trailhead). At the end of the Section, lodgings and meals can be obtained in Swiftcurrent village (or at the elegant, and more expensive, Many Glacier Hotel); and some spaces at the large Many Glacier campground are reserved for the use of through hikers.

It would be possible to proceed north by a shorter and quicker route that bypasses this Section altogether. This would require a climb up the Going-to-the-Sun Road for 4.7 miles to Logan Pass and then a very fine walk beneath the Garden Wall, along the Highline Trail for 8.0 miles, to Granite Park. This alternative is not recommended, however, because of its highway location.

U.S.G.S. Maps: **Logan Pass** and **Many Glacier**.
Also: our Map **3**.

Detailed Trail data are:

The Section begins a few feet below the Jackson Glacier Overlook on the Going-to-the-Sun Road. At the upper end of the parking area, walk through the tunnel and climb in forest; the next mile receives little use and may be poorly maintained. Keep straight at 1.3, where the Siyeh Bend Cutoff Trail turns off to the left. A large avalanche chute opens the forest at 1.9. A bridge with handrails marks Siyeh Creek, at 2.6, where the water steps down several flat limestone ledges. Travel becomes more enjoyable as the forest—here some whitebark pines mixed in with the spruces and firs—thins out.

Preston Park, at 2.9, is a wonderful place to stop and take in the view. Blackfoot Glacier, to the south, is especially prominent (though much of it is obscured by the nearer bulk of Citadel Mountain); on the Continental Divide beyond the glacier you can identify pointed Mt. Logan as well as massive flat-topped Blackfoot Mountain and Mt. Jackson. Take the left fork at the junction in Preston Park and cross the little log bridge. (The Siyeh Pass Trail, a high route to St. Mary Lake, bears off to the right.) As you traverse around Siyeh Creek you will be able to pick out thin, high Piegan Falls tumbling down the side of Piegan Mountain; bighorn sheep and mountain goats frequent the basin below.

Reach the high point of the Section at Piegan Pass, at 4.7. Despite the elevation, snow is unlikely to linger in the area, except in patches, past the end of June. The pass is situated in the prominent broad black band of igneous rock that circles around the cliffs beneath the Continental Divide. The views at the summit are restricted, so follow the tread a bit farther before taking your break. Again there are good prospects for observing mountain goats. Flowers are magnificent in the open terrain, of course—limestone columbine, sky pilot, white dryad, creeping sibbaldia, fernleaf candytuft, moss campion, mountain forget-me-not, and homely buttercups among them.

Pass some small creeks as the Trail descends, with a few switchbacks, to timberline. Boulderhop a fork of Cataract Creek at 6.7. This is a pretty area, with picturesque cascades and chutes along the stream, and with polychromatic rock beyond—blue, green, orange, and red layers in addition to the black band high up on the cliffs.

The descent to the valley floor switchbacks several times. As snow will persist into July, and the slopes are fairly steep, you may need to be especially careful; if the surface is hard and icy, an ice axe would come in handy.

Switchback sharp right as you approach impressive Morning Eagle Falls. Cross Cataract Creek by bridge at 8.3. (However, the bridges over the creek are removed during the winter and put back in place after the peak of the snowmelt; early in the season it may be necessary to ford the frigid water.) Cross Cataract Creek again at 8.8. (*Note:* according to the topographic map, it would be just as convenient to follow an alternate route by taking a trail to the left, at 8.9, to Grinnell Lake and then continuing via the west shore of Lake Josephine, rejoining the designated route at 12.6, on Swiftcurrent Lake. One advantage of the alternate route is that it has no horse traffic.)

The next landmark is delicate Feather Plume Falls, which sprays its water in ribbons that drop hundreds of feet down the cliff face; pass a side creek at 9.2, near the base of these falls. In about a mile, there is a view, to the left, of Grinnell Glacier, with the Garden Wall section of the Continental Divide beyond it.

Leave the contouring main trunk of the Piegan Pass Trail at a junction at 10.7; turn left and descend toward the Oastler Shelter on the shore of Lake Josephine. (It is a leanto that provides cover for persons waiting for the Lake Josephine boat.) Bypass the shelter by remaining right at each of the trail junctions nearby.

The Trail from 11.0 parallels the lakeside, well back from the shore, sometimes on boardwalks, with occasional creeks. A short side trail at 11.8 that angles back to the left, to the outlet of Lake Josephine, offers a fine view of Grinnell Falls and The Salamander. Continue straight at 11.9, where the main Piegan Pass Trail comes downhill from the right and converges with the route. Stump Lake, to the left, is mostly blocked by trees. Walk along Cataract Creek, keeping left at trail junctions at 12.2 and 12.4. (The routes to the right are shortcuts to Many Glacier Hotel.)

After the large bridge over Cataract Creek at 12.4, proceed around Swiftcurrent Lake to the boat dock at 12.6. (The alternate route from Feather Plume Falls reunites with the designated route at the trail junction here.) Skirt the south end of the lake, noting the shrubs—such as menziesia, alder, and snowberry—that are identified by nature trail signs.

Cross Swiftcurrent Creek by bridge at 13.0. The Section ends at 13.3, at the picnic area (the Grinnell Glacier Trailhead) on the paved road between Many Glacier and Swiftcurrent village. See the introductory text for Section 1 for information concerning Many Glacier (to the right) and Swiftcurrent village and ranger station (to the left).

Distances and elevations are:

0.0	Going-to-the-Sun Road	5250
1.3	Siyeh Bend Cutoff Trail Junction	6300
2.6	Siyeh Creek	6850
2.9	Preston Park (Siyeh Pass Trail Junction)	7000
4.7	Piegan Pass (7570)	7550
6.7	Creek	6300
8.3	Cataract Creek	5300
8.8	Enter Many Glacier Quadrangle	5200
10.7	Trail junction	5100
12.4	Cataract Creek	4900
13.3	Grinnell Glacier Trailhead	4900

GLACIER NATIONAL PARK SEGMENT
Section 1
MANY GLACIER TO INTERNATIONAL BOUNDARY
Designated (Waterton) Route: 34.1 Miles
Interim (Chief Mtn.) Route: 28.0 Miles

The designated route in this Section offers an exceptional backpacking experience. Its superb alpine scenery and tundra flora are unequaled anywhere along the Trail in Montana. But severe snow and ice conditions limit travel there to a few weeks—early July to early September; at other times it is best to use the alternate (interim) route described below.

Northbound travelers are advised that they must clear Canadian customs when crossing the boundary. Customs officers are not always stationed in Waterton Townsite, and in their absence one must check in with the Royal Canadian Mounted Police. Be sure to carry personal identification. Until and unless administrative matters pertaining to customs are resolved, the Chief Mountain Route (here called the "interim route")—which is located entirely in the United States—will serve as the primary official route for the Continental Divide National Scenic Trail. The goal is to have the Waterton route established as the primary route as soon as possible.

Swiftcurrent village, at the beginning of the Section, provides all needed services. Leaving civilization behind, the Trail gradually ascends the Swiftcurrent valley for several miles, past a chain of lakes, before climbing more strenuously to Swiftcurrent Pass at 7.4. There are magnificent vistas as the route drops to intersect and pick up the Highline Trail at 8.1, near the Granite Park Chalet. Snow-topped Vulture, Longfellow, and Heavens Peaks are perhaps the most prominent mountains, but the number of summits is beyond counting. (For an even more spectacular view, make a side trip from Swiftcurrent Pass to lofty Swiftcurrent Mountain.)

The route contours northward, on a high shelf beneath towering cliffs. Ahern Creek and Cattle Queen Creek have cut deep side valleys that are traversed at about 12.4 and 15.0, respectively. The Trail reaches its high point on the Section as it crosses the Divide below Mount Kipp at 18.9 and for the last time leaves the Pacific slope.

Continuing across tundra past Fifty Mountain Camp (at 19.9), with its outstanding views, the Trail descends steadily along the flanks of Cathedral Peak from 21.1 to 24.4. For the next several miles, the route follows the valley along the east bank of the Waterton River to Goat Haunt Ranger Station, on Waterton Lake, at 30.2. From there to the Canadian boundary at 34.1, the route follows the lakeshore north.

The heavy winter snowfall makes normal backpacking impractical outside of a few weeks in summer. There is a permanent snowbank at 11.0 that is steep, hazardous to cross until a good path has been cut, and not readily avoided by detour. This is the Ahern Drift, and until it has been worked on in early July you may be discouraged or prohibited from going through (though allowance can be made for experienced hikers equipped with ice axe). By the time the Ahern Drift is open, snow elsewhere should be limited to small patches. Use caution, though, if snow covers a streambed—especially at Cattle Queen Creek—as you could plunge through a weak spot. (Streams are otherwise bridged, where necessary, and should not pose any problem.)

Unless you have obtained a camping permit farther south, be sure to stop at Many Glacier Ranger Station (on the route at 0.3) before setting out. The designated areas in the Section are at Granite Park, Fifty Mountain, Kootenai Lakes, Goat Haunt, and Waterton River. (Wood fires are not allowed at Granite Park or Fifty Mountain.) Through hikers will also be allowed to stay at Many Glacier Campground, near Swiftcurrent. Water sources are frequent throughout the Section.

Meals, lodging, groceries, telephone, and laundry are available at Swiftcurrent. You can buy a good trail lunch at the historic (75-year-old) Granite Park Chalet during its season from July 1 to Labor Day; don't count on spending the night, though, as it starts taking reservations at New Year's and quickly fills its books for the entire season. Sometimes they have a cancellation, so you might contact them to inquire (see address for Belton Chalets in background information). Public transportation (tour bus service) is available at Many Glacier Hotel, a short distance from the start of the Section.

U.S.G.S. Maps: **Many Glacier**, **Ahern Pass**, **Mount Geduhn**, and **Porcupine Ridge**.

Also: our Maps **1** and **3**.

Detailed Trail data are:

The Section begins in the picnic area at the trailhead for the Grinnell Glacier Trail. Turn left, west, on the paved road. The ranger station and campground are off to the left on the side road at 0.3. Swiftcurrent village, described in the introduction, is at 0.5.

Pick up the footpath at the end of the parking area. Cross Wilbur Creek by bridge at 0.6. A pack trail joins from the right near the register box at 0.7. The next mile, past Fishercap Lake, is in forest and is of little interest. However, at 1.9, where the Trail uses a plank bridge to cross a side stream, there is a nice view out over Redrock Lake. A pool of eddying waters—a local ranger called it The Giant Jacuzzi—is at 2.5, just above the pretty cascades of Redrock Falls.

Much of the Swiftcurrent valley, along the route, was burned by a devastating fire in 1936. The scrubby growth that has come in—largely aspens and small conifers—may conceal bears that sometimes frequent the area; so it might be wise to make noise to alert them to your presence.

After circling around to the north of Bullhead Lake, and crossing a couple of side creeks, the Trail at 4.5 starts its long climb from the valley floor. It is a pleasant hike, though, with nice views over the chain of lakes. The grotesquely contorted strata of the headwall are worthy of note at 5.0, where the Trail switchbacks to the right. There are some stunted subalpine fir, but gradually the terrain opens up completely. Switchback to the right again at 5.7, just before a pair of high cascading streams. The hillside is rocky, and marmots abound.

Swing sharply around a spur ridge—called the Devil's Elbow because of the bend and the steep dropoff below—at 6.1; over a thousand feet downhill lies Windmaker Lake. Contour around to the right, passing a small creek at 6.3, and switchback left at 6.5. As you look down Swiftcurrent valley, you can pick out Many Glacier Hotel on Swiftcurrent Lake, with Lake Sherburne beyond it and Duck Lake way out in the haze on the plains.

A small pond lies in the little basin at 6.9. Boulderhop the shallow creeks there and climb more steeply. Approaching the Divide, pass a couple of spring-fed creeks at 7.2.

A large cairn at 7.4 marks Swiftcurrent Pass. Continue over the crest to the junction with the Swiftcurrent Lookout Trail at 7.5. Although the Continental Divide Trail itself affords magnificent views over Granite Park and over the upper McDonald valley towards snowy Heavens Peak, all reports indicate that the 1.4-mile side trip to the lookout (at 8436 feet) ought not to be missed; its 3000-foot plunge to Windmaker Lake must be a dizzying sight. The subalpine meadows as you descend from here are ablaze with globeflowers, glacier lilies, springbeauties, cinquefoils, purple mountain heath (a shrub), shootingstars, false asphodel, veronica, Sitka valerian, and penstemons.

Turn right on the Highline Trail at the junction at 8.1. (Or, turn left if you want to detour to nearby Granite Park Chalet. From the chalet, you can descend on the Granite Park Trail until you intersect a side trail that leads, to the right, to the Granite Park Campground. Sheltered among scattered trees, it lacks water; so either carry some from the chalet or use the creek, on the side trail, some 300 yards beyond the campground.)

Cross a creek at 8.2, passing a onetime (but now closed) route from there to the campground. With the Granite Park Chalet still in sight to the rear, a side trail descends from a junction at 8.5. (It is 0.4 mile on the side trail to the campground. About halfway there you walk to the right of a patrol cabin, where you can obtain water from a reliable creek.) Hike in open country, crossing a short stretch of talus at 9.9.

Enter the Ahern Creek basin at 10.7. The Trail passes under a sheer cliff at 11.0. The Ahern Drift here is a permanent steep snowbank. Even after it is opened for travel—some time in the first half of July—hikers will need to tread carefully when traversing it. During the summer it is necessary from time to time to cut new crossings as the snow gradually moves down the slope.

The principal branch of Ahern Creek is at 12.4; here a signed trail leads off to the right 0.4 mile to Ahern Pass (elevation 7100), which looks out over Helen Lake and the Belly River country. A small stream at 12.9 plummets down the hillside over black rock steps, presumably an outcrop of the igneous Purcell Sill.

The Trail near Fifty Mountain Camp. Sperry Glacier is visible in the distance, between Mt. Cannon and Heavens Peak.

At 13.6, as the Trail leaves the Ahern basin, there are excellent views of the high peaks in the northwest part of the Park and also mountains to the west and south; the Ahern Drift stands out as a white stripe crossing the cliffs on the far side of the cirque.

The Trail begins to descend to Cattle Queen Creek. Across the Mineral Creek valley, two impressive high waterfalls can be observed on the flank of Flattop Mountain. Cattle Queen Creek, at 15.0, may be covered by a snowbank; be careful, as the surface may have been so undercut by the flowing water that it can support little weight. The Trail continues a circuit around this basin, crossing several runoff streams along the way. Leave the Cattle Queen drainage at 16.2. Pass another side stream at 17.6. Climb in open country, with the attractive glacial valley of upper Mineral Creek below.

Our northernmost crossing of the Continental Divide is at 18.9, at a small saddle beneath Mt. Kipp. Mt. Carter, Vulture Peak, Mt. Geduhn, Longfellow Peak, Heavens Peak, and Mt. Cannon, as well as many more mountains, provide an unexcelled panorama. At the Continental Divide, a marked trail leads off to the right, ascending 0.4 mile to the Sue Lake Observation Point (elevation 7750, with excellent views of jagged Stoney Indian Peaks and Mt. Merritt, as well as Pyramid Peak and Mt. Cleveland; Sue Lake is directly below.)

Some small snowpatches may be encountered as the Trail descends, but they are unlikely to present any difficulty. Switchback down to the left at 19.5. (There was once a trail straight ahead, bypassing Fifty Mountain Camp, but it has been abandoned and blocked.)

Descend through tundra carpeted with glacier lilies to Fifty Mountain Camp, at 19.9. The site has magnificent views—perhaps even 50 summits—as well as good water and some trees for shelter. Hike from here on the Waterton Valley Trail, ascending. (An intersecting trail crosses Flattop Mountain and then descends to Going-to-the-Sun Highway in the upper part of the McDonald valley.) The former, but now abandoned, bypass route may still be visible as it joins from the right at the crest of a spur ridge at 21.1.

Vulture Peak remains prominent to the southwest as the Trail descends. Patches of snow may linger, but again should not be an obstacle. Descending in subalpine forest, cross a creek (which may be dry in late summer) at 21.8 and again at 22.0. There is a good creek at 23.6, just below a waterfall, as the path drops down the scrubby slope.

Reach the Waterton valley at 24.4. (Here a faint valley trail, now abandoned, joins from the left.) Cross a side stream at 24.6, once more just below a small waterfall. Follow the narrow gorge carved by cascades of the Waterton River from 24.6 to 25.0. Pass Creek, tumbling over the colorful red boulders of the Grinnell Formation, crosses the route at 25.3.

Rise a bit to the junction with the Stoney Indian Pass Trail (which ascends to the right) at 25.5. From 25.7, descend slightly through brush and then cross a couple of small creeks. Traces of the old Valentine Fire Trail, which led off to the left at 26.5, may still be visible. Openings in the forest afford good views, to the north, of the four jagged pinnacles of Citadel Peaks on Porcupine Ridge.

The Trail crosses a marsh outlet on a low bridge at 27.2. Look ahead from time to time to Mt. Cleveland, the highest mountain in Glacier National Park (10,466 feet). Cross Camp

Creek at 27.8. Just before the creek, a side trail leads 0.3 mile to the left to a campground on one of the Kootenai Lakes; moose are often observed there. Small wet meadows occasionally break the forest. Continue north, crossing several more creeks.

Arrive at Goat Haunt Ranger Station at 30.2. (Following the shoreline of Waterton Lake 0.2 mile east, a paved path leads to a boat landing and exhibit area; nearby are two cabins, each divided into several concrete-floored open-faced hikers' shelters equipped with picnic table and fireplace.)

For the remainder of the Section, the route employs the Waterton Lake Trail, circling around the west shore of the lake. Cross Cleveland Creek by bridge at 30.3. A horse ford at 30.4 crosses the Waterton River to the grassy campground on the far side. Traveling by foot, keep to the left and walk upstream.

Cross the Waterton River by suspension bridge at 30.6. (A side trail to the left, before the bridge, leads 0.4 mile to Rainbow Falls.) A spur trail leads directly from the far side of the bridge to the campground. On the principal route, though, you pass by the junction with the Boulder Pass Trail (which turns left, away from the lake) at 30.9. Turn left at 31.0, where another spur trail from the riverside campground comes in from the right. Proceed with little change of elevation, passing small side creeks at 31.1 and 32.2.

Stay right at 33.7, where the North Boundary Trail heads left, to the west, to Cameron Lake in Canada. Cross Boundary Creek at 33.8 on a sturdy footbridge. The creek here shoots with impressive force through a narrow notch. (There is also a horse ford downstream.)

Canada awaits you at the monuments on the boundary at 34.1. Congratulations! Enjoy the grandeur of the lakeside setting and savor the moment. And do come back as soon as you can to the Continental Divide National Scenic Trail.

Distances and elevations are:

0.0	Grinnell Glacier Trailhead	4900
0.6	Wilbur Creek (4928)	4950
1.9	Creek (5078)	5100
2.3	Redrock Lake	5050

4.5	Leave valley	5300
5.5	Enter Ahern Pass Quadrangle	6000
6.1	Devil's Elbow	6500
6.3	Creek	6550
6.9	Basin	6850
7.4	Swiftcurrent Pass (7185)	7200
8.1	Highline Trail Junction	6750
8.5	Trail junction (campground 0.4 mile)	6650
8.8		6800
9.5		6550
10.0		6800
10.3		6700
10.7	(6765)	6750
11.0	Ahern Drift	6600
11.6		6500
12.4	Ahern Creek	6650
13.6	Ridge	6800
15.0	Cattle Queen Creek	6000
15.3		5800
18.9	Continental Divide (Sue Lake Trail Jct.)	7450
19.5	Switchback	7000
19.9	Fifty Mountain Campground	6700
21.1	Ridge (enter Mount Geduhn Quadrangle)	7000
22.0	Creek	6450
23.4	Enter Porcupine Ridge Quadrangle	5450
23.6	Creek	5250
24.4	Trail junction	4600
25.3	Pass Creek	4500
25.5	Stoney Indian Pass Trail Junction	4550
26.1		4400
26.5	Trail junction	4450
27.8	Camp Creek (campground 0.3 mile)	4400
30.2	Goat Haunt Ranger Station	4200
30.6	Waterton River	4250
30.9	Boulder Pass Trail Junction	4250
31.0	Waterton River Campground (0.2 mile)	4200
32.2	Creek	4250
33.7	North Boundary Trail Junction	4200
33.9		4250
34.1	International boundary	4200

Interim (Chief Mountain) Route

As has already been noted, the interim route enables north-bound travelers to avoid potential difficulties in clearing Canadian customs. Its other advantages are convenient access and the longer season. And although it has noteworthy charms—especially the glacier views from Redgap Pass—it would be a shame to miss the scenery of the Highline Trail and Waterton Lake.

Starting in the developed area at Many Glacier, you would make a wide sweep to the east, over low Swiftcurrent Ridge at 5.7, in order to get around the high mass of Apikuni Mountain. The route then ascends the valley of Kennedy Creek, past Poia Lake at 8.0; it is pleasant enough, but without distinction.

The second half of the Section, beginning with Redgap Pass at 13.8, is much more interesting. The views from the crest are especially fine, but the scenery is rewarding all the way down to lovely Elizabeth Lake at 18.2. Dawn Mist Falls, where the Belly River plummets with tremendous power, demands a pause at 19.7. There are meadows along the valley, from which you can often admire sheer-walled mountains in all directions. The Trail ends at 28.0, after climbing a couple of miles in forest, on the Chief Mountain Highway (Mont. 17) at the international boundary.

Note: there is a shortcut from Many Glacier to Elizabeth Lake, via the Ptarmigan Tunnel. It is not described here, as it is assumed that most people taking this route will be traveling during the snowier months, when the Ptarmigan Tunnel is closed.

Water crossings should present no problem, as all the larger streams have bridges in place. Snow will persist at Redgap Pass into June, and can be expected again in September, but the grades are moderate and should be easier to negotiate than those south of Many Glacier.

Designated campsites in this Section are at Poia Lake, Elizabeth Lake, and in the lower Belly valley (at Belly River Ranger Station and at Threemile Camp). Through hikers will also be allowed to stay overnight at the developed campground at Swiftcurrent, at the start of the Section.

During the tourist season, public transportation (tour bus service) is available each day from the customs station at the border to Many Glacier and on to East Glacier. (This is the bus that connects Waterton Townsite and Glacier National Park.)

U.S.G.S. Maps: **Many Glacier, Lake Sherburne,** and **Gable Mountain.**

Also: our Maps **2** and **3**.

Detailed Trail data are:

The Section commences at the picnic area by the Grinnell Glacier trailhead, between Swiftcurrent village and the Many Glacier Hotel. (The Swiftcurrent ranger station and campground are 0.3 mile, on paved road, to the west. Some spaces are available at the campground for through hikers. Just beyond the campground lies Swiftcurrent village, with lodging, meals, a store, phones, and laundromat.)

Turn right from the picnic area, toward Many Glacier. Swiftcurrent Lake is soon to your right. Walk along it, enjoying the mountain scenery beyond, for a quarter of a mile. At 0.6, at the outlet of the lake, a side road turns right and goes uphill to the Many Glacier Hotel.

Continue eastward along the Many Glacier Road to the Grinnell Glacier observation point at 1.8. Take the marked trail that angles off to the left. Lake Sherburne, as well as the peaks with their glaciers, offers many a rewarding view to the south as you climb. Pass a section with several short boardwalks at 2.7.

Cross permanent Windy Creek on a bridge of logs at 3.5. You might observe a varied thrush in the cottonwoods along the creek. After some more meadows, come to the junction with the Sherburne Cutoff Trail (which joins from the right) at 4.9.

Rise to Swiftcurrent Ridge Lake at 5.3. From the west end of the lake, follow the north shore to 5.4; there you can look out over the water and admire the summits in the distance.

As the crest of Swiftcurrent Ridge, at 5.7, lacks a view, you might just as well keep going without a pause. On the descent, pass some wet spots, crossed by boardwalks, at 6.1 and 6.5; bog-orchids are quite common. There is a nice patch of tall spruces and Douglas firs at one point. A trail formerly led off to the right at 6.6, but it has been abandoned and is overgrown. Step over a small creek at 6.9.

The beaver pond at 7.3 marks the end of the descent and the beginning of the climb up the valley of Kennedy Creek. As you walk, look for stonecrop, buckwheat, and gray daisies among the many flowers on the sunny slope. Note how Kennedy Creek twists and cascades about.

The Poia Lake Campground, situated in dense forest and back from the lake, is at 8.0. The campground is not attractive, but there is a nice view from the shore up the valley and to the glacier in the distance, beyond Redgap Pass; and a hermit thrush might serenade you.

Walk along the foot of the lake to its outlet (Kennedy Creek) at 8.2. Cross the stream on a stout bridge and, curving left, continue to skirt the water. The terrain is open—some willow thickets and then grassy meadows.

Return to forest at about 9.7. A log bridge takes you over a side creek at 10.1. Beavers may have flooded some of the path at 10.6, where the Trail is close to the bank of Kennedy Creek.

The next three miles involve a climb, gently to 11.0 and then more steeply, to gain over 1500 feet. Starting at 11.6, switchback three times across a single creek; and then cross another tumbling one, near the upper end of its falls, at 11.9. Subalpine fir and whitebark pine are the predominant trees as the Trail switchbacks up to timberline.

Approaching Redgap Pass, ascend gradually along the south slopes of Seward Mountain. Water can be obtained from the creek at 13.4. A nice feature is the view south over the pristine little basin of Kennedy Lake to a snow-capped summit (Mt. Gould, probably) beyond. You can also pause to admire the terrain left behind—the forested bottom of Kennedy Creek beneath the rounded bare slopes of Apikuni Mountain.

A magnificent vista awaits at Redgap Pass. Two glaciers are prominent to the west—Ahern on the left and Old Sun (on the slopes of Mt. Merritt). Farther to the right is 10,466-foot Mt. Cleveland, the highest peak in Glacier National Park, with bands of snow along its horizontal rock bands. Elizabeth Lake sits in the valley 2500 feet below, though only its lower half is in clear view. An idol-like rock formation known as Ruggles of Red Gap is said to smile on the west side of the pass, but Ruggles eluded this observer. The flowers sparkle in their customary variety—moss campion, sky pilot, white dryad, fernleaf candytuft, sandwort, mountain forget-me-not, alpine crazyweed, cinquefoil, silky phacelia, and cutleaf daisy among them.

As can be surmised from the name of the pass, the soil and rock along the descent are rusty-hued. Cross a gully at 14.4 and again, after several switchbacks, at 14.7; as it is spring-fed, there's a good chance that it will provide some water. After passing timberline, swing around more to the right. A snowbank at 15.5 may linger well into July, but should not be an obstacle.

Intersect the Ptarmigan Trail, which comes in from the left, at 16.2. (The Ptarmigan Trail is a shorter, alternate, route from Many Glacier; but, as mentioned in the introductory text, it is routed through a tunnel and is open only during the summer season.) Continue to enjoy the mountain scenery as you descend past the scree slope at 16.4; look for stonecrop and spotted saxifrage along with the scrubby aspen. There are good views over Elizabeth Lake toward Helen Lake and Ahern Pass (on the Continental Divide).

Take the suspension bridge over the calm Belly River at 18.1. The campsite at the foot of Elizabeth Lake is situated at the trail junction at 18.2. The campground has a magnificent view south toward the Ptarmigan Wall; it is a popular spot, so permits may be hard to come by. Turn right at the trail junction and descend the Belly valley in forest. You might keep an eye and ear cocked for signs of the winter wren, cedar waxwing, and red-breasted nuthatch.

Dawn Mist Falls is a greater cataract than any that can be found along the entire length of the proper Continental Divide Trail route—not the highest, perhaps, but the most powerful. The Belly River is about 25 feet wide at the brim of the falls; there the water tumbles about 60 feet in a single leap, with a couple of shorter steps below that. The falls can be observed from the top, along the Trail at 19.5, but it is far better to take the side trail at 19.7 that leads (after 0.1 mile) to the base.

Remain on the footpath at 19.9, where a pack trail descends to the right to a horse ford. Turn right at the signed junction at 20.2 and, after 50 feet, cross the Belly River by suspension bridge. Turn left at the junction at 20.3. (The trail to the right is the connecting route from the horse ford.)

Hike in mixed forest, with minor elevation changes. Along with thimbleberry and white geranium, you might watch for queencup, sweetpea, vetch, and—in deep shade by a side creek—a pink pyrola or two. And bunchberry, a diminutive dogwood with showy white bracts, has a limited distribution in Glacier in places such as this.

The next authorized camping area is the Belly River Ranger Station Campground, on the edge of the river; its access is a side trail that descends at a sharp angle to the left at 21.5. As you walk around the perimeter fence of the ranger station, you have a view of the sheer ramparts of Mt. Cleveland. Keep going at the junction at 21.8, where the Cosley Lake Cutoff Trail bears off to the left. Pass through an opening in the ranger station fence at 21.9.

The Trail is close to the stream at a bend of the river at 23.0. Cross some side creeks by means of log bridges. The grassy meadows at 23.9 afford excellent views up the Mokowanis (southwest) valley as well as back up the Belly valley to the south. Also note landmark Chief Mountain to the east. The route edges close to the water again at the bends of the river at 24.4 and 24.6.

The small Threemile Campground is to the left of the Trail, along the Belly River, at 24.8. The valley is a broad open bottom, with a wide path for travel. Walking is very enjoyable so long as you have grass, but much of the vegetation consists of rank herbs (such as cow parsnip) that can be a nuisance. Before leaving the valley, there is a wooden causeway across a wet place; there is also a parallel route, with a ford, for horses to use.

At 25.8, begin the ascent out of the valley. Cross several little side creeks on short bridges as you climb in forest. From the aspen thicket at 27.0, you can look southwest toward 10,004-foot Mt. Merritt.

Reach the trailhead at a parking lot, on the west side of Chief Mountain International Highway (Montana Route 17), at 27.8. Turn left, passing the United States customs office, to the end of the Trail at the boundary, at 28.0.

Distances and elevations are:

0.0	Grinnell Glacier Trailhead	4900
0.6	Many Glacier Hotel (0.3 mile)	4900
1.2	(4849)	4850
1.8	Trailhead	4900
2.2	Enter Lake Sherburne Quadrangle	5000
3.5	Windy Creek	5400
4.9	Sherburne Cutoff Trail Junction	5900
5.4	Swiftcurrent Ridge Lake	6100
5.7	Swiftcurrent Ridge	6200
7.3	Beaver pond	5500

7.9		5850
8.0	Poia Lake Campground	5800
9.3	Enter Many Glacier Quadrangle	5850
10.1	Creek	5900
11.9	Creek	6500
13.4	Creek	7400
13.8	Redgap Pass	7550
14.7	Gully	6850
15.5	Enter Gable Mountain Quadrangle	6500
16.2	Ptarmigan Trail Junction	6050
18.2	Elizabeth Lake Campground	4900
19.7	Dawn Mist Falls (0.1 mile)	4700
20.2	Belly River	4650
21.5	Belly River Campground	4700
21.8	Cosley Lake Cutoff Trail Junction	4650
23.0	River bend	4650
23.9	Meadow	4700
24.8	Threemile Campground	4600
25.8	Leave valley	4550
27.8	Montana Highway 17	5350
28.0	International boundary	5300

APPROACH TRAIL
INTERNATIONAL BOUNDARY TO WATERTON
4.7 Miles

Mountain-rimmed Waterton Lake is splendid hiking country. The Trail parallels the western side of the lake, generally some distance back from and above the shoreline. Although there are some small rises and dips, the elevation changes are nowhere of any consequence. While much of the route is in lodgepole pine forest, there are several viewpoints. The Section ends at a bridge over Cameron Brook, immediately below the notable Cameron Falls, at the western edge of Waterton Park Townsite, Alberta.

All persons entering Canada are required to go through customs. As customs officials may not be stationed permanently in Waterton Townsite, travelers should immediately make their presence known to the Royal Canadian Mounted Police, who can take care of any necessary arrangements. Be sure to carry personal identification documents.

The entire Section lies within Waterton Lakes National Park, which is administered by the Department of Indian Affairs and Northern Development. The headquarters for the Park is in the town.

Water is available from streams. Although camping is permitted at two primitive campsites, this requires prior registration with the Park Superintendent, which may not be practicable for a northbound party.

There is daily bus service during the summer to East Glacier from Waterton Park (with an intermediate stop at Many Glacier). This scenic coach route departs from the Prince of Wales Hotel, just north of the townsite, from which there is a commanding view over the entire seven-mile length of Upper Waterton Lake. Additional summer bus or limousine service may be available to Calgary and to Lethbridge.

The town has numerous motels and restaurants, as well as a large trailer campground. Various publications, including a Park brochure, list of accommodations, map of the townsite showing the trailhead, and topographic map of the national park can be obtained (though they are not needed) by writing the Park Superintendent.

Detailed Trail data are:

The Section begins at the international boundary, which is marked by two obelisks. A locked cabin is located on the Canadian side. Camping is authorized here, at a grassy campsite next to a creek, if a permit has been obtained.

Climb to 0.4 before dropping back to the shore of the lake. Follow the shore closely, climbing with switchbacks to a crest at 1.2. Cross a small brook at 1.4 before reaching the beach again at 1.7. Climb in forest to 2.4; then descend to the lake fairly steeply, crossing a short scree slide and briefly following an undercut and exposed trail. An authorized campsite is situated here, at 2.8, with scenic views of Waterton Lake; permission to camp must be obtained in advance.

Cross Bertha Brook on a bridge at 3.0. Climb to a trail junction, where the Bertha Lake Trail comes in from the left, at 3.6. Remaining to the right, come immediately to a viewpoint with a good vista back down Waterton Lake to the south.

Descend gradually on excellent footpath to meet a secondary road at 4.4. Follow this road northward, passing the start of the Carthew Trail (which leads to the left) at 4.6. Curve down to paved Cameron Falls Drive and walk to the bridge across Cameron Brook, where the Section ends at 4.7. Cameron Falls is directly upstream. (It is about half a mile to Park Headquarters, on Mount View Road, on the northern edge of Waterton Lake Townsite.)

Distances and elevations are:

0.0	International boundary	4200
0.4		4300
0.9	Waterton Lake	4200
1.2		4350
1.4	Brook	4300
1.7	Waterton Lake	4200
2.4		4500
2.8	Waterton Lake	4200
3.0	Bertha Brook	4200
3.6	Bertha Brook Trail Junction	4550
4.4	Road	4300
4.6	Carthew Trail Junction	4300
4.7	Cameron Brook	4250

Maps

Maps

Legend

Map Number	**17**
Continental Divide	
Recommended Route	
Alternate Route	- - -
Terminal Point of Segment	
Terminal Point of Section	
Section Number	2
Topographic Map (1:24000)	Caribou Peak
Corner of Topographic Map	+
Segments and Sections on Map	Scapegoat 4
Scale of Miles (1/2" = 1 Mile)	0 1 2 3

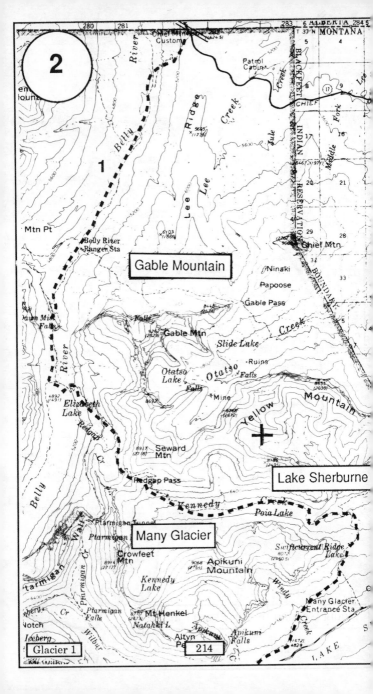

215

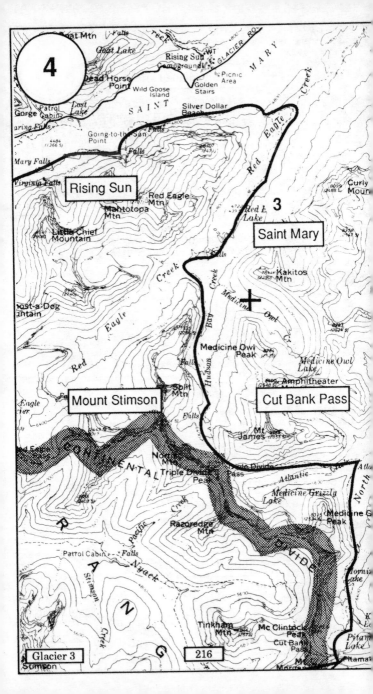

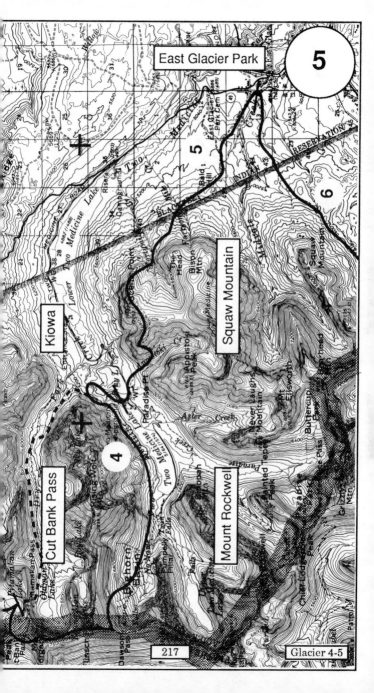

East Glacier Park

5

Kiowa

Squaw Mountain

Cut Bank Pass

Mount Rockwel

4

Glacier 4-5

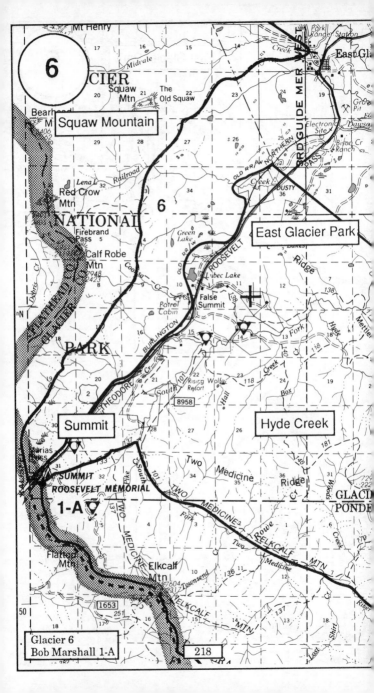

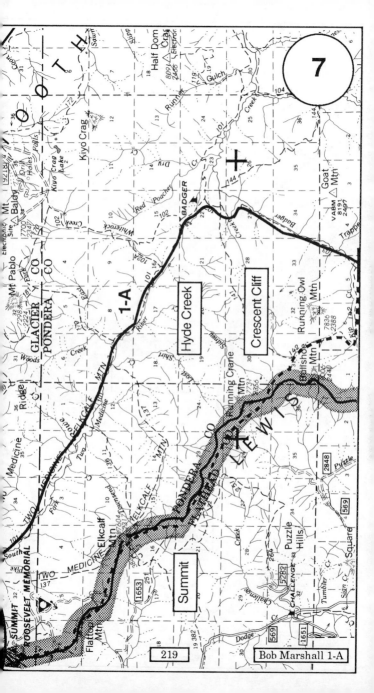

Goat Mtn
VABM △
8191
2497

Bruin Pks
7581 7728
2311 2356

Goofy Gulch

Curly Bear
Mtn
7923
2415

Spotted Eagle
Mtn
8054
2455

Morningst
M

STA
833

Sc
Mt

Elbow Mtn
7131
2174

Lost Horse Camp

A N D

1-B

Blue L

Emeral
Lak
28
Fa
8086
2465

Beaver
Lake

FLATH

Crescent Cliff

Morningstar Mtn.

Bear Pk
6990
2131

Cap Mtn
7512
2290

Wapiti
Park

Gooseberry Park

2

Winter
Pts
7180
2189

ir Mtn

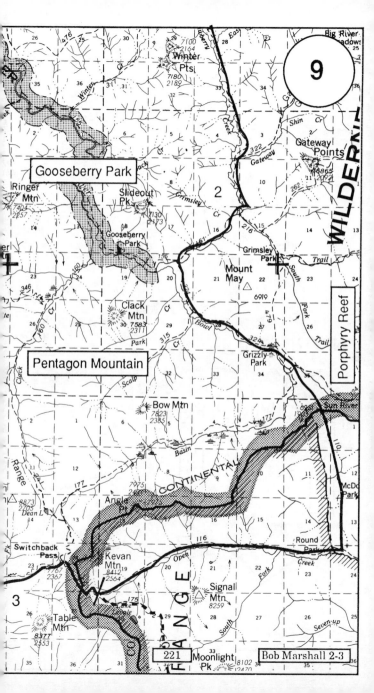

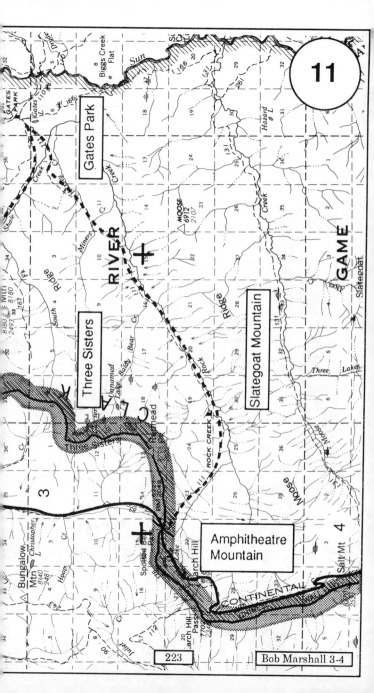

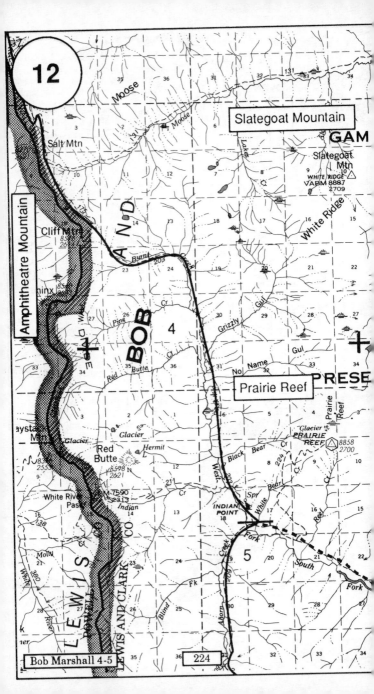

Slategoat Mountain

GAM

Amphitheatre Mountain

Prairie Reef

Bob Marshall 4-5

224

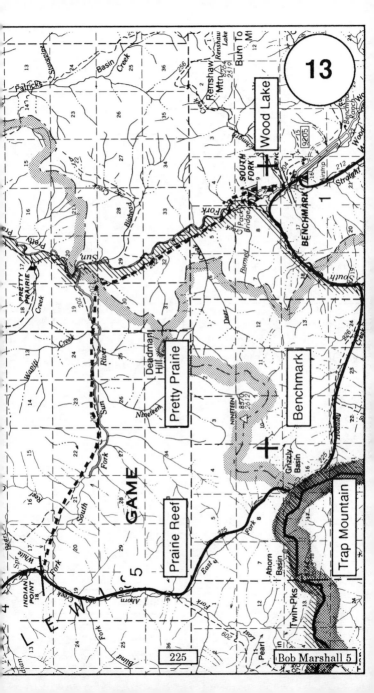

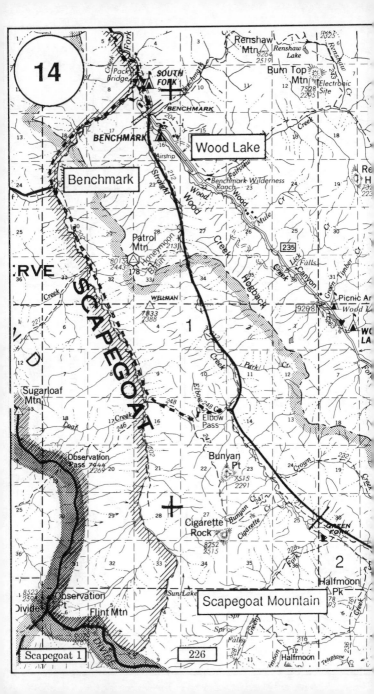

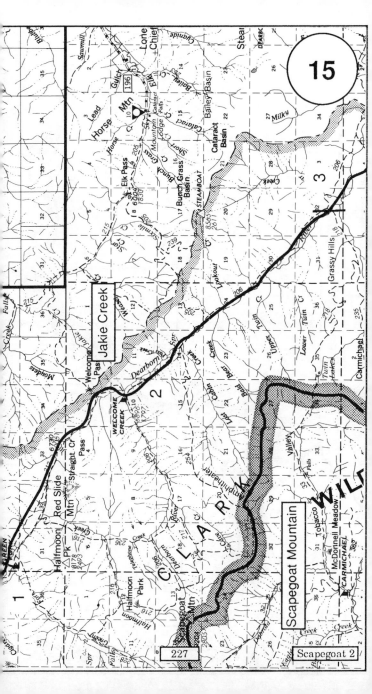

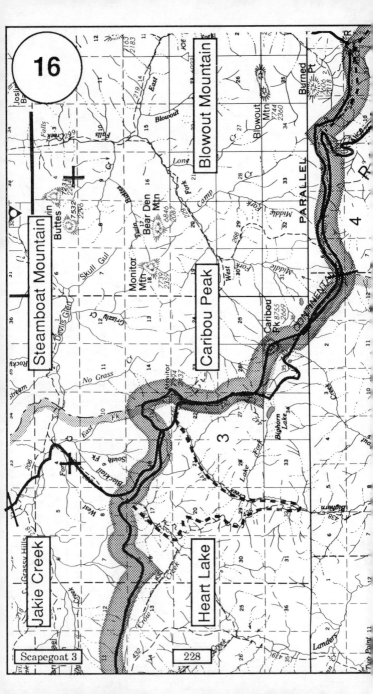

Steamboat Mountain

Blowout Mountain

Caribou Peak

Jakie Creek

Heart Lake

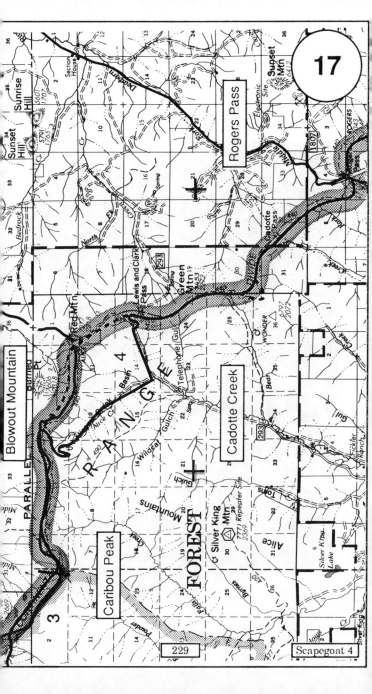

Virginia Falls.

Background

Information

The CDT insignia.

The Continental Divide Trail

America is gradually developing a network of trails for the use and enjoyment of the public. The charter for this effort is the National Trails System Act of 1968 (P.L. 90-543). A principal aim of this law is the establishment of national scenic trails, which are defined as "extended trails so located as to provided for maximum outdoor recreation potential and for conservation and enjoyment of the nationally significant scenic, historic, natural, or cultural qualities of the areas through which such trails may pass."

Congress determined in 1968 that the existing Appalachian Trail and the Pacific Crest Trail measured up to the standard and designated them as national scenic trails. Both had been laid out as a result of epic volunteer efforts, which in the case of the Appalachian Trail stretched back nearly 50 years.

Congress also recognized the potential of several other routes, with the Continental Divide Trail placed at the top of the list. These routes were to be studied, with the findings then to be submitted for legislative review.

The report for the Continental Divide Trail, completed in 1976, endorsed formal destination. Among the findings were these:

- Spectacular scenery of the quality and magnitude along the proposed CDT route is not available anywhere in the continental United States other than in the North Cascades area along the Pacific Crest Trail or in the Yellowstone-Teton area of Wyoming.

- The areas through which the trail would pass are also rich in the heritage and life of the Rocky Mountains and the southwestern United States.

- The hiker of the proposed route of the CDT would encounter a great variety of terrain, geology, climate, and plant and animal life. This would include the unique and unusual character of Glacier, Yellowstone, and Rocky Mountain National Parks and the backcountry solitude of numerous wilderness areas, as well as the living quality of the Red Desert in Wyoming.

After hearings, the Continental Divide Trail was officially designated a national scenic trail on November 10, 1978, when the National Parks and Recreation Act of 1978 (P.L. 95-625) was signed into law. The responsibility for proceeding with development is entrusted to the Secretary of Agriculture (the overseer of the Forest Service) with the assistance of an advisory council representing public and private interest groups.

Progress toward making the Trail a reality has been uneven. Several years were required to accomplish the first major task—preparation of a comprehensive plan to govern the siting, marking, and development of the route. Although this plan was several years in the making, it is now in place and provides workable guidelines. The comprehensive plan contemplates that the Trail will be a simple facility for the hiker and horseman. There should be no significant alteration of the land or vegetation. Limited vehicle use would be permitted on certain existing primitive roads (as in the Great Divide Basin of Wyoming). As a general principle, the Trail is to be as close to the Continental Divide as possible; but deviations are acceptable to provide for safe travel and general recreation appeal, to achieve economic feasibility, and to keep environmental impacts to a minimum. Public lands or existing public rights-of-way are to be used as much as possible. Primary consideration is to be given to snow-free use; where snow travel is feasible and reasonably safe, however, it would not be curtailed.

The first (and, to date, the only completed) official route selection covers the route of the Continental Divide Trail in the states of Montana and Idaho—between the Canadian boundary and Yellowstone National Park. This landmark was celebrated by gala dedication ceremonies at Chief Joseph Pass, on the Divide in southern Montana, on June 21, 1989. Most of the selected travelway is actually constructed and available for use, but some portions remain to be cleared and marked. This book identifies the official route in Glacier National Park and on south through the Bob Marshall and Scapegoat Wildernesses. As noted in the Introduction, however, the official route is not necessarily always the best; and alternative ways are recommended wherever that seems appropriate.

The Environment

Weather

The Trail in northern Montana starts out at the Canadian border in a region of high precipitation and great snowfall and gradually leads to a considerably drier, and slightly warmer, country as it approaches Rogers Pass. The hiker's primary weather-related concern in Glacier National Park is likely to be snow; other concerns are high water in the Bob Marshall Wilderness, and water availability in the Scapegoat Wilderness. Because of the high latitude, daylight (sunrise to sunset) in late June reaches about 16 hours.

Snowfall can amount to more than 300 inches a year in Glacier, with snowpacks often exceeding 100 inches in April. The deepest snow, in the northern portion of the Park, may prevent through travel from Waterton Lakes (our preferred route) until early July. By mid-September, new snow may once again block the route. Spring snow is likely to be a problem into June at higher elevations near the Continental Divide in other parts of Glacier and the Bob Marshall Wilderness as well. Hiking in most sections is feasible into November, though snow storms can be expected with greater frequency and severity in the later weeks.

The season of maximum runoff from melting snow runs through mid-June. During this period it may be difficult to cross the rivers and larger creeks in the Bob Marshall and Scapegoat Wildernesses.

Annual precipitation ranges from about 120 inches in parts of Glacier down to about 20 inches near Rogers Pass. May and June are relatively wet months throughout, July and August usually being much less moist. Most precipitation during the summer is in the form of rain showers, sometimes accompanied by hail or snow. However, a cold front may bring several consecutive days of bad weather with drenching rain and fog. The Trail is generally well below the peaks and so travel, though unpleasant at times, need rarely be impeded by storms. (Hikers should be familiar with the causes and symptoms of hypothermia, and should be prepared to keep dry and warm under all circumstances.)

During July and August, temperatures are excellent for hiking. Typically, nights are in the 40's and days in the low 70's in the Bob Marshall. Glacier is slightly cooler and the Scapegoat a bit warmer, but the variation is not great. Toward the end of August the weather turns markedly colder, with overnight temperatures at higher elevations frequently dropping below the freezing mark. Mean temperatures are on the order of 60° during July and August, 50° in September, and 40° in October.

Geology

The outcropping rocks of the cliffs and mountainsides along the Trail were formed, almost entirely, from sediments of mud and sand deposited long ago in seas or shallow waters. These sediments were compacted to form shales or sandstones or—in the case of seas teeming with calcium-bearing organisms— thick bands of limestone.

Starting less than 100 million years ago there began a long turbulent epoch when movements within the earth pushed the crust upward, causing it to buckle and tilt. One dramatic consequence was the rupture of the crust and the subsequent thrusting of the thick upper layers more than 15 miles eastward over the older plains. In due course much of the uplifted material eroded away from the area of Glacier National Park; what remains is Precambrian rock, about 600 million years old or so, and lacking animal fossils. The most colorful of the common rocks in Glacier is the Grinnell Formation, a conspicuous red argillite (hardened shale). Just below it is the Appekunny Formation, a greenish argillite; and above the Grinnell is the Siyeh Limestone, a thick cliff-forming mass of a pale buff shade. In addition to the sedimentary rocks, one is bound to take note of the prominent black diorite sill (a horizontal band that was formed by intrusion of lava into the rocks of the Siyeh limestone) and perhaps some outcrops of an old free-flowing lava (the Purcell lava) at the top of the Siyeh.

South of the Park one travels mostly through a land of limestones of Paleozoic origin (540 million to 200 million years old), exposed as a result of the same uplifting forces, mentioned above, that created the Rocky Mountains generally. The spectacular cliffs of the Bob Marshall Wilderness, such as the Chinese Wall, are typically composed of limestones dating from early Paleozoic times. The fossils of primitive animals known as trilobites (forebears of crabs and lobsters) are common in the shales and limestones of this age. One of the principal fossil-bearing strata, the Pentagon shale, has its "type locality" where the Trail crosses the Divide near Kevan Mountain between sections of unsurmountable limestone cliffs; numerous trilobite species are found here.

The most dramatic erosional force in recent geologic time has been that of the mighty glaciers that have covered the entire region of the Trail in several distinct ice ages. The enormous scouring force of ice and rock, assisted by freezing water in newly-exposed cracks, results in the landscape of deep U-shaped valleys, amphitheaters and hanging valleys on mountain slopes, and knife-edged ridges marking the meeting-point of adjacent glacial masses. The sculpting of steep cliffs, such as the Chinese Wall, is attributed to the action of glacial ice.

Glaciers in the national park today are but a tiny remnant of former ice sheets. In fact, the twentieth century has been a period of rapid shrinkage for the remaining glaciers, which have not received enough new snow to make up for the snowmelt during the period. Thus Sperry Glacier, estimated to cover 810 acres in 1901, was reduced to 287 acres by 1960. It may be too early to write them off, though, for meteorologists speculate that colder or wetter weather might lie ahead in the next decades. But even if the glaciers decline, the national park's name will remain fitting because the story of the rocks everywhere testifies to their power and artistry.

Birds

Only a few species of birds are commonly seen along the Trail, although many more may be spotted occasionally by the careful observer.

The *American robin*, abundant below timberline, needs no description. Others that are often found at low to middle elevations include the *dark-eyed junco*, a small dusky bird with very conspicuous white outer tail feathers and the *chipping sparrow*, another small species with brown back, white breast, reddish cap, and trilling song. You will often hear, though less often see, a couple of diminutive blue-gray tree-loving birds—the *red-breasted nuthatch*, with a black nape and clear pink-tinged front and the *mountain chickadee*, which is marked by a black cap and bib and a white breast. Watch, too, for the *spruce grouse*, a chicken-like bird that is likely to lure the hiker down the trail so as to get as far away from its chicks as possible.

The *gray jay*, familiarly known as the camprobber because of its fearless behavior, is robin-size and is common in the forests. A somewhat similar bird is *Clark's nutcracker*. The nutcracker, like the jay, is predominantly gray and white; but it occurs at higher elevations, around timberline, and displays distinctive bold black-and-white patterns in its wing and tail. The easiest sparrow to recognize, the *white-crowned sparrow*, is also usually found around or above timberline. It can often be approached closely enough for a good look at the white and black stripes on the head.

The most common ducks are *goldeneyes*—both the *common* and *Barrow's*, which are differentiated (in the male) by the shape of the white spot in front of the eye. *California gulls* can also be found near water, especially around the larger lakes. The *spotted sandpiper* is frequently seen along streams and lakeshores; it is readily identified by its spotted breast, incessant bobbing up and down, and its stiff-winged flight. Fast-running mountain streams are home to the gray *dipper*, likely to be viewed as it flies rapidly up the course of the water.

Mammals

Of the approximately 60 species of mammals found along the Trail, most are so secretive in their habits or few in numbers as to be unobserved by the hiker. The few large or common mammals that may be encountered can be described briefly.

Both the *grizzly bear* and the *black bear* occur along the Trail—not only in Glacier National Park, but in the Bob Marshall Wilderness and the Scapegoat Wilderness as well. *(National Park Service publications, distributed free to visitors, contain useful advice for safe travel in bear country. They should be studied carefully, and their recommendations should be heeded, because of the potential hazards that are involved.)*

The grizzly bear can be distinguished from its cousin, the black bear, by its larger size, its dished-in facial profile, the hump at its shoulders, and the long claws on its front feet. Other carnivores—members of the dog, cat, and weasel families—also occur, but are infrequently seen.

The *moose* is found in the lower valleys of Glacier National Park, but would not be expected elsewhere. Its relatives include the *elk*, about five feet tall at the shoulder, which spends the summer in the mountains in fairly open situations, and the much smaller *mule deer* and *white-tailed deer*. (The mule deer has a rope-like black-tipped tail and a bounding gait; the white-tailed deer lacks the black tail color and runs with more of a gallop.)

The *mountain goat*, with its shaggy white coat, is unmistakable. It is a common species on rocky slopes above timberline in Glacier National Park; in the Bob Marshall Wilderness, goats are said to range along the Chinese Wall and elsewhere. *Bighorn sheep* are also at home in the mountains, but are not so conspicuous as the goats. Massive curved horns are the impressive hallmark of the rams.

The most abundant of all the wild mammals is the little red-nosed *Columbian ground squirrel*. It is found in open areas along the length of the Trail, never venturing far from its burrows; its loud alarm chirp is a familiar sound. The *mantled ground squirrel*, identified by a broad white stripe along its flank, usually chooses rockier and more wooded sites. *Chipmunks* occurring along the way, of several species, resemble the larger mantled ground squirrel in that they too have stripes; with chipmunks, however, the face is also marked with stripes instead of a round eye ring.

Look for *red squirrels* on branches of coniferous trees along the Trail. Their coloration is a solid brownish-red, except for a white belly and eye ring. Their scolding chatter is easily learned and often heard.

Among the larger rodents, the *hoary marmot* is the only one commonly observed. It prefers rocky slopes such as those near Granite Park and Swiftcurrent Pass in Glacier National Park, where it can be inspected at close range. Marmots look like large ground squirrels, grey to brown on the back, with the face marked with black and a conspicuous white nose patch.

The presence of *beavers* is manifested by their dams, but the animals themselves are rather elusive.

The *yellow-haired porcupine*, though mostly nocturnal is sometimes seen during the day in dense forest along the Trail. With its coat of quills, it requires no further description.

Rabbits and hares do not seem to be much in evidence. One species, the *pika*, is worth special mention because of its superficial resemblance to the rodents. It is a small tailless rabbit with short ears, seen (more often, only heard) exclusively at the rockslides which shelter its nest.

Trees

Changes in tree types are the most obvious indicators of the life zones characteristic of the Trail. The alpine zone is completely devoid of trees. The remainder of the Trail is essentially all high forest. At the subalpine elevations, one finds Engelmann spruce and subalpine fir predominating, with some limber and whitebark pine and subalpine larch. This gradually changes to pure lodgepole pine stands lower down, with Douglas fir on sheltered sites.

Two common species of the subalpine zone have needles attached singly rather than in bundles. the *subalpine fir* is easily identified by its smooth silvery bark; its needles are flat and about an inch long. The *Engelmann spruce* (and the similar, but quite uncommon, white spruce) has a dark scaly bark, rather like a lodgepole pine's; its needles, attached singly, are stiff, sharp-tipped, and round or angular (not flat) in cross-section.

The typical subalpine trees with needles in bundles—five in a bundle—are the confusing *limber pine* and *whitebark pine*. The whitebark is said to have stouter twigs than the limber pine's, even the outermost ones thicker than a pencil. The stout purple cones of the whitebark quickly disintergrate; the elongated cones of the limber pine persist on the ground. (The identification in the text of the trail descriptions may occasionally have these two mixed up.) The long-lived whitebark pine has been dying off in recent years, in alarming numbers, for reasons that are not entirely clear.

The *subalpine larch*, which sheds its foliage yearly, is recognized by its lacy appearance. The needles, about one to two inches long, are clustered in bundles of about 20 to 40. It grows at Larch Hill, just to the north of the Chinese Wall, in the Bob Marshall Wilderness; it can also be found in the vicinity of the Trail near Preston Park, south of Many Glacier.

While spruce, fir, and limber pine may also occur at somewhat lower elevations, the predominant conifers on the lower slopes are *lodgepole pine* and *Douglas fir*. The abundant lodgepole is our only species with two needles to a bundle; the dark bark is flaky or shallowly furrowed. Rarely will it exceed a diameter of 18 inches (as contrasted with the two to three foot diameter of mature spruce). The flat needles of Douglas fir are attached singly to the twigs. The deep furrowing of the dark bark immediately distinguishes mature Douglas firs; generally the cones, characterized by sharp-pointed bracts between the scales, are found in good numbers on the ground beneath these trees.

Large deciduous trees occur only at the lower elevations. The most conspicuous is the *quaking aspen*, easily recognized by its smooth whitish bark and finely toothed long-stalked leaves that tremble in even the lightest breeze. Closely related are the cottonwoods, particularly the *black cottonwood*, which grows along creeks and lake shores. Its leaves are longer and narrower than the aspen's and the grayish bark is deeply furrowed.

The *paper birch*, its white bark peeling in thin shreds, may be found in the Waterton valley, but is unlikely elsewhere.

Other deciduous species along the Trail are small in stature and best regarded as shrubs rather than trees. These include alders, serviceberry, willow, black hawthorn, chokecherry, pin cherry, and Douglas maple. A few small shrubs are notable for their showy or pretty flowers—among them the *thimbleberry* (white flowers, maple-like leaves); white and pink *spirea* (dense flat-topped flower clusters and elliptic leaves, found in meadows and openings, mostly in moist locations); *shrubby cinquefoil* (yellow flowers and leaves divided like the fingers of a hand); *wild roses* (prickly stems, red flowers, and leaves divided with segments arranged on a long axis); *alpine laurel* (pink saucer-shaped flowers and opposite leaves, encountered in wet meadows at higher elevations); *puple mountain heath* (a matted shrub with small red urn-shaped flowers and with stems densely covered with needle-like leaves); and *black twinberry* (yellow and red flowers in pairs, each pair supported on a stalk from the leaf axil).

Wildflowers

The other volumes in the guidebook series have included keys for the identification of wildflowers along the Continental Divide. Such keys can be helpful for the casual visitor as well as the backpacker; and so this time the detailed information will be issued as a separate publication. It will include all the conspicuous genera that are represented, in summer, along the Trail in northern Montana. All of the flowers mentioned in this book will be described in the key.

Among the **monocotyledons** (flower parts in 3's or 6's, not 4-parted or 5-parted; leaves not divided, lobed, or toothed, with veins parallel rather than branched), the following are especially likely to attract attention:

Glacier lily (*Erythronium grandiflorum*). Showy yellow flower, on a leafless stem, near melting snowbanks.

Beargrass (*Xerophyllum tenax*). A tall plant, with very narrow leaves and many small flowers in an elongated cluster.

White bog-orchid (*Habenaria dilatata*). Slender, with numerous small white flowers having the familiar characteristics of orchids (the lower petal a spurred pouch).

The largest family of **dicotyledons** is the Aster Family, which includes daisies (*Erigeron spp.*), thistles (*Cirsium spp.*), dandelions (*Taraxacum spp.*), pussytoes (*Antennaria spp.*), and their many relatives. All of these have composite flowers—with compact clusters (heads) of strap-shaped and/or tubular flowers.

If your flower is a dicot, but not in the Aster Family, check to see if it is regular (the parts symmetric like a wheel) or irregular (symmetry 2-sided, not radial). Among the regular flowers, several showy plants in the Buttercup Family are distinguished by the absence of sepals. Some other groups having regular flowers—and with petals separated to their base and no more than 10 stamens—are the Mustard Family (characteristically with four small rounded petals), the Parsley Family (with flowers in an umbrella-like cluster, as in cow parsnip, *Heracleum lanatum*, a thick-stemmed tall plant with leaves divided into three very large segments), the Pink Family (with leaves in pairs, five white or pink petals, and five sepals), and the Saxifrage Family (flowers white or greenish, small, the leaves either all at base of stem or alternating—not paired—along the stem). Regular flowers with numerous stamens and separate petals are apt to be buttercups (*Ranunculus spp.*) or members of the Rose Family (with small sepal-like bracts alternating with sepals—such as cinquefoils, *Potentilla spp.*, in which the flowers are most often yellow and the leaves arranged in palmate fashion, like the fingers of a hand).

Regular flowers with fused petals (joined at least near their base) include bedstraw (*Galium spp.*—flowers small, 4-lobed, the leaves in whorls along the stem), Sitka valerian (*Valeriana sitchensis*, flowers small, 5-lobed, white, densely clustered, leaves paired), western shootingstar (*Dodecatheon pulchellum*, the flower lobes bent backward toward the leafless stalk), and members of the Borage Family (including forget-me-nots and tall bluebells, *Mertensia paniculata*), Harebell Family (especially *Campanula rotundifolia*, roundleaf harebell), Phlox Family (*Polemonium spp.*, with blue flowers and leaves divided into small segments, including Jacob's-ladder and sky pilot), Waterleaf Family (especially *Phacelia sericea*, silky phacelia, with a dense elongated cluster of purplish flowers, their stamens extending well beyond the floral tube), and the Gentian Family.

There are a few irregular flowers with distinct petals. Apart from some violets (in the Violet Family) and larkspurs (in the Buttercup Family), these are members of the Pea Family—including clovers, lupines, vetches, and their relatives. Of the irregular flowers with fused petals, you can distinguish the occasional members of the Mint Family by their characteristic square stems. Most of the flowers in this group belong to the Figwort Family—such as Indian paintbrush (*Castilleja spp.*), elephantshead (*Pedicularis groenlandica*), monkeyflowers (including the red monkeyflower, *Mimulus lewisii*), and penstemons (flowers mostly blue or purplish, with 5 stamens—one of which is sterile—in elongated clusters).

Learning to identify the wildflowers is a challenging and rewarding task—especially enjoyable as an opportunity to pause on a lengthy climb. If you wish to pursue it, work with the key and you should be able to learn them in short order.

History

Man is a newcomer to the Americas. His migration from Asia, by way of a great ice bridge across the Bering Strait, occurred as recently as the last ice age—between 40,000 and 10,000 years ago. Wandering south and east, some of the early nomads and their descendants traveled down the west coast, eventually continuing to the farthest tip of South America, while others spread out on the plains.

It was probably not until about 7,000 years ago that man began to inhabit the Rocky Mountain valleys of Montana. At one stage, characterized by a dry climate, foraging was the principal food source for those ancient people. Later, as the dry period ended and bison herds flourished, buffalo hunting became a way of life. One common method was to stampede the animals over the edge of a steep cliff; many piles of bones, evidence of buffalo jumps years ago, reveal this old practice.

The distribution of Indian tribes in the period preceding white settlement is not fully understood, but the Flatheads (or Salish), Pend d'Oreille (or Kalispel), and Kootenai could be found in northern Montana. The Shoshones—relatives of the Aztecs, long accustomed to a foraging existence in the Great Basin—were among the earliest Indians to acquire horses, which the Spanish had introduced in the southwest; rapidly expanding, their presence was noted in northwestern Montana in the early 1700's. Meanwhile, the Blackfeet were moving into the area from the east as part of a general migration under the pressure of white settlement along the Atlantic.

It was a time of rapid change. Besides the movement of people and the novelty of the horse (which revolutionized the buffalo hunt), the appearance of rifles added another dimension to the turmoil of the age. The Shoshones, no match for armed Blackfeet, retreated from the area by about 1800. The Blackfeet then occupied the entire region on the eastern slopes of the Continental Divide; on the west were the lands of the Kootenai, abutting Canada, and those of the Flatheads south of Flathead Lake and extending on to the Bitterroot Valley. Some of the Pend d'Oreilles had settled in the Flathead area, pretty much between the other two. Buffalo were abundant east of the Rockies and the annual hunts which brought the smaller tribes across the mountains were a constant source of friction and warfare between them and the Blackfeet.

The Lewis and Clark Expedition (1804-1806)

The interior of the continent remained largely unexplored by white men during the eighteenth century, though the possibilities of fur trading and the discovery of a Northwest Passage had stimulated some tentative probing—notably the Verendrye expeditions between 1728 and 1743. No one approached the Continental Divide in Montana during the period, however.

The land east of the Divide, part of "Louisiana," was claimed by France, ceded to Spain in 1762, and then returned to France in 1800. Thomas Jefferson, becoming President the following year, viewed the acquisition of this territory (as well as the Oregon country, subject to British as well as United States claims) as vital to national security and development. Before Jefferson was even inaugurated, in fact, he asked his friend and personal secretary Meriwether Lewis to lead an expedition to explore this unknown foreign soil. The venture's political objective would be to strengthen American claims to the land; the geographic and scientific aims, and even the economic concern with finding a Northwest Passage and studying the prospects of the fur trade were secondary. Actually, by the time the expedition was launched the land had become part of the United States (by virtue of the Louisiana Purchase, a fortuitous side-effect of the wars in Europe) and its political motive was somewhat subordinated.

With a friend and fellow militia officer, William Clark, as co-commander, Lewis set out from St. Louis in May 1804. Spending the winter, from October to April 1805, near present-day Bismarck, North Dakota, they resumed their trip up the Missouri River. Their party of about 30, traveling in eight boats and canoes, included a French-Canadian by the name of Charbonneau and his wife Sacagawea, a kidnapped Shoshone whom he had purchased.

Game was abundant—elk, deer, beaver, buffalo—and at one point there was a terrifying encounter with a charging grizzly bear. On June 2, 1805, the expedition reached the mouth of the Marias River. Soon thereafter, the roaring Great Falls of the Missouri presented a major obstacle, requiring several weeks for portaging, but finally they were able to resume their travel. The party passed the Dearborn River on July 18 and reached the Gates of the Mountains the following day. The land upstream was familiar to Sacagawea and soon friendly contact was established with her people. Following a circuitous route that took them across the Continental Divide at Lemhi Pass and then over the high Bitterroots at Lost Trail and Lolo Passes, Lewis and Clark reached the mouth of the Columbia River in November, remaining there until March 1806.

Heading eastward in the spring, the two commanders divided the party shortly after crossing Lolo Pass again on June 29. Clark explored a route in southern Montana, crossing the Divide at Gibbons Pass and eventually following the Yellowstone River to its junction with the Missouri. Lewis' route took him into the region of this guidebook. Leaving behind his Nez Perce guides, who dreaded the fearsome Blackfeet east of the mountains, Lewis continued up the Blackfoot River past Lincoln. Ascending Alice Creek, his party joyfully reached the Atlantic-bound headwaters of the Dearborn River at Lewis and Clark Pass (in the southernmost section of the Trail described here) on July 7.

The Blackfoot Indians lived up to their reputation, stealing several horses from the party one night. A more serious incident soon followed as Lewis and his men were exploring the upper reaches of the Marias River. On July 26, some 30 miles east of Glacier National Park, they encountered a larger group of Piegans (one of the Blackfoot tribes) who attempted to steal their guns and horses during the night. In the ensuing melee, two Indians were killed, one of them shot to death by Lewis himself. After this, the party beat a rapid retreat eastward to a reunion with Clark on August 12 and a return to St. Louis on September 23. The expedition was remarkably successful in achieving its aims and pointing the way to the subsequent settlement of Montana and the Northwest.

The Fur Trade

In the years following the Lewis and Clark expedition, several fur trading companies began to probe the mountains of Montana. An 1810 sortie by the North-West Company, pushing south from Canada, was probably the first to cross the Divide (most likely at Marias Pass) in the Rockies of northern Montana. The increasing hostility of the Blackfeet over the next 20 years discouraged extensive scouting in the region, though this situation was eased when traders representing John Jacob Astor's American Fur Company negotiated a treaty with the tribe. The briefly-flourishing fur trade was of little permanent consequence, except to the extent that the introduction of smallpox and alcohol contributed to the demoralization of the Indians.

One of the trappers, the Canadian Hugh Monroe, remained in the area, marrying a Blackfoot girl and achieving an exalted position in the tribe under the name of Rising Wolf. He traveled widely in the region, and it is fitting that a mountain in Glacier National Park, just east of the Continental Divide, carries his Indian name.

White Settlement

One sidelight of the fur trade was the introduction of the early missions into western Montana. The Flatheads, intrigued by stories of the power of Catholicism (related to them by Iroquois sent west to instruct the indigenous tribes in trapping techniques), petitioned Church authorities to send them a priest. Their prayers were answered with the arrival of the Jesuit, Father de Smet, and the establishment of the short-lived St. Mary's Mission, in the Bitterroot Valley, in 1841. (In his travels among the Indians, it is believed that Father de Smet may have camped with Hugh Monroe on the grand lakes in Glacier known as the St. Mary's Lakes, presumably having been so named by the priest.) This religious activity was followed in 1854 by the founding of the St. Ignatius Mission, serving the Pend d'Oreilles (Kalispels), in the Mission Valley north of Missoula.

It was gold that brought large numbers of white men into Montana for the first time. Bannack, followed quickly by Virginia City and several others, became a boom town in 1863. In 1864, the riches of Helena were uncovered, bringing still more adventurers westward.

The imprint of prospectors in northern Montana was less significant, as there were no major gold strikes above the Helena region. The country was gradually being opened up, however, as improved travel route were developed between the eastern states and the Pacific Northwest. The first expedition for this purpose was a survey under Isaac Stevens in the early 1850's, which explored the country with a view to selecting a practicable rail route. Stevens recommended a route that would cross the Divide at Cadotte Pass or Lewis and Clark Pass. Although the railroad proposal was not acted upon, one of Stevens' officers by the name of John Mullan returned to the area to direct the construction of a military wagon road in the same area (actually a bit farther south, at Mullan Pass near Helena). The road, finished in 1863, became an important travel route for reaching the gold strikes that were soon to follow.

The next years were a time of frequent skirmishes between the Indians and the whites who were crowding into the area. The Indian attacks, mostly on the plains along the Mullan Road, led to a series of military expeditions culminating in the Custer Massacre at the Little Big Horn in eastern Montana in 1876. The Indians were never numerous—their population at the time was probably only abut 13,000 in Montana—and the battles with the army, the near extinction of buffalo, and crop failures all combined to reduce them both in spirit and in numbers.

However, many of the pioneering American explorers had worked hard to encourage friendly contact with the Indians, and their efforts sometimes led to honorable treaties of peace, without which the bloodshed might have been worse.

One such treaty, negotiated by Isaac Stevens in 1855 with the Flatheads and Blackfeet, granted travel rights to United States citizens and resolved the long-standing feud between the tribes with respect to buffalo-hunting rights. A 1865 treaty, procured by bribing tribal chiefs and never ratified by the United States Senate, aimed at eliminating hostilities on the Mullan Road by restricting the Blackfeet to lands north of the Teton River, a small fraction of their domain as defined just ten years earlier.

In response to continuing Indian raids, a cavalry expedition was sent out in January 1870 and surprised a band camping on the Marias River. Attacking in the middle of the night, the troops massacred 173 Indians, including many women and children, and captured some 300 horses.

A number of unilateral actions, notably a law enacted by Congress in 1874, were even more harsh than the unratified 1865 treaty, taking the lands between Birch Creek and the Teton River without agreement of the Blackfeet or compensation to them. Finally, in 1888, after the plight of the Blackfeet had become pitiable, a treaty was negotiated which defined the boundaries of their reservation as they exist today (except for the subsequent exclusion of lands adjacent to the Divide) and provided for appropriations for various forms of assistance to the Indians.

Considering the impoverished condition of the tribe at the time, the fairness of the 1888 treaty may be questioned. On its face, however, noble sentiments are expressed. The reservation set apart in 1874 is described, in the treaty's words, as "wholly out of proportion to the number of Indians occupying the same, and greatly in excess of their present or prospective wants." The treaty is accordingly adopted, with the Indians being "desirous of disposing of so much thereof as they do not require, in order to obtain the means to enable them to become self-supporting, as a pastoral and agricultural people, and to educate their children in the paths of civilization."

As the Indians were brought under control, whether by treaty or force, the stage was set for the feverish and competitive era of railroad building, spurred onward by the exploitation of the great copper deposits around Butte in the early 1880's. The Northern Pacific (1883) was the first to traverse the state, crossing the Divide (actually tunneling beneath it) at Mullan Pass near the old Mullan Road. Next was the Great Northern, built through Marias Pass and reaching the Pacific in 1893, followed in short order by the Milwaukee Road's route through Pipestone Pass.

Surprisingly, the precise location of Marias Pass, though known to the early mountain men and named on an 1840 map, evaded scouts guided (or deliberately misguided) by Hugh Monroe who searched for it with Isaac Stevens' 1853 survey; they crossed the Divide by 7600-foot Cut Bank Pass in present-day Glacier National Park near Pitamakan Overlook (described in the text), obviously impassable for rail travel. Although another party nearly reached Marias Pass the next year, they were forced to turn back to meet a schedule and the northern route across the Rockies remained undiscovered. It was not until 1889, on a December day with deep snow and temperatures about 40 degrees below zero that John Stevens, accompanied by a single Flathead guide, crossed Marias Pass and found this low and excellent route through the Rockies.

The ruggedness of the terrain, together with the Blackfoot rights east of the Divide, limited settlement in the high mountains. Prospecting continued, with some copper strikes, which led to the 1896 purchase of the Blackfoot lands adjacent to the Divide. The scenic grandeur of the northern lands was gradually recognized, not least by the Great Northern in the interest of developing profitable tourist business, and in 1910 Glacier National Park was established.

Despite the development in the century since Montana became a State, the lands along the Continental Divide remain largely undisturbed. The scenery and wildlife today are very much as they were when the pioneers passed by. And so, when traveling along the Continental Divide National Scenic Trail, the sojourner will be inspired by a natural landscape of grandeur and beauty.

Place Names

Many place names along the Trail commemorate early residents and visitors to northern Montana. Some of the more prominent ones are included here.

Ahern Drift. Lt. George Ahern explored the northern Glacier country in 1838-90. He crossed the Continental Divide in 1890 at Ahern Pass.

Apikuni Mountain. Apikuni was the Blackfoot name conferred on James Willard Schultz, an author who lived among the Indians for some time and wrote extensively about them.

Cadotte Pass. Thomas Canfield (1870) "saw Cadotte himself, who conducted Gov. Stevens, and after whom the pass was named, and he told me he simpl.y followed an old trail." Pierre Cadotte, of an old fur trade family, is variously reported to have died in 1855 or 1873; if the earlier date is correct, the guide may have been Pierre's son, Louis. (See Fort Benton Journal, in *Contributions to the Historical Society of Montana,* vol. 10, 1940.)

Cattle Queen Creek. In addition to her ranching enterprises, Elizabeth Collins prospected near the creek that is named for her.

Mount **Cleveland**. Named for President Grover Cleveland (perhaps in recognition of his setting aside the Glacier area as part of a forest reserve).

Coonsa Creek. Coonsa is sometimes credited with having accompanied John Stevens on his exploration of Marias Pass; but other accounts report his having been murdered before Stevens' trip.

Dawson Pass. For Thomas Dawson, a guide in the earliest days of Glacier National Park.

Dearborn River. Named by Lewis and Clark for Secretary of War Henry Dearborn.

Flinsch Peak. Rudolf Flinsch spent some weeks in 1892 on a hunting trip in the Pitamakan Pass area.

Grinnell Glacier. Starting in 1885, George Bird Grinnell, editor of *Forest and Stream*, explored the Glacier country extensively. Grinnell has been called the "father of Glacier Park" for the role he played in its establishment.

Jackson Glacier. William Jackson, a grandson of Hugh Monroe (Rising Wolf), was a guide during the early days before establishment of Glacier Park.

Kennedy Creek. John Kennedy was an Indian trader with a post at the mouth of Kennedy Creek.

Mount **Kipp**. Son of a famed trader on the upper Missouri, Joseph Kipp was a prospector who had a cabin near the mountain that bears his name.

Logan Pass. For William Richard Logan, the first superintendent of Glacier National Park.

Marias Pass. Marias River, draining this pass, was named by Meriwether Lewis for his cousin, Maria Wood.

Pitamakan Pass. Pitamakan (Running Eagle) was a female war chief of the Blackfeet. She was featured in a 1919 book by James Willard Schultz.

Pumpelly Pillar. Raphael Pumpelly, a renowned geologist, led a scientific expedition that crossed Cut Bank Pass in 1883.

Red Eagle Lake. A Blackfoot medicine man, related by marriage to Hugh Monroe.

Rising Wolf Mountain. The Indian name for Hugh Monroe (1799-1892), who lived with the Blackfeet for his entire adult life.

Rogers Pass. After Major A.B. Rogers, who surveyed it in 1887 for the Great Northern Railroad.

Saint Mary Lake. While St. Mary seems clear enough, the question whether the name was bestowed by Father DeSmet (who may or may not have visited the area) is a matter of controversy.

Mount **Stimson**. Henry Lewis Stimson accompanied Grinnell on early trips to Glacier. He had a distinguished public career, serving as Secretary of War during World War II.

Tinkham Mountain. Lt. A.W. Tinkham, a member of the Isaac Stevens railroad survey, crossed Cut Bank Pass in 1853.

Addresses

Government Agencies

U.S. Geological Survey

Distribution Section, U.S. Geological Survey, Box 25286, Federal Center, Denver, Colorado 80225.

Forest Service

Regional Forester, Rocky Mountain Region, P.O. Box 25127, Denver, Colorado 80225 (for information regarding the Continental Divide Trail as a whole).

Regional Forester, Northern Region, P.O. Box 7669, Missoula, Montana 59807. (406) 329-3511.

Flathead National Forest

Supervisor, Flathead National Forest, 1935 Third Ave. E., Kalispell, Montana 59901. (406) 755-5401.

District Ranger, Hungry Horse Ranger District, P.O. Box 340, Hungry Horse, Montana 59919. (406) 387-5243.

District Ranger, Spotted Bear Ranger District, P.O. Box 310, Hungry Horse, Montana 59919. (406) 752-7345.

Lewis and Clark National Forest

Supervisor, Lewis and Clark National Forest, P.O. Box 871, Great Falls, Montana 59403. (406) 791-7700.

District Ranger, Rocky Mountain Ranger District, P.O. Box 340, Choteau, Montana 59422. (406) 466-5341.

Helena National Forest

Supervisor, Helena National Forest, 301 S. Park, Drawer 10014, Helena, Montana 59626. (406) 449-5201.

District Ranger, Lincoln Ranger District, P.O. Box 219, Lincoln, Montana 59639. (406) 362-4265.

National Park Service

Superintendent, Glacier National Park, West Glacier, Montana 59936. (406) 888-5441.

In Canada

Superintendent, Waterton Lakes National Park, Waterton Park, Alberta. (403) 859-2224.

Other Addresses

Backpackers Inn, P.O. Box 94, East Glacier Park, Montana 59434. (406) 226-9392. Pat and Renee Schur, who operate this economical hostel, close to the post office, will hold packages for arriving guests.

Belton Chalets, P.O. Box 188, West Glacier, Montana 59936. (406) 888-5511 (April to September). For reservations at Granite Park Chalet.

Benchmark Wilderness Ranch, c/o Bud and Beverly Heckman, P.O. Box 190, Augusta, Montana 59410. (406) 562-3336.

Continental Divide Trail Society, P.O. Box 30002, Bethesda, Maryland 20824. (301) 493-4080.

Garland's Town and Country Store, Lincoln, Montana 59639. (406) 362-4244. Call Becky Garland if you need information or assistance.

Glacier Park, Inc., P.O. Box 147, East Glacier Park, Montana 59434. (406) 226-5551. Winter address: Greyhound Tower, Station 1210, Phoenix, Arizona 85077, (602) 248-6000. For hotels, motels, and transportation in Glacier National Park.

Glacier Natural History Association, Inc., P.O. Box 327, West Glacier, Montana 59936. (406) 888-5756.

Intermountain Bus Co., 326 1st Ave. S., Great Falls, Montana 59434. (406) 453-1541. Bus service between Great Fallls and Missoula, via Rogers Pass and Lincoln.

References

Many fine books describe aspects of the country covered by this volume. In addition to standard field guides—available for birds, mammals, butterflies, wildflowers, etc.—those listed below are recommended for further reading or reference.

Cunningham, Bill. *Montana's Continental Divide*. Helena: Montana Magazine, 1986. An exceptional illustrated overview, including cultural and natural history.

Thompson, Larry S. *Montana's Explorers*. Helena: Montana Magazine, 1985. Lewis and Clark, Father DeSmet, the Pacific Railroad Surveys, and much more. This and the preceding are volumes in the outstanding Montana Geographic Series.

Shaw, Richard J. and Danny On. *Plants of Waterton-Glacier National Parks and the Northern Rockies*. Missoula: Mountain Press Publishing Co., 1979. An unkeyed text, with 220 species illustrated and described. (More technical works will be referenced in our forthcoming wildflower guide.)

Hanna, Warren L. *Montana's Many-Splendored Glacierland*. Grand Forks ND: University of North Dakota Foundation, 1987. Comprehensive survey of all aspects of Glacier National Park, including extensive bibliography.

Ruhle, George C. *Roads and Trails of Waterton-Glacier International Peace Park*. Glacier Natural History Association, 1986 revision. The standard guidebook for the park.

Buchholtz, C.W. *Man in Glacier*. Glacier Natural History Association, 1976. The Indians, explorers, surveyors, politicians, tourists, etc.—an excellent social history.

Alt, David D. and Donald W. Hyndman. *Rocks, Ice and Water*. Missoula: Mountain Press Publishing Co., 1973. Geology of Waterton-Glacier Park.

Parratt, Lloyd P. *Birds of Glacier National Park*. Glacier Natural History Association, 1970 reprint.

Thompson, Margaret. *High Trails of Glacier National Park*. Caldwell ID: Caxton Printers, 1936. A travel account, nicely weaving in nature and history notes. Others in this genre: Mary Roberts Rinehart, *Through Glacier Park*, 1916; Walter Prichard Eaton, *Skyline Camps*, 1922; and Albert L. Sperry, *Avalanche*, 1938.

Holterman, Jack. *Place Names of Glacier / Waterton National Parks*. Glacier Natural History Association, 1985. All the way from "Adair Ridge" to "Zephyr" mining claims.

Schultz, James Willard. *Signposts of Adventure*. Boston and New York: Houghton Mifflin Co., 1926. Explains Indian names for topographical features in Glacier Park.

McClintock, Walter. *The Old North Trail*. Lincoln NE: University of Nebraska Press, 1968 reprint. On the Blackfeet, but with information on Cutbank Pass, Father DeSmet, etc.

Murray, Genevieve. *Marias Pass*. Missoula, State University of Montana, n.d. Detailed examination of nineteenth century travel routes through and near Marias Pass.

Graetz, Rick. *Montana's Bob Marshall Country*. Helena: Montana Magazine, 1985. History and natural history of the Bob Marshall and Scapegoat Wilderness Areas, including 64 pages of color photography. Excellent both for planning and remembering a trip.

Picton, Harold D. and Irene E. Picton. *Saga of the Sun*. Montana Department of Fish and Game, 1975. History of the Sun River elk herd, incidentally treating exploration and settlement of the upper Sun River.

Roth, Dennis M. *The Wilderness Movement and the National Forests*. College Station TX: Intaglio Press, n.d. Includes a chapter on the establishment of the Scapegoat Wilderness.

Sprague, Marshall. *The Great Gates*. Boston: Little, Brown and Co., 1964. A reliable and readable account of the exploration of the Continental Divide in the United States and Canada.

Henshaw, Julia W. *Wild Flowers of the North American Mountains*. New York: Robert M. McBride and Co., 1917. Source of this volume's poetic epigraph. (See her comments on the larch, where she quotes the verse, but without identifying its author.)

About the Author

Jim Wolf has traveled throughout the United States in pursuit of his interests as a backpacker and naturalist. Since 1973, he has scouted the Continental Divide from the Canadian border south to Mexico. He was active in the successful campaign to have Congress designate the route as a national scenic trail. He has continued his efforts on behalf of the Trail—both as Director of the Continental Divide Trail Society and as a member of the Continental Divide National Scenic Trail Advisory Council. This guidebook series records his observations and suggestions concerning the present status and future development of the Trail. His studies of the historical geography of the Continental Divide have appeared in *Annals of Wyoming* and other publications.

He served as president of the Audubon Society of Western Pennsylvania for two years, and has also been an officer of the Environmental Planning and Information Center of Pennsylvania, the Pittsburgh Climbers, and the Explorers Club of Pittsburgh. An attorney by profession, he is currently on the staff of the United States Nuclear Regulatory Commission.

About the Society

The Continental Divide Trail Society is dedicated to the planning, development, and maintenance of the Continental Divide Trail as a silent trail—one laid out with appreciation of its natural environment and sensitivity to yearnings for a sense of contact with the wilderness. It stresses each person's responsibility to be a good steward, with respect for fellow travelers, for proprietors of the land, and for the creatures of the earth.

To further these objectives, the Society:

- Scouts the terrain, identifies possible Trail locations, and—through its publications—describes existing feasible routes.

- Collects bibliographic and photographic materials related to the Continental Divide corridor.

- Monitors land use actions of governmental agencies and participates in administrative review procedures. Typical projects have involved wilderness and scenic river studies, and proposals to construct railroads and power transmission lines through scenic areas along the Trail.

- Serves as a clearinghouse for the suggestions of Trail users and other interested persons.

The Society publishes DIVIDEnds, a semiannual newsletter on matters of current interest. DIVIDEnds is distributed to members of the Society and, on an exchange basis, to other organizations with similar interests.

The *Guide to the Continental Divide* is the Society's major publication. The series so far includes:

Vol. 1: Northern Montana (Canada to Rogers Pass).

Vol. 2: Southern Montana and Idaho (Rogers Pass to Macks Inn, Idaho).

Vol. 3: Wyoming (Macks Inn to Rawlins).

Vol. 4: Northern Colorado (Rawlins to Copper Mountain).

Vol. 5: Southern Colorado (Copper Mtn. to Cumbres Pass).

One or more guides to New Mexico will be issued after the location of the Trail in that State is more clearly defined.

Inquiries and suggestions are welcome and will be greatly appreciated.